Stakeholder Theory

Stakeholder Theory

Impact and Prospects

Edited by

Robert A. Phillips

Associate Professor, University of Richmond, USA

Edward Elgar
Cheltenham, UK • Northampton, MA, USA

Published by
Edward Elgar Publishing Limited
The Lypiatts
15 Lansdown Road
Cheltenham
Glos GL50 2JA
UK

Edward Elgar Publishing, Inc.
William Pratt House
9 Dewey Court
Northampton
Massachusetts 01060
USA

A catalogue record for this book
is available from the British Library

Library of Congress Control Number: 2011924167

ISBN 978 1 84844 533 8 (cased)

Typeset by Servis Filmsetting Ltd, Stockport, Cheshire
Printed and bound by MPG Books Group, UK

Contents

Contributors

Shawn L. Berman, Anderson School of Management, University of New Mexico

Douglas A. Bosse, Robins School of Business, University of Richmond

Thomas Donaldson, The Wharton School, University of Pennsylvania

Heather Elms, Kogod School of Business, American University

R. Edward Freeman, The Darden School, University of Virginia

Jeffrey S. Harrison, Robins School of Business, University of Richmond

Edwin M. Hartman, Leonard N. Stern School of Business, New York University

Michael E. Johnson-Cramer, Bucknell University

Thomas M. Jones, Foster School of Business, University of Washington

Moritz Patzer, Institute of Organization and Administrative Science, University of Zurich

Robert A. Phillips, Robins School of Business, University of Richmond

Andreas Georg Scherer, Institute of Organization and Administrative Science, University of Zurich

Patricia H. Werhane, The Darden School, University of Virginia, and Wicklander Professor of Business Ethics, DePaul University

Preface

2009 marked the 25th anniversary of R. Edward Freeman's *Strategic Management: A Stakeholder Approach* – the *locus classicus* of modern stakeholder theory. The volume you hold contains the reflections of the best stakeholder scholars in the world on the occasion of this anniversary. Though my name is on the front, this book would not have been possible without the contributions of the authors. The vast majority of the credit – and my personal gratitude – goes to them. Each of them is a remarkably accomplished scholar with myriad alternative opportunities for their time and outlets for their work. I am honored by their willingness to contribute to this project.

The collection benefitted importantly from conversations on earlier drafts. In its earliest iteration, several of the authors participated in a symposium at the Academy of Management Annual Meeting in 2009 in Chicago entitled 'Stakeholder Theory's Silver Anniversary: Freeman '84 @ 25'. Later in the process, Ed Freeman was gracious enough to devote a session of his doctoral seminar on stakeholder theory to the work contained in this volume. Participants included Bret Crane, Eugene Geh, Megan Hess, Ali Ishrat, Adrian Keevil, and Lauren Purnell. Tom Jones was visiting the Darden School at the time and attended the session, which, in this case, took place at Freeman's home in the idyllic wooded hills outside of Charlottesville, Virginia. In the words of Adrian Keevil, it was '... one for the front of the brochure'. Many of the ideas from this session were relayed to the authors during the revision process and were helpful to me in the performance of my editorial duties.

Molly Freeman was kind enough to provide the original art for the book's cover. Molly is Ed's daughter and there is a special symmetry to this. As I only recently learned, Maureen Wellen (Ed's wife) drew the original – now ubiquitous – hub-and-spoke stakeholder model for the 1984 book.

I also want to acknowledge the work of those in the trenches. Alan Sturmer and Alexandra Mandzak of Edward Elgar Publishers shared the vision of this volume to such an extent that, when I proposed it, they suggested we also organize a collection of the best previously published work in the area. The result was a reference volume called simply *Stakeholders*.

I am grateful for their enthusiasm and patience. Tricia Fanney and Jessica Bailey here at the University of Richmond were also exceptionally helpful to me during this process.

Finally, I would like to thank Ed Freeman himself. His scholarly work – from before 1984 to present – motivated and provoked an entire field for a quarter of a century. Moreover, many of us have benefitted intimately and personally from his kindness and generosity of spirit. No one has benefitted more from this than me and I'm proud to have him as a mentor, friend and bottom turtle.

1. Bounding the world's miseries: corporate responsibility and Freeman's stakeholder theory

Heather Elms, Michael E. Johnson-Cramer and Shawn L. Berman

Both academic and popular discussions of corporate social responsibility (CSR) commonly reference stakeholder theory as a foundational perspective. In doing so, many specifically cite R. Edward Freeman's (1984) book, *Strategic Management: A Stakeholder Approach*. Much of this referential work, however, neglects Freeman's critical analysis therein of the relationship between stakeholder theory and then-prevalent notions of CSR. Moreover, in his 1984 contribution and elsewhere, Freeman sets out a theoretical foundation that, though far-reaching, remains acutely aware of its boundary conditions. Many stakeholder theorists subsequently trying to build on Freeman's foundation remain similarly circumspect and go to great lengths to delimit stakeholder theory in important ways, paying careful attention to 'what stakeholder theory is not' (for example, Phillips, Freeman and Wicks, 2003). At all turns, these theorists contend that Freeman's stakeholder theory is not 'a basket big enough to hold the world's miseries' (Clarkson, 1994: 9). To date, though, the boundaries between stakeholder research and CSR remain relatively uncharted. Using an empirical analysis of citations of Freeman (1984) as a foundation for CSR in the academic literature as a starting point, we explore these boundaries and identify the benefits of both establishing and crossing them.

FREEMAN'S STAKEHOLDER THEORY AND CSR

Freeman's stakeholder theory has always been an explicitly strategic one (see also Harrison, this volume). *Strategic Management: A Stakeholder Approach* – his first comprehensive formulation of the theory (1984) – was written as a *strategy*, not an ethics, text (see Freeman, 2004 and 2005 for the genesis of the book.) In it, Freeman describes the stakeholder concept as 'enrich[ing] the current state of the art in strategic management' (Freeman, 1984: 1) given that 'The point of strategic management is in some sense to chart a direction for the firm. Groups which can affect that direction and its implementation must be considered in the strategic management process' (Freeman, 1984: 46). Earlier conceptions, defining stakeholders as 'those groups without whose support the organization would cease to exist' (Stanford Research Institute, 1963, cited in Freeman, 1984: 31), argued that the point of understanding the expectations of stakeholders was that without doing so, managers could not formulate strategies which would obtain the support necessary for even the continued survival, let alone competitive advantage, of the firm. Freeman (2005) later attributed stakeholder theory's greater embeddedness in the business ethics literature than in the strategic management literature to his personal career moves around the time the 1984 book was published (in 1983, from Wharton to the University of Minnesota, and in 1986 to the Darden School at the University of Virginia).

Consistent with his strategic perspective, Freeman (1984) harbors ambivalence about the notion of CSR. In particular, he worries that CSR might be understood as an activity separate from the business operations of the firm – when the two should instead be considered inseparable:

> While there have been many criticisms of the research in corporate social responsibility, perhaps the most troubling issue is the very nature of 'corporate social responsibility' as if the concept were needed to augment the study of business policy. Corporate social responsibility is often looked at as an 'add on' to 'business as usual' and the phrase often heard from executives is 'corporate social responsibility is fine, if you can afford it.' (Freeman, 1984: 40)

Further, he notes,

> We need to understand the complex interconnections between economic and social forces. Isolating 'social issues' as separate from the economic impact which they have, and conversely isolating economic issues as if they had no social effect, misses the mark both managerially and intellectually. Actions aimed at one side will not address the concerns of the other. Processes, techniques and theories which do not consider all of these forces will fail to describe and predict the business world as it really is.
>   While the corporate social responsibility literature has been important in bringing to the foreground in organizational research a concern with social and political issues, it has failed to indicate ways of integrating these concerns into the strategic systems of the corporation in a non-ad hoc fashion. (Freeman, 1984: 40)

Regardless of these critical statements (and we provide further details of Freeman's critical perspective on CSR following a discussion of our analysis), we and others have noted the ubiquitous use of Freeman (1984) as a foundation for CSR research. Wokutch and Shepard (1999: 528), for example, note that 'One popular way of understanding CSR is through the stakeholder management model (Freeman, 1984)' and indeed, a recent issue of *The Academy of Management Review* (July, 2007), contains several articles linking Freeman (1984) to CSR (for example, Barnett, 2007; Mackey, Mackey and Barney, 2007; Campbell, 2007). These observations led us to wonder how prevalent this linkage was in the literature, so we conducted a review of the academic literature in an effort to document that prevalence, as well as identify common themes underlying the link. We use the understanding generated by this analysis to attempt to untangle stakeholder theory and CSR, demonstrating how these two literatures represent fundamentally different projects – both important in their own right, but also complementary.

Our intention is one of 'immanent critique' (Walzer, 1994: 47), given the potentially greater power of internal and on-the-ground, rather than external or transcendent, perspectives. 'The work of the critic, when it is maximalist work, is also local and particularist in character' (Walzer, 1994: 61). The authors of this chapter all self-identify as stakeholder theorists. Like many of our colleagues, we as scholars have struggled with the distinctions and links we make here, and the invitation to write this chapter has provided us with an opportunity to come to some conclusions. We hope that our work spurs discussion in our field, as well as similar critiques and discussions of the use of foundational literatures in other fields – for example, agency and resource dependence theories in strategy, and institutional theory in organizational theory. We would also like to emphasize that almost 85 percent of the citations we analyzed were consistent with Freeman (1984). *All* of the citations we analyzed have enabled our understanding of the relationship between stakeholder theory and CSR. Those more interested in our thoughts about that relationship, rather than our literature evaluation, may easily skip to the section titled 'The Three Mischaracterizations'.

LOOKING IN THE LITERATURE: METHODOLOGY

Our literature review included three business and society/ethics journals: *Business & Society (B&S), Business Ethics Quarterly (BEQ)* and *Journal of Business Ethics (JBE)*, and three general management journals: *Academy of Management Journal (AMJ), Academy of Management Review (AMR)* and *Strategic Management Journal (SMJ)*. We utilized several search strategies to identify articles linking Freeman (1984) with CSR. First, to cast a broad net, we searched on 'Freeman' or 'Strategic Management: A Stakeholder Approach' and 'responsibility'. More narrowly, we also searched on 'Freeman' or 'Strategic Management: A

Table 1.1   Search results

Journal	Hits using 'Freeman and responsibility not Hannan and Freeman'	Hits using 'Freeman and CSR'	Actual citations of Freeman (1984)
Academy of Management Journal	87	1	17
Academy of Management Review	130	19	55
Business & Society	102	27	30
Business Ethics Quarterly	182	26	63
Journal of Business Ethics	422	154	200
Strategic Management Journal	30	2	13

Stakeholder Approach' and 'CSR', as well as 'Freeman' or 'Strategic Management: A Stakeholder Approach' and 'corporate social responsibility', 'corporate responsibility' and 'social responsibility'. The *AMJ, AMR, B&S, JBE* and *SMJ* searches encompassed January 1982 through August 2009. We began with 1982 to cover the possibility of authors citing the forthcoming book before it was actually published. *BEQ* did not commence publishing until January 1991 so that search encompassed only January 1991 through August 2009. We feel reasonably confident that together, these search strategies over the date ranges identified yielded all of the citations linking Freeman (1984) to CSR.

In researching the citations for the first journal we examined (*AMR*), it quickly became apparent that the search of 'Freeman' and 'responsibility' captured many extraneous citations. In particular, the results included cites to Michael Hannan and John Freeman's article, also published in 1984, in the *American Sociological Review*. We thus excluded the term 'Hannan and Freeman' from future searches. Thus, the numbers reported here reflect a search on 'Freeman and responsibility not Hannan and Freeman'. While this search did a better job of returning relevant citations, it still returned many extraneous citations. The authors felt that in the interest of making sure we had all relevant cites, however, that we should check all articles this search returned (see the first column of Table 1.1). Table 1.1 also includes search results for 'Freeman and CSR' because some authors only used the CSR acronym (otherwise, these citations would have been picked up by the 'Freeman and responsibility' search.)

The final column of Table 1.1 identifies the number of articles actually referring to Freeman (1984) that together our searches revealed.

Our next step was a two-stage classification of each of the articles citing Freeman (1984). The authors divided up the journals among themselves and each categorized all articles for their journals, discussing any citations about which they had questions with the other authors. The authors first categorized for depth of content, rating the citation in terms of how substantively it dealt with the ideas found in *Strategic Management: A Stakeholder Approach*. We refer to non-substantive citations as 'Generic', and substantive citations as 'Substantive' (see more extensive descriptions of these categories below.) The second step involved further classifying citations on the basis of whether they were consistent with, or mischaracterized, the content of Freeman (1984). We developed four categories to classify the citations: Two categories captured articles which dealt with Freeman's ideas on a non-substantive level: 'Generic/ Title', and 'Generic/Content', while another two categories captured whether the more substantive citations were consistent with, or mischaracterized, Freeman (1984): 'Substantive/Consistent' and 'Substantive/ Mischaracterization'. Articles were always classified by the highest level they reached, but 'Mischaracterization' always dominated 'Consistent' – that is, if the article contained both 'Generic' and 'Substantive' references, it was classified as 'Substantive', and if it contained both 'Substantive/ Consistent' and 'Substantive/Mischaracterization' references it was classified as 'Substantive/Mischaracterization'. The authors did not identify any incorrect 'Generic' references that mischaracterized Freeman (1984). Each category is briefly explained below, and we also include some exemplar quotations demonstrating how citations were categorized in Table 1.3.

Generic/Title

This category includes the least complex references to Freeman (1984). Articles placed in this category merely mention the phrases 'stakeholder theory', 'stakeholder management' or simply state that firms have stakeholders without an elaboration of the term 'stakeholder' and then cite Freeman (1984). The category name 'Generic/Title' refers to the fact that such citations refer to little more content than is included in the title of Freeman (1984).

Generic/Content

This category captures the set of articles that move a bit beyond the generic citation described above. These citations require at least a cursory reading of the book (or at least delving into another publication that provides detail on the content of Freeman (1984) beyond the title of the book). Quotations of, or reference to, a reasonable rewording of Freeman's definition of stakeholders (for example, 1984: 46, 'A stakeholder in an organization is (by definition) any group or individual who can affect or is affected by the achievement of the organization's objectives') qualified an article for this category. Articles that provided a list of potential stakeholders and then cited Freeman (1984) were also classified as 'Generic/Content' citations. Articles in this category showed a deeper understanding of Freeman (1984) than articles in the 'Generic/Title' category but remained limited relative to 'Substantive' citations. Articles that only referred to Freeman (1984) as a seminal work in stakeholder theory were also classified as 'Generic/Content'.

Substantive/Consistent

We reserved this category for articles which demonstrated some depth of understanding of Freeman (1984). This might be represented by using multiple quotations, discussing the application of Freeman's ideas in multiple settings or otherwise significantly engaging with the content of Freeman (1984). In contrast to the other two categories, a citation in this category clearly required an understanding of the book's true content.

Substantive/Mischaracterization

This category includes articles that contributed to the genesis of this chapter. These articles suggested a misunderstanding of the content of Freeman (1984). This might be done by citing Freeman (1984) in a way that mischaracterizes the content of the book, or – perhaps more problematically – by citing Freeman (1984) for content not contained in the book. In many cases, the latter type might have appropriately cited *another* Freeman source, but Freeman (1984) was an inappropriate citation for the point. We return to this issue (and suggest some appropriate alternative citations) in discussing the common themes underlying problematic links between Freeman (1984) and CSR below.

ANALYSIS AND RESULTS

The results of our analysis are presented in Table 1.2, and exemplar quotations are provided in Table 1.3.

Table 1.2   Analysis results

Journal	N	Articles containing Generic/Title citations	Articles containing Generic/Content citations	Articles containing Substantive/Consistent citations	Articles containing Substantive/Mischaracterization citations	Percentage of articles with a Generic citation (%)	Percentage of articles with a Substantive citation (%)	Percentage of substantive citations that were Mischaracterizations (%)
Academy of Management Review	55	20	13	17	5	60	40	24
Academy of Management Journal	17	6	5	6	0	65	35	0
Business & Society	30	7	8	14	1	50	50	<1
Business Ethics Quarterly	63 (62 used)	9	16	18	19	40	60	51
Journal of Business Ethics	200	48	103	28	21	76	24	43
Strategic Management Journal	13	1	8	4	0	69	31	0
Total	377	91	153	87	46	N = 244	N = 133	D = 46
Percentage of total (%)		24	41	23	12	65	35	35

Note: The classification percentages sometimes add up to more than 100% given rounding error.

7

Table 1.3   Exemplar quotations[a]

Generic/Title	'also figures prominently in several other literatures including those on social exchange theory (Blau, 1984) . . . stakeholder theory (Freeman, 1984; Jones 1995)' (Love and Kraatz, 2009: 316); 'as theorized, for instance, in the stakeholder approach (Freeman, 1984; Jones 1995)' (Durand and Calori, 2006: 95)
Generic/Content	'In a seminal paper on stakeholder theory, Freeman (1984) asserts that firms have relationships with many constituent groups and that these stakeholders both affect and are affected by the actions of the firm' (McWilliams and Siegel, 2001: 118); 'Stakeholders have been defined (Freeman, 1984: 46) as those groups that "are affected by and can in turn affect the achievement of the organizational objectives" of the firm' (Hosmer, 1994: 25)
Substantive/ Consistent	'Contractarian or Rawlsian "strategies" (Freeman, 1984) are ultimately driven by concerns of fairness and justice' (Singer, 1994: 197); 'One comprehensive approach to stakeholder management was suggested in an analysis and popularization of the concept a decade ago (Freeman, 1984). This process included four generic steps: (1) stakeholder and stake identification; (2) . . .' (Starik, 1995: 213)
Substantive/ Mischarac- terization	'The stakeholder approach to CSR popularized by Freeman (1984) provides another fruitful theoretical lens, which could help in shedding light on the peculiarities of SMEs in relation to CSR. Freeman's (1984) stakeholder approach to CSR has helped in re-conceptualizing the nature of the firm' (Jamali, Zanhour and Keshishian, 2009: 359); 'some business and society scholars have argued that firms have a duty to society that goes well beyond simply maximizing the wealth of equity holders (Swanson, 1999; Whetten, Rands and Godfrey, 2001). These scholars argue that such a narrow focus can lead management to ignore other important stakeholders – including employees, suppliers, customers, and society at large – and that sometimes the interests of these other stakeholders should supersede the interests of firms' equity holders in managerial decision making, even if this reduces the present value of the firm's cash flows. (Clarkson, 1995; Donaldson and Preston, 1995; Freeman, 1984; Mitchell, Agle and Wood, 1997; Paine, 2002; Wood and Jones, 1995)' (Mackey, Mackey and Barney, 2007: 817)

Note: a. Please see Appendix 1.1 for a complete analysis of *BEQ* citations. Complete analyses for the other journals will be made available by the authors online.

Analysis

The first point revealed by our citation search is that Freeman (1984) is cited a great deal in discussions of responsibility. In the six journals we reviewed, Freeman (1984) is cited in close to 400 articles discussing some dimension of responsibility. Within these articles, Freeman's book appears to have become the standard reference for the term 'stakeholder theory' – the second largest category of references to Freeman (1984) was in this vein (the 'Generic/Title' references). Sometimes references elaborated with Freeman's (1984) definition of stakeholders or a similar description (the 'Generic/Content' references). These two categories ('Generic/Title' and 'Generic/Content') accounted for far more than half (65 percent) of the articles containing citations to Freeman (1984). More problematically, however, when substantive references were made, as many as 51 percent (in *BEQ*) mischaracterized Freeman (1984).[1] Additionally troubling is that the rate of mischaracterization of Freeman's (1984) ideas appears to be increasing in some of the journals. As an example, although Table 1.2 does not break down mischaracterized citations by years, in *JBE*, from the period encompassing 1982–99, there were only five mischaracterized citations of Freeman (1984), but between 1999 and 2009, there were 16. Similar patterns are present for *AMR* and *B&S*.

This dynamic evidence suggests a possible source of the problem. Until shortly after our analysis, *Strategic Management: A Stakeholder Approach* was out of print – and the initial and only printing only included 2500 copies (Freeman, 2009, personal communication). Amazon.com recently had only a single used copy for sale at the remarkable price of $2004.12. An increase in the number of authors citing an, at best, constant number of copies suggests a possible increase in the number of authors who cite the book without having access to a copy. Authors may also have relied on mischaracterizations of the book available in other publications instead of reading the book themselves. Fortunately, this situation may be shortly ameliorated, as Cambridge University Press reissued the book in 2010.

Dynamic issues aside, there remain many references to Freeman (1984) which mischaracterize Freeman's work in relation to CSR. In the following pages, we identify three key mischaracterizations which appear to pervade the literature linking Freeman (1984) to CSR. We begin with (1) the assumption that Freeman (1984 – or in fact elsewhere) approves of CSR, (2) the assumption that Freeman (1984 – or again, any other of Freeman's stakeholder theory contributions) is about firms' relationships with society rather than with specific stakeholders, and (3) the assumption that Freeman (1984) is a normative work. We detail what Freeman really said in 1984 about each of these three issues, and discuss some of his subsequent contributions on each. We then identify several possible boundary markers between stakeholder theory and CSR. We conclude by offering a view of how both projects might be strengthened by a more explicit recognition of their differences.

The Three Key Mischaracterizations

(1) The assumption that Freeman (1984) approves of CSR
We have already noted that even as early as 1984, Freeman is ambivalent about CSR, identifying the tendency to understand CSR as an activity separate from the business operations of the firm as only the '*most troubling*' (our italics) of 'many criticisms of the research in corporate social responsibility' (Freeman, 1984: 40). Freeman's concerns were well founded. By 1984, CSR was already a widely used concept. Bowen (1953: 6), for example, had defined CSR as 'the obligations of businessmen [sic] to pursue those policies, to make those decisions, or to follow those lines of action which are desirable in terms of the objectives and values of our society'. However, Preston and Post (1975: 52) referred to the current state of conceptual development around CSR as 'frothy', 'vague' and 'ill-defined', and discomfort with the concept had already given rise to a movement to focus not on CSR as a benevolent activity, but rather on corporate social *responsiveness* as a set of business practices for responding to societal demands (Frederick, 1978/1994). Subsequent developments in both scholarly and practical circles (for example, Friedman, 1970; Carroll, 1979) encouraged the notion that CSR might be something altogether separate from the core operations of business.

  The foundations of stakeholder theory would rest, instead, on an integrative impulse. Freeman (1984: 40) writes that 'Given the turbulence that business organizations are currently facing and the very nature of the external environment, as consisting of economic and socio-political forces, there is a need for conceptual schemata which analyze these forces in an integrative fashion'. The stakeholder approach is meant to be that schemata (see also Waddock and Graves, 1997; Rowley and Berman, 2000). Freeman and Liedtka (1991: 92) explicitly call for the 'immediate demise' of CSR, and Freeman (1994) for the first time critically names CSR's tendency to treat 'business' as separate from 'ethics' as the 'separation thesis' (but see also Freeman, 2000; Martin and Freeman, 2004; Harris and Freeman, 2008; for non-Freeman authored discussions, see Sandberg, 2008, and Scherer and Patzer, this volume) and even later the separation 'fallacy' (Freeman, Martin and Parmar, 2007; Freeman, 2008a; see also Hart's 2005 'great trade-off illusion'). Instead, Freeman and other theorists recognize that successful (or even just lasting) businesses must meet stakeholder demands for responsible operations. Addressing the tendency to separate 'economic' and 'social' effects, Harrison and Freeman (1999: 483) refer to the distinction as 'arbitrary'. 'Indeed, one of the original ideas behind the stakeholder management approach', they write, 'was to try to find a way to integrate the economic and the social' (Harrison and Freeman, 1999: 483–4). Freeman (2005: 424) notes that 'the idea of "corporate social responsibility" is probably superfluous' if the argument of Freeman (1984) is correct, and Freeman et al.'s recent book (2010: 241), *Stakeholder Theory: The State of the Art,* continues to critique CSR, saying,

> The concept and capabilities of CSR, which rely on a separation between business and society and also a separation of business and ethics, fall short in addressing all the three problems that stakeholder theory aims to solve. The problem of value creation and trade does not fall into within the scope of CSR, unless the way in which a company creates value affects society negatively. CSR has nothing to say about how value is created, because ethics is an afterthought in the value-creation process.
>
> By adding a social responsibility to the existing financial responsibilities of the firm, CSR only exacerbates the problem of capitalism and ethics. The recent financial crises show the consequences of separating ethics from capitalism. The large banks and financial services firms all had CSR policies and programs, but because they did not see ethics as connected to what they do – to how they create value – they were unable to fulfill their basic responsibilities to their stakeholders and ended up destroying value for the entire economy.
>
> Managers need a way to think about these issues that is closely tied to their day-to-day activities. The discourse of CSR is abstracted from managerial concerns and does not embed ethics in the fabric of management. It keeps the description of capitalism and business as amoral and tries to add an ethical safeguard too late in the process. Without redescribing the managerial function as a moral function, the CSR literature perpetuates the interpretation of business that allows moral concerns to be marginalized.

(2)   The assumption that Freeman (1984) is about society

> Many have argued, from Adam Smith (1759) onward, that business is a social institution, but that its role can only be realized by an external environment which allows 'laissez faire capitalism'. Such a policy requires that the dominant mode of thought be oriented towards 'production', while recognizing, or at least saying, that business is a social institution. On the other hand, there have been calls for the nationalization of business activity on the ground that the modern corporation is too far removed from its social roots.
>
> Both approaches seem to miss the mark. (Freeman, 1984: 8)

Instead, Freeman (1984: 8) proposes 'the development of a theory, or picture, of the world which allows us to manage . . . more effectively'. That theory/picture is stakeholder theory – and is focused on stakeholders, not society. In defining stakeholders as 'any group or individual who can affect or is affected by the achievement of the organization's objectives' (1984: 46), and by equating stakeholder and legitimacy ('Stakeholder' connotes 'legitimacy', and while managers may not think that certain groups are 'legitimate' in the sense that their demands on the firm are appropriate, they had better give 'legitimacy' to these groups in terms of their ability to affect the direction of the firm' (1984: 45),[2] perhaps Freeman (1984) gives the initial impression that 'stakeholders' might refer to all of society, but he never equates 'stakeholders' and 'society' in the 1984 book or elsewhere (though several of Freeman's (1984: 101–7) hypothetical 'enterprise strategies' are society-directed – as they are in Freeman and Gilbert, 1988).

Freeman's more recent contributions work hard to delimit the network of stakeholders involved in a firm's value creation activities,[3] with one work stressing that stakeholder theory is not 'everything nonshareholder oriented' (Freeman, Wicks and Parmar, 2004: 365). Writing with John McVea, Freeman reinforces a 'names and faces approach' to firm relations with stakeholders, explicating how 'concrete business problems' can be solved by focusing on individual relationships (McVea and Freeman, 2005: 60). This approach, pioneered by Gilbert (1992: 177), takes its inspiration from Freeman's (1984) insistence on the importance of stakeholders rather than society, which remains apparent even when taking on a group as amorphous as 'community' (cf. Dunham, Freeman and Liedtka, 2006). Other more recent work (Freeman, Velamuri and Moriarty, 2006: 5; Freeman, Harrison and Wicks, 2007: 99) substitutes 'stakeholder' for 'social' in CSR, emphasizing that stakeholder theory is meant to shift attention away from the relationship between the corporation and an amorphous 'society' and focus instead on the nature of its relationships with particular stakeholders. As Freeman et al. (2010: 260) emphasize (their italics),

> Stakeholder theory enters in the CSR debate by suggesting that the managers of the corporations have a responsibility not simply (and vaguely) to serve the *general interests* of society (which society? In today's global economy, where even small firms have dealings involving partners in several countries, with different social, legal, and ethical contexts, the definition of 'society' as if it was a unique entity becomes very problematic), but rather to serve the interests of *the corporation's stakeholders . . .*

Freeman-consistent stakeholder theorists evidence a similar predisposition. A growing stream of literature describes the reciprocal nature of the obligations firms owe to their stakeholders and those owed by stakeholders to firms (Goodstein and Wicks, 2007; Bosse, Phillips and Harrison, 2008; Elms and Phillips, 2009). This work stresses that corporate responsibility requires stakeholders to act responsibly as well, and begins to specify some of those stakeholder responsibilities – as well as corporate responsibilities. Phillips (2003) provides a particularly detailed justification of reciprocal moral responsibilities between firms and stakeholders, and both Goodstein and Wicks (2007) and Elms and Phillips (2009) provide particularly detailed descriptions of some of the content of those obligations. These treatments, and others (Palazzo and Scherer, 2006; Scherer and Palazzo, 2007), all suggest that this content should be established through discourse between and among companies and stakeholders.

(3)   The assumption that Freeman (1984) is a normative work
Freeman (1984) goes to great lengths to avoid making a moral argument concerning how firms should manage stakeholders. Many discerning readers have recognized this effort. In identifying the literature examining the moral foundations of stakeholder theory, for example, Phillips, Freeman and Wicks (2003: 481) do not include Freeman (1984). Langtry (1994: 432) notes: 'In earlier work, Freeman offered a morally neutral definition of a stakeholder. Perhaps the idea was to leave the ground uncluttered as a starting point either for subsequent moral argument or for nonmoral discussion of effective management strategies and techniques.'

Yet, there remains a tendency to look to *Strategic Management: A Stakeholder Approach* for the roots of a moral argument Freeman would later make, under the acknowledged influence of Gilbert (Freeman and Gilbert, 1988; see Freeman, 1994: 420, n12 for this acknowledgment). Indeed, subsequent works – these include Freeman and Gilbert (1988), Evan and Freeman (1989/1993), Freeman (1994) and Wicks, Gilbert and Freeman (1994) – would afford Freeman venues for that moral argument, which has, in turn, given rise to a host of similar attempts to justify stakeholder theory (see Phillips, Freeman and Wicks, 2003: 481 for a list).

One possible explanation for this confusion is that Freeman himself (1984) tended to use the word normative more broadly than the term has subsequently come to be used in the business ethics literature. Recognizing that his prescriptions did not rise to the level of morally absolute categorical imperatives demanded by Kantian ethics (Kant, 1787/1929), Freeman suggests that his prescriptions are normative hypothetical imperatives, based on means–ends rationality. Subsequent writers in the business ethics field have tended to reserve the term *normative* (that is, 'normative theory', 'normative inquiry') for morally laden discourse designed to justify an argument concerning how managers should behave, if they are to behave morally. In an influential article distinguishing normative and empirical research in business ethics, Donaldson (1994: 158–9; see also current volume) offers an elaborate definition of the term:

> If a theory or proposition is normative, then it is action-guiding, or as moral philosophers often say, 'prescriptive.' By saying this I mean to exclude mere factual assertions, including ones that certain means will achieve (or maximize) certain ends. Hence the statement, 'Pull the trigger and you will kill Jones,' is, strictly speaking, a descriptive statement, not a normative one, whereas the statement 'You should pull the trigger and kill Jones,' qualifies as normative.

He continues:

> Often statements appear normative but are disguised empirical statements. Business schools abound with statements specifying means for achieving ends in contexts where the ends are so well-accepted they go unmentioned. For example, the statement: 'Include countercyclical strategic business units in your corporate portfolio,' is usually intended as a prescription to achieve business ends, and hence is a shortened version of the hypothetical statement, 'If . . . (you want more constant corporate earnings) or (higher corporate profits), then . . . include countercyclical strategic business units in your corporate portfolio.' That is to say, the reasoning is 'means-ends' reasoning, and predicts a higher probability of achieving a given end if a certain action or policy is undertaken. It is not, consequently, a normative statement in the sense defined above, and fails in the class Immanuel Kant (1959) called the 'hypothetical imperative.'

In the same special issue on this subject, Weaver and Treviño (1994: 130) simplify the distinction still further, equating *normative* work with 'moral inquiry'. And in applying the oft-cited descriptive-empirical/instrumental/ normative distinction to stakeholder research, Donaldson and Preston (1995: 71) simply define normative stakeholder inquiry as 'the identification of moral or philosophical guidelines for the operation and management of corporations'.

Defining normative inquiry as Donaldson and most subsequent researchers have and equating *normative* with *morally normative,* we can see that Freeman (1984) is not normative. Though Freeman intends to prescribe action, his prescriptions boil down to the simple phrase, 'If you want to manage effectively, then you must take your stakeholders into account in a systematic fashion' (1984: 48). This differs little from the sort of 'disguised empirical statement' that Donaldson refers to. Moreover, by Freeman's (1984) own admission, his prescriptions are not intended to satisfy the demand that the definition of moral absolutes requires.

It is possible, of course, to argue that all prescriptive stances have, at least, implicit moral underpinnings – that, in short, not only are all normative statements prescriptive but all prescriptive statements are normative. Thus, even as Freeman explicitly avoids positing either a moral case for stakeholder responsiveness or elaborating a justification for such an argument, a reader might insist that the prescriptions are nonetheless implicitly moral and, therefore, normative.[4] However, looking for the underlying moral premise of Freeman (1984) in its text often leads to quite perverse outcomes, in which one might ascribe a moral position to Freeman (1984) quite different from where his later normative work points. Freeman (2005: 426) describes just such an experience:

> While I was at Minnesota, Dan Gilbert was a doctoral student. I sat in on one of his classes to assess his teaching, and the class I chose was one in which he was using my book, and arguing to the students that I was a Utilitarian. As an ardent Rawlsian, at the time, I was appalled, and determined to fix this inadequacy in the book, so we began to work on *Corporate Strategy and the Search for Ethics* [1988].

Another plausible gloss on the normative character of Freeman's (1984) prescriptions is that it is actually quite compatible with Friedman's (1962, 1970) notion of managerial effectiveness as an instrumental means to shareholder wealth (Goodpaster, 1991; Donaldson and Preston, 1995). For those relying on Freeman's thinking as a foil to Friedman, citing Freeman (1984) produces results antithetical to those intended.

Of course, all this would seem a mere matter of semantics, if those who mischaracterize Freeman (1984) as normative were not actually ascribing specific moral content to the book. Two more specific claims are that (a) Freeman (1984) is about stakeholder rights and (b) that Freeman (1984) advocates a fiduciary duty to stakeholders. We can look more closely at Freeman (1984) to put these claims into context. On the first, Freeman (1984: 196) does note that: 'The stakeholder approach developed in the preceding chapters advocates that we have a thorough understanding of our stakeholders and calls for the recognition that there are times when stakeholders must participate in the decision-making processes of the firm [also see Freeman and Reed, 1983].' However, neither this statement nor any in the book more comprehensively argues for stakeholder recognition or participation on the basis of stakeholder rights. Evan and Freeman (1989/1993: 76) appears to be Freeman's first use of a rights-based argument:

> We argue that the legal, economic, political, and moral challenges to the currently received theory of the firm, as a nexus of contracts among the owners of the factors of production and customers, require us to revise this concept along essentially Kantian lines. That is, each of these stakeholder groups has a right not to be treated as a means to some end, and therefore must participate in determining the future direction of the firm in which they have a stake.

And: 'if the modern corporation requires treating others as means to an end, then these others must agree on, and hence participate (or choose not to participate) in, the decisions to be used as such' (Evan and Freeman, 1989/1993: 78).

Regarding the second claim, Freeman (1984: 249) explicitly leaves extension of fiduciary duty to stakeholders to future research. Evan and Freeman (1989/1993: 75–6) take up the subject, writing: 'Our thesis is that we can revitalize the concept of management capitalism by replacing the notion that managers have a duty to stockholders with the concept that managers bear a fiduciary duty to stakeholders.' They also go so far as to advocate a stakeholder board of directors 'comprised of representatives of five stakeholder groups, including employees, customers, suppliers, stockholders, and members of the local community, as a well as a representative of the corporation' as a 'structural [mechanism] to make a stakeholder management conception practicable' (Evan and Freeman 1989/1993: 83). Later versions (meaning that much of the text is the same) of Evan and Freeman (1989/1993) – such as Freeman (2002) – continue to argue for stakeholder rights and a fiduciary duty to stakeholders, but remove 'Kantian Capitalism' both from the title of the article and the argument within. Advocacy for a stakeholder board of directors is also eliminated. Even later textbook contributions about stakeholder theory evolve to Freeman's modern focus on his '"pragmatist argument" that suggests we see managing for stakeholders as a new narrative about business that lets us improve the way we currently create value for each other' (Freeman, 2008b: 40; Freeman, 2009: 56). Other post-1984 contributions are consistent. Freeman and McVea (2005: 60–61) write: 'A managerial approach [to stakeholder theory] would not attempt to justify the existence of the firm, similar to many normative theories. Rather, it would focus on how managers make decisions that create value.'

Specifically in reference to organizational democracy, Harrison and Freeman write: 'Organizational democracy should be pursued only if there is some practical or economic reason for doing so' (2004: 52). Freeman (2005: 422) notes that 'Evan saw [the stakeholder] project as a way to democratize the large corporation' – but in re-writing Evan and Freeman (1989/1993) as the sole author and leaving out the stakeholder board of directors and so forth, Freeman does not appear to share this vision of the stakeholder project.

Those who would seek (and cite) the true spirit of Freeman (1984) might, with Langtry (1994), appreciate the morally neutral tone of the book, especially (given this chapter's focus) his treatment of social responsibility as one possible form of enterprise strategy. Freeman's (1984: 90) discussion of enterprise strategy 'that answers the question, "What *should* we do?"' (Freeman's italics) – is based in a previous explicitly *strategic* literature on enterprise strategy including Schendel and Hofer (1979) and Hofer et al. (1980). While Freeman's discussion of enterprise strategy includes reference to explicitly normative enterprise strategies (for example, the Rawlsian), his 1984 treatment of these strategies is illustrative (that is, some firms *might* pursue such strategies) rather than prescriptive (that is, firms *should* choose a particular strategy). On p. 91, Freeman notes that:

> Enterprise level strategy does not necessitate a particular set of values, nor does it require that a corporation be 'socially responsive' in a certain way. It does examine the need, however, for an explicit and intentional attempt to answer the question for 'what do we stand for'.

He writes further (p. 107):

> It is very easy to misinterpret the foregoing analysis [of enterprise strategy] as yet another call for corporate social responsibility or business ethics. While these issues are important in their own right, enterprise level strategy is a different concept. We need to worry about enterprise level strategy for the simple fact that corporate survival depends in part on there being some 'fit' between the values of the corporation and its managers, the expectations of stakeholders in the firm and the societal issues which will determine the ability of the firm to sell its products.

On p. 110, he emphasizes, 'The purpose of analyzing enterprise level strategy . . . has not been to argue for one or another of the five strategies. Rather, I believe it is important for us to understand honestly whatever our enterprise strategy happens to be' And, towards the end of the book (p. 210), he repeats,

> I have shown that the stakeholder approach offers no concrete, unarguable prescriptions for what a corporation should stand for. Rather, it tries to make available the variety of flavors which are available for choice, by surfacing the possible combinations of stakeholders, values, and societal issues. Thus, while the stakeholder approach to strategic management is put forth here as a normative theory, it is not normative in the sense that is prescribes particular positions of moral worth to the actions of managers.

Thus we suggest that while it is possible to cite *other* Freeman publications for an explicitly moral argument about stakeholder responsiveness, that argument is not explicit in Freeman (1984).

EXPLORING THE STAKEHOLDER–CSR FRONTIER

> Good fences make good neighbors only when there is some general agreement on where the fences should go.
>
> Michael Walzer (1994: 66)

Given the focus of the stakeholder research tradition and its ambivalence toward the concept of CSR, the question remains: what is the relationship between stakeholder theory and CSR? If, as we have suggested, there are important differences between these two traditions, where do those boundaries lie? In this section of the chapter, we suggest some possible boundary markers between stakeholder theory and CSR. We then argue that, by demarcating the frontier between the two domains, we can identify important opportunities for future research that might otherwise have been obscured by the overlap between the two concepts.

Boundary #1: Business-centric Versus Society-centric Theory

The first boundary marker concerns the primary level of analysis addressed by work in the respective domains. From the outset, stakeholder theory has been about better business, not a better world – at least, not necessarily or directly. If we take Freeman (1984: 46) seriously, that stakeholder management is primarily intended 'to chart a direction for the firm', then stakeholder theory must be primarily concerned with the firm. As Donaldson and Preston (1995) state the matter, stakeholder theory must be 'managerial', and its aim must be to improve the ways in which a firm engages in the business of creating and distributing value. If stakeholder theory does lead to societal betterment (cf. Walsh, Weber and Margolis, 2003), it will primarily arrive there indirectly through the improvement of a firm's approach to strategic management and the indirect effects that these changes might have on society as a whole.

Turning to the scholarly enterprise, the phenomena of interest to stakeholder theorists are primarily outcomes at what Freeman (1984; referring explicitly to the organization theory of Dill and others) might identify as organization 'set' level phenomena – those that reside in the relationships of individual firms and those groups with which each firm interacts. As our analysis of the literature referencing Freeman (1984) suggests, the vast majority of researchers honor this original focus, both in their selection of outcome variables and in the level of analysis of the explanations they posit for these outcomes. For example, Jones (1995) predicts firm performance as a function of the honesty and integrity of a firm's behavior toward its immediate stakeholders. Freeman, Harrison and Wicks (2007) seek to prescribe ways for firms to collaborate more fully and effectively with their employees, other suppliers, and customers to create new value for all concerned. Frooman (1999; Frooman and Murrell, 2005) explores the sources of conflict in firm–stakeholder relationships and accounts for stakeholder behaviors (that is, strategic choice) as a function of the resource dependencies present in firm–stakeholder relationships. In each instance, the phenomena being explored reside at the organization–stakeholder set level, and the causal accounts, advanced implicitly or explicitly, rely not on macro-social context or individual psychology but rather on dynamics at the set level.

By contrast, CSR research is neither focused on core business activities nor primarily interested in improving business outcomes. Indeed, to the extent that CSR research examines individual firm behaviors, such actions are weighed in the context of interactions with society as a whole, and the outcomes of concern are societal level phenomena as diverse as poverty reduction (Porter and Kramer, 2006), world peace (Fort, 2007; 2008; Fort and Schipani, 2004) and the reduction of other human misery (Margolis and Walsh, 2003). Its focus is rightly on societal outcomes. It sometimes envisions business as a voluntary contributor in the cross-sectoral collaborations that often produce better societal outcomes. More often, it identifies those ways in which business presents an obstacle to societal betterment.

In the early days of stakeholder research, there was still some hope that the stakeholder tradition would come to encompass both of these approaches. At the Toronto Conference, a formative moment in the development of current stakeholder research, Wood (1994) suggested that stakeholder theory might come to encompass both *firm* and *system* levels of analysis.[5] The former would focus on those dynamics that surround firms and their stakeholder sets. Thus, for example, firm-level stakeholder research would focus on why managers prioritize stakeholder claims as they do (Mitchell, Agle and Wood, 1997). The latter level of analysis would concern those impacts and outcomes of stakeholder management at the social system level of analysis. Ostensibly, this is where thinking would occur about the institution of business, its role in society, and the place of multiple constituent interests in societal priorities. Claims, for example, that society must recognize and balance the needs of multiple stakeholders (for example, Alstott and Ackerman, 2000) derive from a system-level stakeholder approach.

There are probably several reasons why this dual-formulation has not been more widely accepted – why, indeed, the boundary between stakeholder and CSR research is so readily discernible. First, though there is a growing demand for the study of societal level impacts of organizational action (Friedland and Alford, 1991; Stern and Barley, 1996), societal and political outcomes like poverty, war, and civic engagement are complex and require the attention of those most readily trained to study them. It is little surprise that some of the most promising streams of research in the CSR domain, concerning notions of citizenship and cross-sectoral collaboration, have attracted the attention of business and society scholars trained primarily as political scientists (for example, Moon, Crane and Matten, 2005) and sociologists (for example, Gray and Wood, 1991).

Second, the decision to focus on managerial theory that will improve a firm's ability to create value and achieve competitive advantage derives from a motivation qualitatively different from the desire to improve society. This has been the subject of critique among those CSR scholars who worry that the managerial focus of stakeholder research borders on outright managerialism (Marens, 2004; Wood, 2008). The explicit commitment to communitarian values evident in some work on CSR (for example, Waddock, 2006) is not as widely shared or as explicitly articulated either in Freeman's work or in those that have built on his work. Quite the opposite is true, in fact. Freeman and Phillips (2002), for example, argue for a form of 'stakeholder capitalism' that is explicitly libertarian and premised on freedom and voluntary action.

Finally, we suspect that a third, more practical consideration has prevented stakeholder researchers from taking up the charge to extend the stakeholder view to the system level. The simple fact is that firm–stakeholder dynamics, at least as they occur at the set level, might not account for very much of the variance of phenomena occurring at the societal system level. Admittedly, there have been few attempts at multi-level theory (Klein, Tosi and Cannella, 1999) to account for societal phenomena as a function of set-level dynamics. However, stakeholder researchers seem to share a tacit belief that the main value of stakeholder theory is to account for the more immediate relationship between a firm's approach to stakeholder management and firm-level outcomes such as performance.

Boundary #2: Identification Theories

An alternative way to conceive of the boundary between stakeholder theory and CSR is to attend to which actors are identified as legitimate claimants on the firm. While Freeman's (1984: 46) widely cited definition of a stakeholder as 'any group or individual who can affect or is affected by the achievement of the organization's objectives' initially seems broad in cast, the practical thrust of the rest of the book clearly identifies a fairly bounded set of actors as stakeholders. For largely pragmatic reasons, he sets forth the familiar hub-and-spoke model with only a handful of familiar stakeholder labels: customers, shareholders, employees and so forth.

Nowhere is this pragmatic predisposition more apparent than in his discussion of how firms might monitor stakeholders. Though he urges managers to be fairly comprehensive, Freeman (1984) acknowledges that there are conditions that demand more active monitoring and those that demand little or none; these depend on (a) how sure managers are about how stakeholders will behave and (b) how critical the stakeholder's support is to success. 'Constant monitoring of the interactions between organization and stakeholder,' he writes (1984: 173) 'is called for in those cases where the manager is rather uncertain about the stakeholder and where the stakeholder's support is crucial. Where there is a higher degree of certainty the manager must keep an open mind, and may even initiate research to validate the model that is being used.' For situations of high certainty and low importance, Freeman urges firms to place monitoring on the 'back burner' (Freeman, 1984: 173). Implicit throughout this prescription is the notion that companies have limited energy and resources for attending to, monitoring and accommodating stakeholders, and some system of priority is essential to any notion of stakeholder legitimacy. If managers need, as Freeman asserts, to accord legitimacy to those stakeholders that can obviously affect them, the implicit corollary is that there must be some boundary condition by which the firm decides not to acknowledge or devote significant resources to groups and organizations that, though technically defined as stakeholders, do not merit managers' attention.

Over the ensuing years since Freeman (1984), stakeholder researchers have similarly posited a fairly limited set of customary stakeholders and accepted that most firm–stakeholder dynamics can be understood as applying within this handful of primary relationships. Given this focus, one of the major tasks of stakeholder theory is not simply to identify who matters, or who should be considered a stakeholder, but to seek boundary constraints defining who might not be considered a stakeholder at all (Mitchell, Agle and Wood, 1997). Phillips (2003) elaborates one possible rationale, arguing that most claims on the firm by secondary actors (for example, NGOs, unions, and so on) merely derive from their relationship to other stakeholders with a more direct, legitimate claim on the firm (customers, employees). The basic assumption in this work is that the set must be bounded and relatively narrow (a) if the term stakeholder is to have any meaning at all (Clarkson, 1995) and (b) if the theory is to be managerial and, thus, practicable (Freeman, 1984).

CSR research, on the other hand, tends to cast its net quite broadly, so as to include groups and individuals that might, ostensibly, have little to do with the operations of the firm but play a key role in society at large. Indeed, insofar as CSR explicitly includes attention to discretionary matters, the purview of CSR research naturally includes many claims, issues and groups that managers and their companies explicitly do not need to attend, though they choose to do so anyway (Carroll, 1979). The very notion of responsibility derives not from the specific claims of singular groups but from the power that companies have accrued to influence a broad range of groups and issues and the general obligation to society as a whole – to stakeholders in the aggregate – to use this power wisely (Davis and Blomstrom, 1975). Thus, for example, CSR discourse in the 1980s frequently included calls for divestment from South Africa, despite the fact that many of the organizations and businesses being criticized had little or no direct impact on or relationship with the apartheid system. Similarly, that today's CSR movement often proscribes investment in arms dealers says little about how these companies treat their employees, customers or suppliers, and much more about the general place in society such industries occupy. It is, perhaps, no coincidence that the defining cases in CSR are often about those matters for which advocates hope companies will come to care, if only because these companies have the ability to make positive changes in society as a whole.

We note, then, two important implications of how the stakeholder and CSR literatures engage with the identification problem. First, because CSR acknowledges such a broad range of claims, it tests the very usefulness of the term stakeholder. It is natural, in fact, to eschew the term stakeholder itself as relatively meaningless and depict problems and concerns as 'social issues', that is those that have import for society as a whole (Clarkson, 1995). The prisoner of conscience in China has no meaningful stake in Microsoft or Google per se, yet CSR advocates might well point to human rights violations as a legitimate and important concern for any firm that would do business there (Santoro, 2000). Within a societal scheme, the meaning of the term stakeholder breaks down, in favor of constituencies within a pluralist system (Epstein, 1969), interested parties relative to a certain issue (Mahon and Wartick, 2003), or members of a much broader social field (Friedland and Alford, 1991). Second, stakeholder and CSR research rest on almost inverted assumptions about why the relationships they identify might be important. Stakeholder research, at its narrowest, urges firms to attend to those groups that have the power to affect them (Freeman, 1984) and, at its broadest, to include those groups that lack the power to mitigate the effects of company behavior (Post, Preston and Sachs, 2002). CSR, on the other hand, urges firms to attend to social issues beyond the scope of company behavior and, in many cases, to do so not because societal actors have the ability to affect firm objectives but because firms have the ability to affect societal objectives (Bowen, 1953).

Boundary #3: Texture

A third way to mark the boundary is to acknowledge the differing textures of stakeholder and CSR research. By texture, we mean specifically the nature of the research enterprise and, in particular, the degree to which research aims toward either a universal conception of its subject or a particular understanding of it. Stakeholder research tends, even at its most abstract, to exhibit a preference for the particular. For example, Jones (1995) pursues an ambitious marriage of economics and ethics in his instrumental stakeholder theory; however, his research propositions are, by no means, statements of universal relationships. Rather, in a way uncommon in management research, he points to specific relationships between firm behaviors (for example, the adoption of poison pills, executive pay levels, and so on) and firm performance that should hold if the general principle of instrumental stakeholder theory holds. For his part, Freeman shares this concern with the particular, dating back to his 1984 book. The familiar hub-and-spoke model placing the firm at the center and major stakeholders around in a circle has received much criticism for being over-simplistic and unrealistic (Rowley, 1997; Werhane, this volume). Of course, Freeman (1984) anticipates this critique and explicitly acknowledges that the generic hub-and-spoke model *is* over-simplistic and unrealistic. He (1984: 54) writes:

> Unfortunately, most attempts at 'stakeholder analysis' end with the construction of Exhibit 3.1 [the hub-and-spoke model]. . . . 'Generic stakeholders' refers to 'those categories of groups who can affect . . .' While 'Government' is a category, it is EPA, OSHA, FTC, Congress, etc. who can take actions to affect the achievement of an organization's purpose. Therefore, for stakeholder analysis to be meaningful Exhibit 3.1 must be taken one step further. Specific stakeholder groups must be identified.

In recent years, Freeman takes this approach a step further and, borrowing a term from Gilbert (1992), urges a 'names and faces' approach to stakeholder management, in which there is growing awareness of whom the firm is dealing with in its stakeholder set. After all, businesses are created and perpetuated by collections of idiosyncratic individuals who create relationships rather than merely occupying roles (McVea and Freeman, 2005). This impulse – to create a stakeholder tradition with a strong preference for the particular and local – gravitates somewhat against the desire for generalizable theory in management. As such, the particularistic project envisioned in Freeman (1984) and re-articulated in McVea and Freeman (2005) remains only partially realized in stakeholder research at large. Yet, it influences even the most ambitious theoretical works (for example, Rowley, 1997; Frooman, 1999; Rowley and Moldoveanu, 2003) to rely on and elaborate specific examples of each theoretical relationship in greater detail than is often found in other literatures.

By contrast, CSR research has a very different texture, characterized by a preference for the universal rather than the particular. The earliest work in CSR was not far removed from the names and faces approach. Individual case studies dominated the literature (Sethi, 1971; Post, 1978), and the early conceptual talk suggested that business might have very specific responsibilities that could be enumerated (Bowen, 1953). While the assertion that CSR mattered was, itself, ambitious, the intellectual enterprise was somewhat more limited in scope. Increasingly, however, a dominant motif in the responsibility literature was the creation of a CSR term that encompassed the many facets of the phenomenon. Frederick (1978/1994; 1998) elaborates a series of reconceptions of CSR to emphasize its different normative and descriptive potentialities. With the advent of the new construct of corporate social performance (CSP), Carroll (1979) takes this theoretical work one step further and imagines a way to locate any given firm in three-dimensional space, such that all of a firm's interactions with society might be described at a glance. Others followed suit (Wartick and Cochran, 1985; Wood, 1991a and b); like Carroll, they explicitly acknowledged a desire to describe the whole of a firm's social performance, including the wide range of issues it faces, the principles to which it adheres, the processes by which it responds to societal demands, and the impacts it has on society. In turn, this gave rise to a burgeoning empirical literature on how a firm's CSP might relate to its financial performance (Griffin and Mahon, 1997; Waddock and Graves, 1997; Margolis and Walsh, 2001; Orlitzky, Schmidt and Rynes, 2003). This empirical work rests on an impulse, present in much earlier work (for example, Moscowitz, 1972) but made much more sophisticated in recent years, not only to create a generalizable description of the entirety of a firm's behavior with respect to society but also to capture this conceptual notion in a single measure. This ambition has drawn methodological and conceptual critiques (Rowley and Berman, 2000; Mattingly and Berman, 2006; see also Jones, this volume, for the role stakeholder theory might play in overcoming these critiques). What remains unquestioned within the tradition, however, is the universalistic aims of the project.

   To acknowledge this boundary, of course, is not to critique one or the other literature as insufficiently rigorous or scholarly. Insofar as stakeholder research has taken up the challenge to explore specific relationships, practices and cases, it has become a stronger, more well-grounded and more managerial theory (cf. Donaldson and Preston, 1995; Wood and Jones, 1995). On the other hand, with its emphasis on the universal and general, CSR research has become well placed to bear the standard for business and society research at large, helping to establish the economic case for why firms should attend to society. This textural contrast may reflect the different motivations and subject matters captured along the previous two boundaries, but it goes further in emphasizing that the two literatures differ not only in *what* and *why* they exist but in *how* they conduct their research.

Boundary #4: The Source of Normative Claims

One thing that stakeholder and CSR research share is a concern not only for understanding and explaining empirical reality but also for exploring normative considerations. They offer insights into how business both *can* and *should* interact with their stakeholders and with society. The explicitly normative nature of these two domains, however, tends to obscure somewhat different moral foundations, as the normative claims of stakeholder theory and CSR derive from very different sources. Of the two, stakeholder theory is the more explicitly normative enterprise. Though Freeman (1984) makes no moral claims, his later work explicitly acknowledges stakeholders and firms as moral agents, obliged to respect each other's dignity and autonomy. This normative stance becomes the so-called normative core around which stakeholder theory is built (Donaldson and Preston, 1995), such that some have held that one of the few propositions uniting stakeholder researchers of all stripes is a belief in the intrinsic worth of stakeholders (Jones and Wicks, 1999). The interplay between normative and empirical research remains one of the defining features of the stakeholder field (Berman and Johnson-Cramer, 2009).

The critical scholarly question, in this regard, is why firms should treat their stakeholders with respect or honor their claims on firm resources. What is the source of this moral obligation? What are its limits? Many stakeholder researchers have offered answers, rooted in feminist (Wicks, Gilbert and Freeman, 1994), Kantian (Evan and Freeman, 1989/1993), contractarian (Donaldson and Dunfee, 1999), Rawlsian fairness (Phillips, 2003) and even libertarian (Freeman and Phillips, 2002) ethical theories. To no small degree, this quest for a normative core for stakeholder theory remains one of the most vital areas of research in business ethics. What unites these diverse efforts is the basic assumption that one of the main sources for normative claims on business behavior is its willing engagement in relationships with stakeholders. In other words, the various obligations on firms and their managers arise from a fairness-based obligation to reciprocate contributions and support from fellow participants in a cooperative scheme (Phillips, 2003). Alternatively, firms and their stakeholders comprise members of a common local moral community, bound by moral norms which they create and constitute together (Donaldson and Dunfee, 1999). Or, by virtue of their common humanity, firms owe duties to their stakeholders to respect their intrinsic worth, dignity and autonomy – neither coercing them nor seeking to behave opportunistically

toward them (Freeman, 1994). In each argument, the source of the normative claims is the obligation that arises from the direct relationship between
the firm and its stakeholders. Put simply, if firms want to participate in a
cooperative scheme with inter-dependent groups like suppliers, customers
and employees, they generate certain obligations to these groups by virtue
of their partnership.

The CSR domain is admittedly less explicitly philosophical. The concept
of responsibility is, of course, morally laden and implies moral obligations. Bowen (1953), among others, referred explicitly to the moral underpinnings of the term. 'It is assumed, however, that as servants of society,'
he writes (1953: 6) '[Business people] must not disregard socially accepted
values or place their own values above those of society. Synonyms for
social responsibility are "public responsibility", "social obligations", and
"business morality".' This concern for the principles of responsibility
undergirds both empirical research and advocacy in the CSR domain. Yet,
the concept remains dramatically under-theorized. The work that has been
done to lay out the ethical case for CSR and to define the responsibilities
of business rests on the simple notion that firms (particularly corporations) have responsibilities to society because they are a legal, economic
and social product of society. The basic logic is the moral equivalent of
grant theory – a legal doctrine holding that corporations exist only as a
'special privilege conferred by the state' and as such could be bound (in
this case, legally) by whatever limitations the state sought to impose to
govern the public purpose for which the charter was granted (Horwitz,
1994: 72). CSR, reasoning by analogy, involves the moral obligations a
corporation has to the society which creates it; those obligations arise
reciprocally in return for the protections and privileges society grants (for
example, liability protection, tax status, speech rights, and so on). These
responsibilities are especially important where society grants the ability to
amass significant corporate power (Davis and Blomstrom, 1975).

As such, the term corporate *social* responsibility is no coincidence, as
CSR implies that the firm owes moral obligations to society rather than
to any particular stakeholder. This contrasts to the notion of corporate
stakeholder responsibility, increasingly in vogue to describe the obligations to stakeholders that obtain by virtue of the collaborations the firm
has entered into. It is no coincidence, then, that recent attempts to conceive of the ethical underpinnings have resorted to ideas like corporate
citizenship. When authors such as Waddock (2006), Wood and Logsdon
(2002), and both Palazzo and Scherer as well as Baumann (for example,
Palazzo and Scherer, 2006; Scherer, Palazzo and Baumann, 2006) appeal
to broad philosophical concepts such as citizenship, it is not to citizenship in a cooperative scheme like the stakeholder set but to citizenship in

society. Similarly, Nien-hê Hsieh's (2004) positive duty of assistance rests morally on Rawls's (1999) law of peoples, which applies to humanity by virtue of its common citizenship in society. Here, then, the boundary is at its starkest: CSR holds that the source of normative claims on the firm rests on the firm's relationship to society; stakeholder theory traces its normative claims to the firm's participation in the cooperative scheme comprised of the stakeholder set (Phillips, 2003). Here is the moral corollary to the society–stakeholder difference highlighted by the first boundary. An arms manufacturer or tobacco firm, for example, might well treat every one of its stakeholders appropriately (satisfying the normative claims on the firm) and yet underperform in CSR terms by failing to make society better, more healthy or more peaceful. By contrast, societal improvement is incidental to stakeholder theory; if firms create value and treat their immediate stakeholders appropriately, they might well contribute to societal well being, but there is no guarantee.

CROSSING CSR–STAKEHOLDER BOUNDARIES

> Before I built a wall I'd ask to know
> What I was walling in or walling out,
> And to whom I was like to give offence.
> Robert Frost (1969: 34)

To this point, we have identified four ways in which stakeholder research differs from CSR. These boundaries have their naissance in Freeman's seminal work (1984), and they are important both to understanding the legacy of that work and to assessing the current state of both fields (see Table 1.4). However, once we have demarcated these boundaries clearly, we may also find it helpful to explore the complementarities between the two domains. If fences sometimes make good neighbors, we may occasionally wonder, with Frost, what we may have chosen to constrain or rule out by building fences too high or drawing boundaries too sharply. And ironically, it may be when the two domains are most clearly distinguished that their potential for fruitful interchange is most obvious. This interchange may work in both directions and entail both normative and empirical research streams.

The Potential Influence of Stakeholder Theory on CSR

There are at least two ways in which distinguishing stakeholder and CSR research might help to advance the CSR domain. First, it may prompt further normative reflection about the concept of CSR. As we have argued,

Table 1.4   Possible boundary markers

	CSR	Stakeholder theory
Level of analysis	Systemic impacts on society (Wood, 1991a, 1991b, 1994)	Outcomes within organization set (Freeman, 1984; Post, Preston and Sachs, 2004; Freeman et al., 2010)
Identification theories	Broad (Carroll, 1979, 1989; Starik, 1994)	Narrow (Freeman, 1984; Clarkson, 1995; Phillips, 2003)
Texture	Universal (Waddock and Graves, 1997; Orlitzky, Schmidt and Rynes, 2003)	Particular (Freeman, 1984; McVea and Freeman, 2005)
Source of normative claims	Obligations to society (Wood and Logsdon, 2001; Hsieh, 2004, 2009)	Obligations to members of cooperative scheme (Jones and Wicks, 1999; Werhane and Freeman, 1999; Phillips, 2003)

CSR research remains normatively under-theorized. In part, this is because CSR researchers have relied so heavily on stakeholder theory for theoretical arguments justifying attention to actors not directly related to the business mission of the firm. It is, after all, Freeman's stakeholder theory (1994; Evan and Freeman, 1989/1993) to which CSR advocates turn to refute Friedman's (1962; 1970) assertion that the firm owes no obligation to society beyond the generation of economic returns. Yet, as the case for stakeholder responsibility stops short of positing a responsibility to society as a whole (Clarkson, 1995; Freeman, 2008a), it leaves CSR advocates to do their own normative theorizing on how moral obligations to society might exist above and beyond the obligation to treat particular stakeholders well.

Second, as CSR empirical research focuses on the societal outcomes of business behavior, stakeholder theory might become a valuable explanatory tool. To date, a common refrain in work on the relationship between corporate social performance and financial performance – the locus of much empirical CSR research – is that the stakeholder concept is primarily an organizing device. It offers a convenient list of relationships, a familiar shorthand describing the most convenient dimensions of a firm's relationship with society (Rowley and Berman, 2000). This shorthand obscures the real contribution of stakeholder theory, which has much to say about how firm–stakeholder relationships actually do and should unfold. As such it may be reasonable to propose that some society-level outcomes (for example, poverty, demographic shifts, civic engagement) – the phenomena of interest to CSR scholars – might be a function of the ways that firms tend to interact with their stakeholders in that society. At a minimum, recognizing the complexities of stakeholder theory will lend greater scholarly rigor and thus credibility to CSR research.

The Potential Influence of CSR on Stakeholder Theory

In the other direction, there are also at least two ways CSR research might serve as a resource for stakeholder theorists. First, just as distinguishing between CSR and stakeholder theory might encourage CSR theorists to engage in further normative reflection about CSR, it may also encourage additional normative reflection by stakeholder theorists. While we have argued that stakeholder theory is the more normatively developed domain, that development remains incomplete. The field is, for example, just beginning to move past a discussion focused on the *establishment* of a moral obligation to stakeholders (for example, Phillips, 2003), to a discussion of the content of those obligations (for example, Goodstein and Wicks, 2007; Elms and Phillips, 2009). Additional examination of the content of CSR programs in practice might help further advance the latter discussion. Distinguishing CSR from stakeholder theory might, however, also help stakeholder theorists to better identify the boundaries of the firm, and thus, clarify further to whom the firm owes a normative obligation.

Second, understanding a firm's approach to CSR may play a role in shaping specific firm–stakeholder relationships. How a firm responds to more general obligations to society may serve as an important signal to individual stakeholder groups about what sorts of treatment they can expect toward them. There is, for example, some evidence that overall corporate social performance influences employee and customer attitudes toward a firm (Turban and Greening, 1997; Sen and Bhattacharya, 2001; Luo and Bhattacharya, 2006). Extending these insights, we may wish to explore whether a firm's general reputation for CSR overshadows its behavior toward a particular stakeholder group in determining that group's satisfaction. Overall CSR might well moderate the commonly assumed relationship between stakeholder management and outcomes within the stakeholder set (satisfied stakeholders, reduced likelihood of stakeholder action and even financial returns). Already, stakeholder theorists have started to explore this possibility of a spill-over effect of unfairness toward one stakeholder in the attitudes of another (Bosse, Phillips and Harrison, 2009), and it would take little to argue that such justice considerations might extend beyond the bounds of the stakeholder set to unmet social needs which the firm has the capacity to address but fails to do so. Here, by drawing a boundary between the stakeholder preoccupation with the particular (including attention to specific stakeholder groups such as employees and customers) and the CSR tendency to direct attention to the universal (in terms of larger obligations to society), we potentially arrive at insights that draw upon both.

CONCLUSION

This chapter begins the conceptual work of tracing clear boundaries between stakeholder theory and CSR. But, in a much larger sense, this chapter, like the others in this volume, offers a meditation on the impact of Freeman's (1984) book on some of the central concepts in the field of business and society studies. Though often mischaracterized by later work, that book marks a seminal moment in the development of the field. For stakeholder theorists, the book legitimates inquiry into dynamics at the firm–stakeholder set level, a field of research which, 25 years later, we have only just started to understand. And for CSR theorists, the book represents a challenge to which the domain has not yet fully responded. Yet, the legacy of Freeman (1984) is much more complex than one chapter can convey. Freeman's viewpoint, initiated in 1984 but evolving in his prolific work since then, is complex, and mischaracterizations (including our own) are inevitable. The subtleties of Freeman's developing thought almost necessitate a road map. For us, this chapter is our attempt to offer one. For us, it has been a worthwhile project. The impact of Freeman's thinking on the field and on our own scholarly development has been profound. Thus, we think it fitting to conclude by offering our thanks and by expressing our certain expectation that, when 25 more years have passed, Freeman (1984) will still hold the relevance and inspiration for business and society studies that it does today.

ACKNOWLEDGMENTS

The authors would like to thank James P. Walsh for inspiring our methodology at the University of Washington Business School Stakeholder Theory Conference in 2006.

We would also like to thank Robert A. Phillips for the invitation to write this chapter, as well as for extensive comments on a previous version. We thank R. Edward Freeman for his encouragement, and Thomas M.

Jones and Megan Hess for comments associated with a discussion of this chapter in a doctoral seminar at the University of Virginia's Darden School of Business in 2010. We presented the earliest versions of this chapter at the 2009 annual meetings of the International Association for Business and Society and the Academy of Management, and are appreciative of participants' comments at each. All errors remain our own. Heather Elms gratefully acknowledges the support provided by a Kogod Research Professorship. Shawn Berman thanks Samuel Kunzman for assistance with the literature review and Brittany Crail for assistance with the production of the tables.

NOTES

1. In thinking about the relatively high rate of 'Substantive/Mischaracterization' references in *BEQ*, the authors hypothesized that this outcome might be associated with an expected relatively higher rate of normative arguments in *BEQ*, and thus a greater likelihood that Freeman (1984) would be referred to as a normative work (a substantive mischaracterization of Freeman (1984)). Arguably 17 of the 19 'Substantive/Mischaracterization' *BEQ* citations of Freeman (1984) appear to ascribe a normative position to Freeman (1984).

2. Freeman (1984) suggests that we understand this 'very weak sense' of legitimacy (1984: 23) 'in a managerial sense implying that it is "legitimate to spend time and resources" on stakeholders regardless of the appropriateness of their demands' (1984: 45). 'For the present time I shall put these questions [about a broader notion of legitimacy – including the relative legitimacy of stakeholder claims] aside, not because they do not bear fruitful research, but rather, I believe that first we must understand the weaker sense of "stakeholder legitimacy": if you want to be an effective manager, then you must take stakeholders into account.' (1984: 45). He also notes that 'Such a broad notion of "stakeholders" will include a number of groups who may not be "legitimate" in the sense that they will have vastly different values and agendas for action from our own. . ... For instance, some corporations must count "terrorist groups" as stakeholders. As unsavory as it is to admit that such "illegitimate" groups have a stake in our business, from the standpoint of strategic management, it must be done. Strategies must be put in place to deal with terrorists if they can substantially affect the operations of the business' (1984: 53). We note these details of Freeman's (1984) understanding of legitimacy partly because some references to Freeman (1984) suggest a stronger sense of the legitimacy of stakeholder interests.

3. Freeman and McVea (2001: 192) note specifically with respect to the CSR literature that 'there has been some confusion in the corporate responsibility literature around the priorities of stakeholders. There is one point of view that all stakeholders are equally important, simply because all have moral standing. It is difficult to document this position in the writings of stakeholder theorists, for instance in Freeman (1984), yet this idea that all stakeholders, defined widely, are equally important has been a barrier to further development of this theory.'

4. Thanks to Thomas M. Jones for bringing this point to our attention.

5. Wood (1994) is one of several papers from the Toronto Conference included in a special issue of *Business & Society*. The conference also resulted in two books (Clarkson, 1998; Clarkson Center for Business Ethics, 1999). See also Jones (current volume).

REFERENCES

Alstott, B.A. and Ackerman, A. 2000. *The Stakeholder Society.* New Haven, CT: Yale University Press.

Barnett, M.L. 2007. Stakeholder influence capacity and the variability of financial returns to corporate social responsibility. *Academy of Management Review,* **32**: 794–816.

Berman, S.L. and Johnson-Cramer, M.E. 2009. Stakeholder theory: seeing the field through the forest. Unpublished Working Paper.

Blau, P.M. 1964. *Exchange and Power in Social Life.* New York: Wiley.

Bosse, D.A., Phillips, R.A. and Harrison, J. 2009. Stakeholders, reciprocity and firm performance. *Strategic Management Journal,* **30**: 447–56.

Bowen, H. 1953. *The Social Responsibilities of the Businessman.* New York: Harper & Bros.

Campbell, J.L. 2007. Why would corporations behave in socially responsible ways? An institutional theory of corporate social responsibility. *Academy of Management Review,* **32**: 946–67.

Carroll, A.B. 1979. A three dimensional model of corporate performance. *Academy of Management Review,* **4**: 497–505.

Carroll, A.B. 1989. *Business and Society: Ethics and Stakeholder Management.* Cincinnati, OH: South-Western Publishing.

Clarkson Centre for Business Ethics. 1999. *Principles of Stakeholder Management.* Toronto: Clarkson Center for Business Ethics.

Clarkson, M.B.E. 1994. *A Risk-based Model of Stakeholder Theory.* Toronto: The Centre for Corporate Social Performance and Ethics.

Clarkson, M.B.E. 1995. A stakeholder framework for analyzing and evaluating corporate social performance. *Academy of Management Review,* **20**: 92–117.

Clarkson, M.B.E. 1998. *The Corporation and its Stakeholders: Classic and Contemporary Readings.* Toronto: University of Toronto Press.

Davis, K. and Blomstrom, R.L. 1975. *Business and Society: Environment and Responsibility.* New York: McGraw-Hill.

Donaldson, T. 1994. When integration fails: the logic of prescription and description in business ethics. *Business Ethics Quarterly,* **4**: 157–69.

Donaldson, T. and Dunfee, T.W. 1999. *Ties that Bind: A Social Contracts Approach to Business Ethics.* Cambridge, MA: Harvard University Press.

Donaldson, T. and Preston, L. 1995. The stakeholder theory of the corporation: concepts, evidence, and implications. *Academy of Management Review,* **20**: 65–91.

Dunham, L., Freeman, R.E. and Liedtka, J. 2006. Enhancing stakeholder practice: a particularized exploration of community. *Business Ethics Quarterly,* **16**: 23–42.

Durand, R. and Calori, R. 2006. Sameness, otherness? Enriching organizational change theories with philosophical considerations on the same and the other. *Academy of Management Review,* **31**: 93–114.

Elms, H. and Phillips, R.A. 2009. Private security companies and institutional legitimacy: corporate and stakeholder responsibility. *Business Ethics Quarterly,* **19**: 403–32.

Epstein, E.M. 1969. *The Corporation in American Politics.* Englewood Cliffs, NJ: Prentice Hall.

Evan, W.M. and Freeman, R.E. 1989/1993. A stakeholder theory of the modern corporation: Kantian capitalism. Reprinted in T.L. Beauchamp and N.E. Bowie (eds), *Ethical Theory and Business,* 4th edition, Englewood Cliffs, N.J.: Prentice-Hall, pp. 75–84.

Fort, T. 2007. *Business, Integrity and Peace: Beyond Geopolitical and Disciplinary Boundaries.* New Haven, CT: Yale University Press.

Fort, T. 2008. *Prophets, Profits, and Peace: The Positive Role of Business in Promoting Religious Tolerance.* Cambridge, UK: Cambridge University Press.

Fort, T.L. and Schipani, C.A. 2004. *The Role of Business in Fostering Peaceful Societies.* New York: Cambridge University Press.

Frederick, W.C. 1978/1994. From CSR1 to CSR2: the maturing of business-and-society thought. *Business & Society,* **33**: 150–64.

Frederick, W.C. 1998. Moving to CSR4: what to pack for the trip. *Business & Society,* **37**: 40–59.

Freeman, R.E. 1984. *Strategic Management: A Stakeholder Approach.* Marshfield, MA: Pitman Publishing Inc.

Freeman, R.E. 1994. The politics of stakeholder theory: some future directions. *Business Ethics Quarterly,* **4**: 409–21.

Freeman, R.E. 1999. Response: divergent stakeholder theory. *Academy of Management Review,* **24**: 233–6.

Freeman, R. E. 2000. Business ethics at the millennium. *Business Ethics Quarterly,* **10**: 169–80.

Freeman, R.E. 2002. Stakeholder theory of the modern corporation. In T. Donaldson, P.H. Werhane and M. Cording (eds), *Ethical Issues in Business: A Philosophical Approach,* 7th edition. Upper Saddle River, NJ: Pearson Education Inc.

Freeman, R.E. 2004. The stakeholder approach revisited. *Zeitschrift für Wirtschafts- und Unternehmensethik,* **5**: 228–41.

Freeman, R.E. 2005. The development of stakeholder theory: an idiosyncratic approach. In K. Smith and M.A. Hitt (eds), *Great Minds in Management: The Process of Theory Development.* New York: Oxford University Press.

Freeman, R.E. 2008a. Ending the so-called 'Friedman–Freeman' debate. In B.R. Agle, T. Donaldson, R.E. Freeman, M.C. Jensen, R.K. Mitchell and D. Wood (contributors), Dialogue: toward superior stakeholder theory. *Business Ethics Quarterly,* **18**(2): 153–90.

Freeman, R.E. 2008b. Managing for stakeholders. In T. Donaldson and P.H. Werhane (eds) *Ethical Issues in Business: A Philosophical Approach,* 8th edition. Upper Saddle River, NJ: Pearson Education Inc.

Freeman, R.E. 2009. Managing for stakeholders. In T. Beauchamp, N.E. Bowie and D.G. Arnold (eds), *Ethical Theory and Business,* 8th edition. Upper Saddle River, NJ: Pearson Prentice Hall.

Freeman, R.E. and Gilbert, D.R. 1988. *Corporate Strategy and the Search for Ethics.* Englewood Cliffs, NJ: Prentice-Hall, Inc.

Freeman, R.E. and Liedtka, J. 1991. Corporate social responsibility: a critical approach. *Business Horizons,* **34**: 92.

Freeman, R.E. and McVea, J. 2001. A stakeholder approach to strategic management. In M.A. Hitt, R.E. Freeman and J.S. Harrison (eds), *The Blackwell Handbook of Strategic Management.* Oxford, UK: Blackwell Publishers Ltd., pp. 189–207.

Freeman, R.E. and McVea, J. 2005. A names-and-faces approach to stakeholder management: how focusing on stakeholders as individuals can bring ethics and entrepreneurial strategy together. *Journal of Management Inquiry,* **14**: 57–69.

Freeman, R.E. and Phillips, R.A. 2002. Stakeholder theory: a libertarian approach. *Business Ethics Quarterly*, **12**: 331–49.

Freeman, R.E. and Reed, D. 1983. Stockholders and stakeholders: a new perspective on corporate governance. In C. Huizinga (ed.), *Corporate Governance: A Definitive Exploration of the Issues*. Los Angeles, CA: UCLA Extension Press.

Freeman, R.E., Harrison, J.S. and Wicks, A.C. 2007. *Managing for Stakeholders: Survival, Reputation, and Success*. New Haven, CT: Yale University Press.

Freeman, R.E., Martin, K. and Parmar, B. 2007. Stakeholder capitalism. *Journal of Business Ethics*, **74**: 303–14.

Freeman, R.E., Velamuri, S.R. and Moriarty, B. 2006. *Company Stakeholder Responsibility: A New Approach to CSR*. Charlottesville, VA: Business Roundtable Institute for Corporate Ethics.

Freeman, R.E., Wicks, A.C. and Parmar, B. 2004. Stakeholder theory and 'The corporate objective revisited'. *Organization Science*, **15**: 364–9.

Freeman, R.E., Harrison, J.S., Wicks, A.C., Parmar, B. and De Colle, S. 2010. *Stakeholder Theory: The State of the Art*. New York: Cambridge University Press.

Friedland, R. and Alford R.R. 1991. Bringing society back in: symbols, practices, and institutional contradictions. In W.W. Powell and P.J. DiMaggio (eds) *The New Institutionalism in Organizational Analysis*. Chicago, IL: University of Chicago Press, pp. 232–63.

Friedman, M. 1962. *Capitalism and Freedom*. Chicago, IL: University of Chicago Press.

Friedman, M. 1970. The social responsibility of business is to increase its profits. *New York Times Magazine*, September 13.

Frooman, J. 1999. Stakeholder influence strategies. *Academy of Management Review*, **24**: 191–205.

Frooman, J. and Murrell, A. 2005. Stakeholder influence strategies: the roles of structural and demographic determinants. *Business & Society*, **44**: 3–31.

Frost, R. 1969. *The Poetry of Robert Frost: The Collected Poems, Complete and Unabridged*. New York: Henry Holt & Co.

Gilbert, D.R. 1992. *The Twilight of Corporate Strategy: A Comparative Ethical Critique*. New York: Oxford University Press.

Goodpaster, K.E. 1991. Business ethics and stakeholder analysis. *Business Ethics Quarterly*, **1**: 53–73.

Goodstein, J.D. and Wicks, A.C. 2007. Corporate and stakeholder responsibility: making business ethics a two-way conversation. *Business Ethics Quarterly*, **17**: 375–98.

Gray, B. and Wood, D.J. 1991. Collaborative alliances: Moving from practice to theory. *The Journal of Applied Behavioral Science*, **27**: 3–22.

Griffin, J.J. and Mahon, J.F. 1997. The corporate social performance and corporate financial performance debate: twenty-five years of incomparable research. *Business & Society*, **36**: 5–31.

Harris, J. and Freeman, R.E. 2008. The impossibility of the separation thesis. *Business Ethics Quarterly*, **18**: 541–8.

Harrison, J.S. and Freeman, R.E. 1999. Stakeholders, social responsibility, and performance: empirical evidence and theoretical perspectives. *Academy of Management Journal*, **42**: 479–85.

Harrison, J.S. and Freeman, R.E. 2004. Special topic: democracy in and around organizations. *Academy of Management Executive*, **18**: 49–53.

Hart, S. 2005. *Capitalism at a Crossroads*. Upper Saddle River, NJ: Wharton School Publishing.

Hofer, C., Murray, E., Charan, R. and Pitts, R. 1980. *Strategic Management: A Casebook in Business Policy and Planning*. St. Paul, MN: West Publishing Co.

Horwitz, M.J. 1994. *The Transformation of American Law, 1870–1960: The Crisis of Legal Orthodoxy*. New York: Oxford University Press.

Hosmer, L.T. 1994. Strategic planning as if ethics mattered. *Strategic Management Journal*, **15** (Summer): 17–34.

Hsiesh, N-h. 2004. The obligations of transnational corporations: Rawlsian justice and the duty of assistance. *Business Ethics Quarterly*, **14**: 643–62.

Hsieh, N-h. 2009. Does global business have a responsibility to promote just institutions? *Business Ethics Quarterly*, **19**: 251–73.

Jamali, D., Zanhour, M. and Keshishian, T. 2009. Peculiar strengths and relational attributes of SMEs in the context of CSR. *Journal of Business Ethics*, **87**: 355–77.

Jones, T.M. 1995. Instrumental stakeholder theory: a synthesis of ethics and economics. *Academy of Management Review*, **20**: 404–37.

Jones, T.M. and Wicks, A.C. 1999. Convergent stakeholder theory. *Academy of Management Review*, **24**: 206–21.

Kant, I. 1787/1929. *Critique of Pure Reason*. New York: St. Martin's Press.

Kant, I. 1959. *Foundations of the Metaphysics of Morals*. L.W. Beck (trans.). New York: Liberal Arts Press.

Klein, K.I., Tosi, H. and Cannella, A.A. 1999. Multilevel theory building: benefits, barriers, and new developments. *Academy of Management Review*, **24**: 243–8.

Langtry, B. 1994. Stakeholder and the moral responsibilities of business. *Business Ethics Quarterly*, **4**: 431–43.

Love, E.G. and Kraatz, M. 2009. Character, conformity, or the bottom line? How and why downsizing affected corporate reputation. *Academy of Management Journal*, **52**: 314–35.

Luo, X. and Bhattacharya, C.B. 2006. Corporate social responsibility, customer satisfaction, and market value. *Journal of Marketing*, **70**(4): 1–18.

Mackey, A., Mackey, T.B. and Barney, J. 2007. Corporate social responsibility and firm performance: investor preferences and corporate strategies. *Academy of Management Review*, **32**: 817–35.

Mahon, J.F. and Wartick, S.L. 2003. Dealing with stakeholders: how reputation, credibility and framing influence the game. *Corporate Reputation Review*, **6**: 19–35.

Marens, R. 2004. Wobbling on a one-legged stool: the decline of American pluralism and the academic treatment of corporate social responsibility. *Journal of Academic Ethics*, **2**: 63–87.

Margolis, J.D. and Walsh, J.P. 2001. *People and Profits? The Search for a Link Between a Company's Social and Financial Performance*. Mahwah, NJ: Lawrence Erlbaum Associates, Inc.

Margolis, J.D. and Walsh, J.P. 2003. Misery loves companies: rethinking social initiatives by business. *Administrative Science Quarterly*, **48**: 268–305.

Martin, K. and Freeman, R.E. 2004. The separation of technology and ethics in business ethics. *Journal of Business Ethics*, **53**: 353–64.

Mattingly, J.E. and Berman, S.L. 2006. Measurement of corporate social action:

discovering taxonomy in the Kinder Lydenburg Domini ratings data. *Business & Society*, **45**: 20–46.

McVea, J.F. and Freeman, R.E. 2005. A names-and-faces approach to stakeholder management: how focusing on stakeholders as individuals can bring ethics and entrepreneurial strategy together. *Journal of Management Inquiry*, **14**: 57–69.

McWilliams, A. and Siegel, D. 2001. Corporate social responsibility: a theory of the firm perspective. *Academy of Management Review*, **26**: 117–27.

Mitchell, R.K., Agle, B.R. and Wood, D.J. 1997. Toward a theory of stakeholder identification and salience: defining the principle of who and what really counts. *Academy of Management Review*, **22**: 853–86.

Moon, J., Crane, A. and Matten, D. 2005. Can corporations be citizens? Corporate citizenship as a metaphor for business participation in society. *Business Ethics Quarterly*, **15**: 429–53.

Moscowitz, M. 1972. Choosing socially responsible stocks. *Business and Society Review*, **1**: 71–5.

Orlitzky, M., Schmidt, F.L. and Rynes. S.L. 2003. Corporate social and financial performance: a meta-analysis. *Organization Studies*, **24**: 403–41.

Paine, L.S. 2002. *Value Shift*. New York: McGraw-Hill.

Palazzo, G. and Scherer, A.G. 2006. Corporate legitimacy as deliberation: a communicative framework. *Journal of Business Ethics*, **66**: 71–88.

Phillips, R.A. 2003. *Stakeholder Theory and Organizational Ethics*. San Francisco, CA: Berrett Koehler Publishers, Inc.

Phillips, R.A., Freeman, R.E. and Wicks, A.C. 2003. What stakeholder theory is not. *Business Ethics Quarterly*, **13**(4): 479–502.

Porter, M.E. and Kramer, M.R. 2006. Strategy and society: the link between competitive advantage and corporate social responsibility. *Harvard Business Review*, December.

Post, J.E. 1978. Research on patterns of corporate response to social change. In L. Preston (ed.), *Research in Corporate Social Performance and Policy*. Greenwich, CT: JAI Press, pp. 89–112.

Post, J.E., Preston, L.E. and Sachs, S. 2002. *Redefining the Corporation: Stakeholder Management and Organizational Wealth*. Stanford, CA: Stanford Business Books.

Preston, L.E. and Post, J.E. 1975. *Private Management and Public Policy*. Englewood Cliffs, NJ: Prentice-Hall.

Rawls, J. 1999. *A Theory of Justice, Revised Edition*. Cambridge, MA: Harvard University Press.

Rowley, T. 1997. Moving beyond dyadic ties: a network theory of stakeholder influences. *Academy of Management Review*, **22**: 887–909.

Rowley, T. and Berman, S. 2000. A brand new brand of corporate social performance. *Business & Society*, **39**(4): 397–418.

Rowley, T.J. and Moldoveanu, M. 2003. When will stakeholder groups act? An interest- and identity-based model of stakeholder group mobilization. *Academy of Management Review*, **28**: 204–19.

Sandberg, J. 2008. Understanding the separation thesis. *Business Ethics Quarterly*, **18**(2): 213–32.

Santoro, M.A. 2000. *Profits and Principles: Global Capitalism and Human Rights in China*. Ithaca, NY: Cornell University Press.

Schendel, D.E. and Hofer, C.W. 1979. *Strategic Management: A New View of Business Policy and Planning*. Boston, MA: Little, Brown.

Scherer, A. and Palazzo, G. 2007. Toward a political conception of corporate responsibility: business and society seen from a Habermasian perspective. *Academy of Management Review*, **32**: 1096–120.

Scherer, A.G., Palazzo, G. and Baumann, D. 2006. Global rules and private actors: toward a new role of the transnational corporation in global governance. *Business Ethics Quarterly*, **16**: 505–32.

Sen, S. and Bhattacharya, C.B. 2001. Does doing good always lead to doing better? Consumer reactions to corporate social responsibility. *Journal of Marketing Research*, **38**: 225–43.

Sethi, S.P. 1971. *Up Against the Corporate Wall: Modern Corporations and Social Issues of the Seventies*. Englewood Cliffs, NJ: Prentice-Hall.

Singer, A.E. 1994. Strategy as moral philosophy. *Strategic Management Journal*, **15**: 191–213.

Smith, A. 1759/1976. *The Theory of Moral Sentiments*. Stanford, CA: Stanford University Press.

Starik, M. 1994. The Toronto conference: reflections on stakeholder theory. *Business & Society*, **33**: 89–95.

Starik, M. 1995. Should trees have managerial standing? Toward stakeholder status for non human nature. *Journal of Business Ethics*, **14**: 207–17.

Stern, R.N. and Barley, S.R. 1996. Organizations and social systems: organization theory's neglected mandate. *Administrative Science Quarterly*, **41**: 146–62.

Swanson, D.L. 1999. Toward an integrative theory for business and society: a research strategy for corporate social performance. *Academy of Management Review*, **24**: 506–21.

Turban, D.B. and Greening, D.W. 1997. Corporate social performance and organizational attractiveness to prospective employees. *Academy of Management Journal*, **40**: 658–72.

Waddock. S.A. 2006. *Leading Corporate Citizens: Vision, Values, Value-added*. New York: McGraw-Hill.

Waddock, S.A. and Graves, S.B. 1997. The corporate social performance–financial performance link. *Strategic Management Journal*, **18**(4): 303.

Walsh, J., Weber, K. and Margolis, J.D. 2003. Social issues and management: our lost cause found. *Journal of Management*, **29**: 859–81.

Walzer, M. 1994. *Thick and Thin: Moral Argument at Home and Abroad*. Notre Dame, IN: University of Notre Dame Press.

Wartick, S.L. and Cochran, P.L. 1985. The evolution of the corporate social performance model. *Academy of Management Journal*, **10**: 758–69.

Weaver, G.R. and Treviño, L.K. 1994. Normative and empirical business ethics: separation, marriage of convenience, or marriage of necessity? *Business Ethics Quarterly*, **4**: 129–43.

Werhane, P. and Freeman, R.E. 1999. Business ethics: the state of the art. *International Journal of Management Review*, **1**: 1–17.

Whetten, D.A., Rands, G. and Godfrey, P.C. 2001. What are the responsibilities of business to society? In A. Pettigrew, H. Thomas and R. Whittington (eds), *Handbook of Strategy and Management*. London: Sage, pp. 373–410.

Wicks, A.C., Gilbert, D.R. and Freeman, R.E. 1994. A feminist reinterpretation of the stakeholder concept. *Business Ethics Quarterly*, **4**: 475–97.

Wokutch, R.E. and Shepard, J.M. 1999. The maturing of the Japanese economy: corporate social responsibility implications. *Business Ethics Quarterly*, **9**: 527–40.

Wood, D.J. 1991a. Corporate social performance revisited. *Academy of Management Review*, **16**: 691–718.

Wood, D.J. 1991b. Social issues in management: theory and research in corporate social performance. *Journal of Management*, **17**: 383–406.

Wood, D.J. 1994. *Business and Society*. New York: HarperCollins.

Wood, D.J. 2008. Corporate responsibility and stakeholder theory: challenging the neoclassical paradigm. In B.R. Agle, T. Donaldson, R.E. Freeman, M.C. Jensen, R.K. Mitchell and D. Wood (contributors), Dialogue: toward superior stakeholder theory. *Business Ethics Quarterly*, **18**(2): 153–90.

Wood, D.J. and Jones, R.E. 1995. Stakeholder mismatching: a theoretical problem in empirical research on corporate social performance. *International Journal of Organization Analysis*, **3**: 229–67.

Wood, D.J. and Logsdon, J.M. 2002. Business citizenship: from individuals to organizations. *Business Ethics Quarterly*, **12**: 59–94.

APPENDIX 1.1 ANALYSIS OF *BEQ* CITATIONS

Year	Author	Title	Categorization	Content used for classification (unless in 1984: p. # format, page numbers are from *BEQ* article citing Freeman, 1984)
1991	Goodpaster, K.	Business ethics and stakeholder analysis	Substantive/ Consistent	Quotes stakeholder definition (p. 54) and then suggests 'Professor Freeman (1984, cited above) appears to adopt some form of strategic stakeholder synthesis' (p. 59). Also, 'Professor Freeman, quoted earlier, contemplates what I am calling the multi-fiduciary view at the end of his 1984 book under the heading The Manager As Fiduciary To Stakeholders' (p. 62) and then quotes Freeman (1984: 249). (There are also multiple other Freeman, 1984 quotations throughout.)
1992			No citations of Freeman 1984	
1993	Shaw, B. and Zollers, F.E.	Managers in the moral dimension: what Etzioni might mean to corporate managers	Generic/ Content	Quote stakeholder definition (p. 159).
1994	Boatright, J.R.	Fiduciary duties and the shareholder–management relation: or, what's so special about shareholders?	Substantive/ Mischarac-terization	Characterizes Freeman (including 1984) as including the extension of fiduciary duties to include all constituencies (p. 393, and first citation in footnote 3 on p. 406 is Freeman (1984)): 'More recently, R. Edward Freeman has popularized the stakeholder approach, in which every group with a stake in a corporation has claims that rival those of stockholders. Consequently, the fiduciary duties of management include serving the interests of employees, customers, suppliers, and the local community in addition to the traditional duties to shareholders.'

Year	Author	Title	Categorization	Content used for classification (unless in 1984: p. # format, page numbers are from *BEQ* article citing Freeman, 1984)
	Freeman, R.E.	The politics of stakeholder theory: some future directions	Substantive/ Consistent	Suggests he 'made a rather limited attempt' to articulate principles to govern individuals/human beings/moral beings in Freeman (1984) (pp. 411/420).
	Maitland, I.	The morality of the corporation: an empirical or normative disagreement?	Substantive/ Mischaracterization	Implies Freeman (1984) extends fiduciary duty to stakeholders by quoting and footnoting (#12) Freeman (1984: 249) – but this page is Freeman's suggestions for future research: 'In its weaker version, the stakeholder model would leave in place the basic governance of the corporation, but it would extend management's fiduciary or quasi-fiduciary obligations to all stakeholders, not just stockholders.' It would replace 'the notion that managers bear a fiduciary relationship to stockholders or the owners of the firm . . . by a concept of management whereby the manager must act in the interests of the stakeholders in the organization.' (pp. 447/456)
	Langtry, B.	Stakeholders and the moral responsibilities of business	Substantive/ Consistent	'In earlier work, Freeman offered a morally neutral definition of a stakeholder. Perhaps the idea was to leave the ground uncluttered as a starting point either for subsequent moral argument or for nonmoral discussion of effective management strategies and techniques.' (p. 432).
	Schlossberger, E.	A new model of business: dual-investor theory	Generic/ Content	Quotes Edward R. Freeman (sic) (1984) for narrow *vs.* wide definitions of stakeholder (pp. 460–61/472).
	Wicks, A.C., Gilbert, D.R. and Freeman, R.E.	A feminist reinterpretation of the stakeholder concept	Substantive/ Consistent	Recognize Freeman's (1984) framework as 'dramatically different' from his later work, including that stakeholders are not clearly recognized as ends in Freeman (1984) (p. 476).

	Author	Title	Type	Notes
	Dienhart, J.W.	Responsibility and community: a theory of public cooperation	Substantive/Consistent	'Freeman (1984) argues, for example, that private companies can act in ways that are consistent with the interests of their stakeholders independently of forum-like organizations' (p. 229).
	Hosmer, L.T.	Why be moral? A differerent rationale for managers	Generic/Content	Quotes stakeholder definition (pp. 193/203).
1995	Calton, J.M. and Lad, L.J.	Social contracting as a trust-building process of network governance	Generic/Content	Quote stakeholder definition (p. 277).
	Shepard, J.M., Shepard, J., Wimbush, J.C. and Stephens, C.U.	The place of ethics in business: shifting paradigms?	Generic/Title	For 'stakeholder management model' – no quotation (p. 593).
	Dunfee, T.W. and Donaldson, T.	Contractarian business ethics: current status and next steps	Generic/Content	Cite Freeman (1984) for 'elaboration and extension of the [stakeholder] concept in the business ethics literature' (p. 174), though we note that Freeman intends (1984: 1) as a contribution to strategy, and explicitly describes enterprise strategy – one of the key foci of the book – as NOT 'another call for corporate social responsibility or business ethics' (1984: 107). Note also that Dunfee and Donaldson do not cite Freeman (1984) as one of their examples of 'the greatest elaboration[s] of the stakeholder approach' (p. 175) but do include a 1982 Freeman citation there that is not included in the references.
	Shaw, B.	Virtues for a postmodern world	Generic/Content	As describing corporation as a 'battleground of stakeholder interests' (pp. 852/861).

Year	Author	Title	Categorization	Content used for classification (unless in 1984: p. # format, page numbers are from *BEQ* article citing Freeman, 1984)
	Hazera, A.	A comparison of Japanese and US corporate financial accountability and its impact on the responsibilities of corporate managers	Substantive/ Mischarac- terization	For stating 'that managers are responsible to a wider variety of "stakeholders"' (pp. 479/491). Freeman (1984) speaks critically of 'corporate social' responsibility, and otherwise refers to responsibility in reference to the 'responsibility for managing stakeholder relationships', not in the sense of 'responsibility to stakeholders', e.g., Freeman (1984: 215): 'Responsibility for managing stakeholder relationships, even in the sense of recognizing only employees, customers, stockholders and suppliers, has traditionally been the arena of functional managers.'
1996	Burton, B.K. and Dunn, C.P.	Feminist ethics as moral grounding for stakeholder theory	Substantive/ Mischarac- terization	Describe Freeman as 'legalistic, particularly in its emphasis on stakeholder rights' (p. 133).
	Fort, T.L.	Business as mediating institution	Generic/ Content	For 'firm as a location for the interests of many stakeholders' (pp. 150/161).
	Liedtka, J.M.	Feminist morality and competitive reality: a role for an ethic of care?	Generic/Title	For stakeholder theory – no quotation (p. 182).
1997				No citations of Freeman, 1984

Year	Author	Title	Classification	Comments
1998	Hasnas, J.	The normative theories of business ethics: a guide for the perplexed	Generic/Content	For 'effective management requires the balanced consideration of and attention to the legitimate interests of all stakeholders' (pp. 25/38), though Freeman (1984) is explicit about legitimacy only in the 'very weak sense' of whether or not stakeholders are legitimate 'to spend time worrying about' (1984: 23), 'regardless of the appropriateness of their demands' (1984: 45).
	Vidaver Cohen, D.	Motivational appeal in normative theories of enterprise	Not classified	Cites Freeman (1984) in bibliography but not in text so do not know for what content – this citation dropped from summary analysis below.
	Margolis, J.D.	Psychological pragmatism and the imperative of aims: a new approach for business ethics	Generic/Title	For stakeholder theory (p. 411).
1999	Wokutch, R.E. and Shepard, J.M.	The maturing of the Japanese economy: corporate social responsibility implications	Generic/Title	'One popular way of understanding CSR is through the stakeholder management model (Freeman, 1984).' (p. 528) True, though might critique this use!
	Hoch, D. and Hamilton, J.B.	The hope and limits of legal optimism: a comment on the theories of Orts and Nesteruk regarding the impact of law on corporate ethics	Substantive/Mischaracterization	For 'corporate responsibility extends beyond shareholders' (p. 679).

Year	Author	Title	Categorization	Content used for classification (unless in 1984: p. # format, page numbers are from *BEQ* article citing Freeman, 1984)
	Marens, R. and Wicks, A.C.	Getting real: stakeholder theory, managerial practice, and the general irrelevance of fiduciary duties owed to stakeholders	Generic/Content	For 'seminal book on stakeholder theory' – though refer to it as 'Freedman's (1984) seminal book' (p. 274).
	Weaver, G.R. and Treviño, L.K.	Compliance and values oriented ethics programs: influences on employees' attitudes and behavior	Generic/Content	'When ethical awareness is part of employees' role identity, we should find a greater range of potential issues and problems being attended to in decision-making processes; decision processes should take into account a greater array of stakeholder concerns (Freeman, 1984)' (p. 322).
2000	Bishop, J.D.	A framework for discussing normative theories of business ethics	Substantive/Consistent	'Most stakeholder theories, including Freeman's 1984 seminal version, are instrumental' (p. 573).
	Epstein, E.M.	Contemporary Jewish perspectives on business ethics: the contributions of Meir Tamari and Moses L. Pava: a review essay	Substantive/Mischaracterization	'Current stakeholder theory implicitly adopts [a Judaistic] view, recognizing that a firm may have varying levels of responsibility to various constituencies impacted by its actions (see, e.g., Clarkson, Freeman, and Wood)' (p. 534) (and only Freeman included in references is 1984).

Year	Author	Title	Classification	Reason
	Freeman, R.E.	Business ethics at the millennium	Substantive/ Consistent	For the history of the stakeholder idea (p. 179).
	Goodstein, J.D.	Moral compromise and personal integrity: exploring the ethical issues of deciding together in organizations	Generic/ Content	For 'the involvement of multiple stakeholders in many business decisions' (pp. 806–7).
2001	Van Buren, H.J.	If fairness is the problem, is consent the solution? Integrating ISCT and stakeholder theory	Substantive/ Consistent	For being seminal, strategic, descriptive/empirical and instrumental more than normative (p. 482).
	Carroll, A.B.	Models of Management Morality for the New Millennium [SBE presidential address]	Substantive/ Consistent	For enterprise strategy (p. 368).
	Hendry, J.	Missing the target: normative stakeholder theory and the corporate governance debate	Substantive/ Mischarac- terization	As '[began] to address status of stakeholders as moral agents' (p. 162).

45

Year	Author	Title	Categorization	Content used for classification (unless in 1984: p. # format, page numbers are from *BEQ* article citing Freeman, 1984)
	Ryan, L.V. and Buchholtz, A.K.	Trust, risk, and shareholder decision making: an investor perspective on corporate governance	Substantive/Mischaracterization	For 'Managers' responsibility to shareholders has been characterized as . . . one of many stakeholder responsibilities' (p. 177).
	Hosmer, L.T. and Chen, F.	Ethics and economics: growing opportunities for joint research	Generic/Title	For stakeholder theory (p. 615).
	Wicks, A.C.	The value dynamics of total quality management: ethics and the foundations of TQM	Substantive/Mischaracterization	For 'Stakeholder theorists generate accounts of the firm that offer moral concepts as the driving forces of the organization, create parameters requiring firms to treat their various key stakeholders in an ethically positive manner, and try to establish that such approaches will enable firms to succeed' (p. 503).
	Dalton, D.R. and Daily, C.M.	Director stock compensation: an invitation to a conspicuous conflict of interests?	Generic/Content	As seminal book (but do not include in references, only in text) (p. 91).
2002	Logsdon, J.M. and Wood, D.J.	Business citizenship: from domestic to global level analysis	Substantive/Mischaracterization	As about 'linking CSR . . . to the stakeholder environment of the firm' (p. 182).

Author	Title	Category	Description
Freeman, R.E. and Phillips, R.A.	Stakeholder theory: a libertarian defense	Substantive/Consistent	For 'managerial and libertarian roots' of stakeholder theory (p. 331), for 'a managerial conception of organizational strategy and ethics' (p. 333), for coming from the strategy discipline (p. 333), and for plea for voluntarism (p. 337).
Orts, E.W. and Strudler, A.	The ethical and environmental limits of stakeholder theory	Generic/Content	Quote stakeholder definition and note that 'often described as a landmark' (pp. 218/230).
Gallagher, J.A. and Goodstein, J.	Fulfilling institutional responsibilities in health care: organizational ethics and the role of mission discernment	Generic/Title	For 'corporate stakeholder theory' (p. 438).
Sollars, G.G.	The corporation as actual agreement	Substantive/Mischaracterization	As one of a set of 'examples of different viewpoints regarding the moral status of the corporation' (pp. 351/365).
Jensen, M.C.	Value maximization, stakeholder theory, and the corporate objective function	Substantive/Consistent	'Stakeholder theory as stated by Freeman (1984) . . . contains no conceptual specification of how to make the tradeoffs among stakeholders that must be made' (p. 242). Also quotes stakeholder definition (p. 254), including that 'some corporations must count "terrorist groups" as stakeholders' (Freeman, 1984: 53) – though while including them in the same quotation, Jensen changes the order in which Freeman presents these points.

Year	Author	Title	Categorization	Content used for classification (unless in 1984: p. # format, page numbers are from *BEQ* article citing Freeman, 1984)
2003	Phillips, R., Freeman, R.E. and Wicks, A.C.	What stakeholder theory is not	Substantive/ Consistent	As recognizing the importance of procedural justice (p. 487). Also describes Donaldson and Preston (1995) as the 'most commonly quoted work of stakeholder theory since Freeman (1984)' (p. 495), and Freeman (1984) NOT included in table of normative justifications for stakeholder theory, although Wicks, Gilbert and Freeman (1994), Evan and Freeman (1993) and Freeman (1994) are (p. 481).
	Phillips, R.A.	Stakeholder legitimacy	Substantive/ Consistent	'Stakeholder legitimacy has been a central concern at least since Freeman's (1984) ground breaking discussion. Though concerned with questions of legitimacy, Freeman chose to "put aside" such matters' (p. 27; quoting Freeman, 1984: 45). Also for consideration of stakeholder legitimacy's importance (p. 27), for stakeholder definition (pp. 28, 30, 38, 39) – including terrorists and competitors (p. 28) – and for power and legitimacy (p. 32).
2004	Roberts, R.W. and Mahoney, L.	Stakeholder conceptions of the corporation: their meaning and influence in accounting research	Substantive/ Mischarac-terization	'Organizational-level theorists argue that managers have discretion in decision-making such that current shareholder returns can and should be reduced (in essence diverting potential short-term profits to other stakeholders) in order to improve long-term returns to shareholders (Freeman 1984)' (p. 404).
	Wei-Skillern, J.	The evolution of Shell's stakeholder approach: a case study	Generic/ Content	As emphasizing 'a focus on a broad set of stakeholder relationships rather than a narrow set of purely economic relationships' (p. 715).
	Norman, W. and MacDonald, C.	Getting to the bottom of 'triple bottom line'	Substantive/ Mischarac-terization	Characterize as believing that 'attention to social responsibility and ethics help a firm sustain profits in the long run' (pp. 247/259).

Year	Authors	Title	Type	Notes
2005	Van Buren, H.J.	An employee-centered model of CSP	Substantive/Mischaracterization	As source for 'Stakeholders have a right to participate in organizational policy setting' (p. 696).
	Moon, J., Crane, A. and Matten, D.	Can corporations be citizens? Corporate citizenship as a metaphor for business participation in society	Substantive/Mischaracterization	For 'stakeholder democracy' (p. 443) – only the words 'corporate democracy' used in Freeman (1984: 196 and elsewhere).
	van de Ven, B. and Jeurissen, R.	Competing responsibly	Substantive/Mischaracterization	For, 'It is widely accepted in business ethics that a moral evaluation of firm behavior should focus on the impact of the firm on the rights and legitimate interests of its stakeholders' (pp. 299/315).
	Hosmer, L.T. and Kiewitz, C.	Organizational justice: a behavioral science concept with critical implications for business ethics and stakeholder theory	Substantive/Mischaracterization	For, 'The "can affect" portion meant that the rights and interests of those groups had to be considered by the management of the firm' (p. 83).
2006	Scherer, A.G., Palazzo, G. and Baumann, D.	Global rules and private actors: toward a new role of the transnational corporation in global governance	Generic/Content	'Freeman pointed out that managers not only have to satisfy the expectations of of the company's shareholders or contractors, but must also recognize various stakeholder interests' (p. 513).

Year	Author	Title	Categorization	Content used for classification (unless in 1984: p. # format, page numbers are from *BEQ* article citing Freeman, 1984)
	Sobczak, A.	Are codes of conduct in global supply chains really voluntary? From soft law regulation of labour relations to consumer law	Generic/Title	As 'providing an in depth description of this stakeholder theory' (p. 177).
	Harting, T.R., Harmeling, S. and Venkataraman, S.	Innovative stakeholder relations: when 'ethics pays' (and when it doesn't)	Substantive/Consistent	'In 1984, Freeman's seminal treatise on stakeholder theory declared that a successful business must treat the parties affected by the firm's actions as constituents to be consulted rather than spectators to be ignored (Freeman 1984)' (p. 43).
	Dunham, L., Freeman, R.E. and Liedtka, J.	Enhancing stakeholder practice: a particularized exploration of community	Substantive/Consistent	'In it, Freeman proposes stakeholder theory as a strategic management approach aimed at enabling the firm to survive in turbulent times by becoming more responsive to the many constituencies that could play a role in the firm's success' and for stakeholder definition (p. 25).
	Heath, J.	Business ethics without stakeholders	Substantive/Mischaracterization	'[Freeman, 1984] identifies [social responsibility] quite explicitly as a set of obligations that fall upon managers, as part of their professional role' (p. 553) (no page number provided for where Freeman is quite explicit).

Year	Author	Title	Type	Description
2007	Goodstein, J. and Wicks, A.C.	Corporate and stakeholder responsibility: making business ethics a two-way conversation	Substantive/ Consistent	As about corporate responsibility (pp. 375/395). True – the book does talk about corporate responsibility, but is critical and does not make link to stakeholder theory.
	Gilbert, D.U. and Rasche, A.	Discourse ethics and social accountability: the ethics of SA 8000	Generic/Title	For stakeholder theory (p. 208).
2008	Wood, D.J.	Corporate responsibility and stakeholder theory: challenging the neoclassical paradigm, in Dialogue: toward superior stakeholder theory	Substantive/ Mischaracterization	'Next, stakeholder theory began to offer specifics about to whom a company should be responsible and about what specific interests and rights were at risk (Freeman, 1984. . .)' (p. 161).
	Neron, P-Y. and Norman, W.	Citizenship, Inc.: do we really want businesses to be good corporate citizens?	Generic/ Content	'The roots of most modern stakeholder theories grow from Freeman (1984)' (p. 19).

Year	Author	Title	Categorization	Content used for classification (unless in 1984: p. # format, page numbers are from *BEQ* article citing Freeman, 1984)
	Howton, S.D., Howton, S.W. and McWilliams, V.B.	The ethical implications of ignoring shareholder directives to remove antitakeover provisions	Substantive/ Consistent	'Freeman (1984) provided original arguments on the importance of a stakeholder perspective in corporate strategy. Subsequent research has reexamined Freeman's stakeholder theory to develop the ethical implications' (p. 323).
2009	Elms, H. and Phillips, R.A.	Private security companies and institutional legitimacy: corporate and stakeholder responsibility	Substantive/ Consistent	For being about stakeholder legitimacy (p. 403) and being explicitly managerial (p. 406).
	Tashman, P.A. and Fort, T.L.	Book review of Johnson, K.W. and Abramov, I., *Business Ethics: A Manual for Managing a Responsible Business Enterprise in Emerging Market Economies*	Generic/Title	As being about stakeholder management (pp. 307/318).

Summary:		%	Additional details
Total articles citing Freeman, 1984:	63	100	(only 62 of the 63 were actually classified – see below)
Generic/Title citations	9	15	
Generic/Content citations	16	26	All Generic references = 25/62, or 40%
Substantive/Consistent citations	18	29	Generic/Content and Consistent/Substantive = 34/62 or 55%
Substantive/ Mischaracterization citations	19	31	Mischaracterization as % of Substantive = 19/37 or 51%

(One citation fell out as it was included in the bibliography but not cited in text, so could not be classified. We thus used 62 as the denominator in the above calculations as these were the only citations classified. The classification percentages add up to 101 given rounding error.)

53

2. The nature of firm–stakeholder relationships: realizing the potential of an underappreciated contribution of Freeman's 25-year-old classic

Thomas M. Jones

It is widely acknowledged that *Strategic Management: A Stakeholder Approach*, R. Edward Freeman's 1984 classic explication of the stakeholder concept, is a very important scholarly work. Although, by his own account, Freeman intended this book to be a textbook (Freeman, 2009), it has garnered literally thousands of citations in academic journals, many of them read primarily, perhaps exclusively, by other scholars. Although many of the key extensions of this book are related to the practice of management, my focus in this chapter is on a contribution to an important academic issue – the relationship between 'being good' and 'doing well' – that has been a common research theme among scholars in the Social Issues in Management Division (SIM) of the Academy of Management for over three decades. Ultimately, of course, empirical work in this area should have implications for practicing managers, but not until more definitive answers regarding the relationship can be found.

KEY CONTRIBUTIONS OF FREEMAN'S 1984 BOOK

Before beginning an in-depth examination of this question, let me review some contributions that underpin the topic at hand by offering three answers to the question: how did Freeman's 1984 book put SIM scholars on a path to better research in general? First, it presented a refined version of the stakeholder model. By Freeman's own account, he was not the first to think of corporate operations in terms of stakeholders; indeed, he gives ample credit to his predecessors in the development of the stakeholder concept. His own contribution in this realm was to clarify, refine, elaborate on and expand the meaning of stakeholder thinking. Many of us now take the stakeholder model for granted, but we must remember the work that led us to this consolidation.

Second, the book forced us to focus on the relationship between the firm and its stakeholders by making clear the impact that good (or bad) firm–stakeholder relationships can have on corporate operations. Although there are many facets to Freeman's admonition to think in terms of such relationships, I will elaborate on only two – corporate policies and actions with respect to stakeholders, and the actual nature of those relationships – in my evaluation of his contribution to the empirical literature involving the corporate social performance (CSP)/financial performance (FP) relationship.

Third, the book offered substantial clarification of an important empirical question that had already been investigated at some length in the SIM literature – the relationship between CSP and FP (CSP–FP). Since Freeman's main purpose was to inform managers and future managers of the value of stakeholder thinking, this insight is not presented as directly as SIM scholars might have preferred. Instead, it is embedded in Freeman's overall argument regarding the value of good relationships with stakeholders to the success of the company. I will focus my chapter on this insight.

RESEARCH ON THE CSP–FP RELATIONSHIP: PRE- AND POST-1984

On page 1, Freeman presents the *raison d'être* of his work: 'managers need new concepts, tools, and techniques, and new theories if they are to be successful in the current business environment.' These opening lines could have introduced any number of written responses to the economic issues of the day. At that time (the early 1980s), government regulations, media attacks on business, the emergence of articulate critics of the corporate system and specific companies within that system, and serious competitive threats from Europe and the Far East (Japan in particular) presented significant challenges to the executives who ran large firms. These challenges had not gone unnoticed by management consultants, business scholars and other observers of the corporate economy. Everyone, it seemed, had a solution to the problems facing American business, many of them drawing lessons from other countries. Better management of people, reduced governmental regulation, industrial policy (a form of governmental planning) and labor concessions were among the touted solutions.

Hence Freeman was not alone in noting these problems. He was, however, among the prescient few who sensed the need for a more comprehensive response. The result was 'the stakeholder approach', and its impact continues to expand. However, as noted above, Freeman's answer to these manifold problems was not immediately apparent. Later in the book, he demonstrates how a high level of 'stakeholder management capability' (p. 78) holds the key to effectively addressing the challenges of that era and, we now understand, many of the challenges of the current era.

CSP–FP Research: The Pre-1984 Period

Research on the relationship between CSP and FP was well underway by 1984. Numerous studies had been published and countless others were trying to claim coveted journal space. Several theoretical explanations were available to authors of these studies, although some options were infrequently employed. Findings in these individual papers featured either a positive or a negative relationship between CSP and FP; that is, socially responsible firms were also profitable or socially responsibility and profitability were not compatible. In the case of a positive relationship, two causal explanations were available. Authors could claim that good social performance leads to good financial performance – that is, the market rewards socially responsibility and punishes social irresponsibility or social indifference. Alternatively, authors could claim that strong financial performance gives firms the resources to engage in socially responsible behavior, an option denied to financially strapped companies.

Two causal explanations were also available in cases involving the finding of a negative relationship. Researchers could conclude that socially responsible practices drain the firm's resources, resulting in less profitable operations than shareholder-oriented behavior. Or, it could be argued that firms with poor financial performance try to compensate with better social performance, while profitable firms feel no need to polish their images with social responsibility. Put differently, there was a theoretical explanation for any empirical finding, heightening the need for a strong and coherent theoretical framework. Of course, some projects found no relationship whatsoever between CSP and FP, obviating the need for a theoretical explanation. Against this background, the title of Ullmann's 1984 paper 'Data in search of a theory: a critical examination of the relationship among social performance, social disclosure, and economic performance' seemed to capture the state of the art of CSP–FP research at the time.

Although Freeman is clear that his primary intent in publishing his 1984 book was something else – that is, a textbook for students and managers – the insights that it contained lent substantial structure to empirical work on the CSP–FP relationship for those scholars who chose to discover it. Taken in its entirety, Freeman's model can be seen as a clear empirical statement: high stakeholder management capability can lead to success in the current business environment. In simplified form, it could be read as: *Good stakeholder management leads to improved firm financial performance.*

The simplicity and clarity of this statement set it apart from much (certainly not all) work in this area. The valence is clear: good stakeholder management and financial performance are *positively* related. The direction of *causality* is also clear: good stakeholder management *results in* improved financial performance. The major remaining ambiguity is the extent to which good stakeholder management and corporate social performance are synonymous.

CSP–FP Research: The 1984–2009 Period

Twenty-five years into the stakeholder theory era, virtually all of the scholarly research done on the CSP–FP relationship, including a number of studies done by scholars calling themselves stakeholder theorists, have employed measures representing *corporate policies and/or actions* with respect to stakeholders to operationalize CSP. This is an approach that Freeman endorsed, at least as part of his detailed prescription for improved management in economically parlous times: 'Managers in organizations with high Stakeholder Management Capability think in "stakeholder serving" terms' (1984: 80). Furthermore, as a first order approach, focusing on policies and actions makes good sense. Stakeholders are unlikely to be good partners if the formal policies and specific actions that frame their relationships with the corporation result in their being treated poorly.

In addition, a very important factor in the choice of variables of this type was the emergence of the Kinder Lydenberg and Domini (KLD) database. In an area of research for which the generation of good social performance data is a difficult and often tedious process, KLD offered several indicators of CSP in terms of assessments of *strengths* or *weaknesses* in such key areas as employee relations, environmental protection, workplace diversity, product issues and community relations. The addition of this well-assembled database put additional wind in the sails of CSP–FP researchers.

Problems remained, of course. Scholars had no compelling way to generate an overall score for CSP; simply adding up the individual scores was not a very convincing means of establishing a company's commitment to corporate social responsibility. Although various weighting schemes were tried, none really captured the attention of more than a few authors, and the cumulative value of CSP–FP research remained modest. The title of

Griffin and Mahon's 1997 literature review article 'The corporate social performance and corporate financial performance debate: twenty-five years of incomparable results' may have been offered partially in jest, but it did reflect the state of research at the time fairly well. Nonetheless, the KLD indices accelerated the rate at which progress was made in research that empirically linked CSP and FP.

Given the current state of affairs of CSP–FP empirical research, it is reasonable to ask if we have missed something in our quest to fully address this important research question. I believe that answers to this question can be found by looking at: (1) the results of existing studies; (2) the nature of the KLD database; and (3) insights from Freeman's (1984) original work.

Where do we currently stand with respect to this area of research that has generated so much attention from scholars in the SIM field? First, scores of individual studies have been done to date. Extrapolating from a 2007 tally by Joshua Margolis (personal communication, 2007), who, along with co-author James Walsh, has examined this literature extensively, I would estimate that the total number of studies may be closing in on 200 overall. If one looks at individual studies as a group, the results, as always, are highly diverse. Nonetheless, progress is being made in terms of drawing some more general conclusions. First, a meta-analysis by Orlitsky, Schmidt and Rynes (2003) identified positive, but not strong, relationships in both directions. CSP positively affects FP, but FP also positively affects CSP.

In addition, a study by Hillman and Keim (2001) moved the conversation forward by differentiating between policies that affect stakeholders, which they identified as 'stakeholder management', and policies that are unrelated to stakeholder management, which they called 'social issues participation'. Using KLD data, they found that stakeholder management leads to better financial performance and that social issues participation is negatively linked to improved financial results. Both findings are in line with their theory-based predictions. One problem mars this study's results, however. The authors disaggregated their stakeholder management data and found that, of the five variables designated as elements of stakeholder management – employee relations, diversity, environment, product and community relations – only community relations was positively linked to good financial performance. Thus, while Hillman and Keim's (2001) overall results make intuitive sense, not many stakeholder theorists would predict, *a priori*, that community relations are likely to be a major driver of financial performance. Thus, some important issues with respect to the CSP–FP relationship are not really settled; we have more explaining to do. How should we proceed?

Drawing the Right Conclusions

Despite significant improvements in theory and methods, we must ask ourselves whether we have really identified the elements of stakeholder management that are likely to result in superior financial performance. To answer this question, we need to take a closer look at the KLD measures, the source of CSP data for many studies. As noted above and as detailed in Appendix 2.1, KLD rates companies on five dimensions of relationships with 'stakeholders' – employee relations, diversity, environment, product and community relations. Within these individual categories, criteria are mostly, but not entirely, functions of either company policies or specific corporate actions. For example, a main criterion under diversity is 'notable progress in the promotion of women and minorities'. While progress with respect to promoting women and minorities is a worthy goal of corporate social policy, in the absence of much better developed theory, there is no reason to expect it to advance the financial goals of the firm. It is reasonable to assume that promoted women and minorities perform as well as, but no better than, white men. Why then would we expect *better* financial returns in firms that regularly promote women and minorities?

Similarly, under the category of environment, one criterion is 'environmentally superior property, plant and equipment'. Again, earning a KLD rating of 'strength' is certainly good for the environment and for those of us who breathe the air and drink, swim in or eat fish from the water, but there is no particular reason to expect that investments in superior property, plant and equipment will reap significant financial rewards for the firm. With respect to community, 'innovative philanthropy' is a factor in a 'strength' rating. Although philanthropy in general is valued and innovation is often beneficial, without some specific theory linking innovative philanthropy to financial returns, we have no reason to expect the firm to make more money than it would with more mundane programs for contributions to charities. Most other KLD criteria are similar to those described above; they refer to *policies enacted or actions taken* (by the company in question) that have to do with stakeholders.

What is wrong with this approach? Why have we not answered the questions surrounding stakeholder relations more decisively? First, let us assume for discussion purposes that the three most critical stakeholder groups in addition to shareholders are customers, employees, and suppliers. Relationships with each of these groups are certainly essential to the ongoing success of virtually all firms. Yet suppliers are not included on the KLD list of stakeholders. Furthermore, actual relationships with customers and employees are addressed only tangentially. *Customers* surely stand to benefit if a company has a 'strength' in the *product* category because of 'relatively high levels of R&D expenditures, new product development, or unusual inventiveness', but without some indication of how these virtues came about, we can draw few conclusions regarding the value of firm–customer relationships. A firm that spends a disproportionate amount on research and development, for example, may not fully recover these expenditures with additional sales or improved market positioning.

The overriding problem may be that the policies and actions addressed by the KLD indicators may have little or nothing to do with the kinds of firm/stakeholder relationships that might result in significantly improved financial performance. What is needed is some measure of how the firm and its customers work together to make the firm's products better for its customers. Keeping in mind that not all customers are retail customers – that is, a lot of buying and selling goes on in business-to-business relationships – how can firms and their customers 'relate' better to assure that the firm's products (or services) meet customer needs on an ongoing basis? It would appear that research that examines the actual nature of the relationships in question, and that does not involve KLD indicators (or similar measures), will have to be done.

Finally, Freeman's (1984) own work gives us a clue about what we might be missing. In fact, his notion of 'stakeholder serving' policies is only one facet of firm/stakeholder relationships in his model. Freeman was primarily concerned with these relationships at what he then called the 'transactional' level. Scholars now frequently distinguish between transactions and relationships, but in 1984, no such distinction seemed necessary. In Freeman's own words, transaction level issues focused on the question: 'How do the organization and its managers interact with stakeholders?' (1984: 69). I believe that the greatest gains in our understanding of the relationship between good stakeholder management and improved financial performance will be found at this level of analysis.

In short, it is my belief that most stakeholder theory researchers have yet to fully understand what constitutes good stakeholder management; that is, management that results in financial benefits for the firm and, in many cases, benefits for the stakeholder group. Instead of examining company policies and specific actions, researchers should be examining the content and nature of the relationships themselves, and identifying features that make the relationships work better. Although most stakeholder theory scholars have yet to adopt this approach, there are numerous examples of such work in the literatures of other fields. I will now turn to these examples.

EXTANT SCHOLARSHIP ON FIRM–STAKEHOLDER RELATIONSHIPS

Relationships with stakeholders have the potential to generate value for the firm in several areas of corporate operations. Dyer and Singh (1998) set the stage for establishing a relational view of the process of generating superior performance. They argue that performance advantages often span firm boundaries and lie in the relationship between and among 'independent' firms. These authors point to, among other things, knowledge-sharing routines and effective governance. In this chapter, I analyze research that covers these and other potential relational sources of superior performance. Recognizing that the categories overlap, the examples offered below describe studies involving firm–supplier relationships, buyer–seller relationships, alliances/joint ventures, knowledge sharing, and firm–employee relationships.

Firm–Supplier Relationships

As noted above, firm–supplier relationships might be one source of potential competitive benefits for firms that manage them well. As early as 1992, the marketing literature featured analyses and empirical work on the norms that govern firm–supplier relationships. In particular, Heide and John (1992) note the deficiencies associated with the assumption of opportunism in transactions cost economics and suggest that optimal relationship governance may be neither market nor hierarchy, the two choices offered by transactions cost economics. Instead, *relational norms,* the actual standards of behavior that guide relational partners, are key elements. These authors also conducted empirical work and showed that supportive norms are important even when one of the partners to the relationship would seem to be powerful enough to impose the terms of relational governance. Clearly, the marketing literature has insights to offer stakeholder theorists.

The strategic management literature is also a potential source of such insights. A study by Dyer and Chu (2003) is a fine example of research that can shed light on good stakeholder management. This study examined the role of trust between automotive suppliers and automobile companies in Korea (Hyundai, Daewoo and Kia), Japan (Toyota and Nissan) and the United States (General Motors, Ford and Chrysler). In all, 344 bilateral relationships were studied. Using carefully chosen informants within each of the supplier firms, these authors assessed the level of trustworthiness of the automakers with whom the supplier dealt. They found substantial differences in transactions costs among these two-way relationships. Indeed, the authors estimated that the transactions costs involved in dealing with a supplier's least trusted customer (auto manufacturer) was about *five times* as great as the cost of dealing with its most trusted customer. This is a very large difference by any standard; firm–supplier trust could make a substantial contribution to improved financial performance. Also of great interest are the reasons for the extreme disparities in transactions costs. Suppliers spent significantly more time in contract negotiations, haggling face-to-face with their least trusted customers.

The study discussed above follows a study by Dyer (1997) that examined firm–supplier relations based on the observation that transaction costs can vary significantly depending on the form of 'safeguards' chosen. In this paper, the author addressed an anomalous situation in which *higher* relation-specific investments were associated with *lower* transaction costs, a result that directly contradicts the predictions of transaction costs economics (Klein, Crawford and Alchian, 1978; Williamson, 1985). According to transaction costs economics, additional asset specificity increases the risk of opportunism to those who invest in such assets. Hence, they must demand more (and more expensive) protections. After reviewing a number of types of governance safeguards, this author empirically examined the relationship between asset specificity and transaction costs among auto companies and their suppliers in Japan and the United States, and attempted to explain the anomaly in terms of different forms of relational safeguards. Clearly, Dyer's (1997) article represents an important example of how good stakeholder management can lead to improved financial performance.

Buyer–Seller Relationships

The marketing literature holds considerable potential as a source of useful information on the key elements of buyer–seller relationships. Marketing scholars have been aware of the importance of trust and commitment in such relationships for several years. Morgan and Hunt (1994) developed and tested a model of relationship marketing, an area of marketing that by 1994 had spawned no less than ten forms of the genre. Using the assumption that cooperation within a network is a key to competitive success, these authors offer what they call a commitment–trust theory of relationship marketing, and provide some encouraging empirical support for it. The details of the commitment–trust model are important to stakeholder theorists in their quest to define 'good stakeholder management'. Partners must: (1) provide 'resources, opportunities, and benefits that are superior to the offerings of alternative partners'; (2) maintain 'high standards of corporate values' and choose exchange partners with similar values;

(3) communicate 'valuable information, including expectations, market intelligence, and evaluations of the partner's performance'; and (4) avoid 'malevolently taking advantage of their exchange partners' – that is, avoid opportunistic behavior (Morgan and Hunt, 1994: 34). With its high level of detail, this paper, and its progeny, should yield valuable insights to stakeholder theorists.

Strategy scholars also have much to contribute to the development of theories of 'good stakeholder management' in the area of buyer–seller relationships. A good example drawn from the strategy literature is an article by Zaheer, McEvily and Perrone (1998), who focus on interorganizational exchange. In trying to parse the effects of trust on negotiation costs, interorganizational conflict and corporate performance, these authors develop a model that links interpersonal trust to trust between organizations. These constructs are distinct, and both play key roles in the processes of negotiation, avoidance of conflict and, ultimately, organizational performance. Although their results are complex and defy easy interpretation, these authors unambiguously conclude that trust clearly does matter to successful interorganizational exchange. Perhaps the complexity of elements of their findings could supply the grist for more refined developments in the 'good stakeholder management' model.

Alliances/Joint Ventures

Work on interfirm alliances can also shed light on our understanding of what constitutes 'good' stakeholder management practices; that is, practices that create additional value for the firm. Arino, de la Torre and Ring (2001) shed considerable light on this issue in their discussion of 'relational quality' in alliances and joint ventures. The strategic management literature has featured a number of other articles on alliances that should be useful to stakeholder theory scholars as well. Other early work includes Doz's (1996) study of three 'partnership cycles', each being a joint venture/alliance involving two large corporations. This study should be particularly useful to stakeholder theorists who are trying to identify practices that represent good stakeholder management, simply because the differences between the successful partnership and the two unsuccessful partnerships represent fertile ground for drawing important conclusions. The first failure was a joint venture between AT&T and Olivetti, and involved an attempt to design and build a minicomputer in the mid-1980s. Trust never developed between the two companies. Fears that information was being withheld and that one of the firms was planning to 'go it alone' once key advances had been made virtually assured that the cooperation necessary to make the requisite advances never materialized. The venture foundered and was eventually suspended, resulting in financial losses for both companies.

Another failed partnership, a drug development venture that spanned the late 1970s and early 1980s, involved Ciba-Geigy and Alza. Again the two firms could not trust each other enough to engage in the cooperative efforts required to make the venture succeed. This partnership also collapsed due to a lack of interfirm trust.

The one successful partnership in the trio studied by Doz involved General Electric and SNECMA, jet engine manufacturers based in the United States and Europe, respectively. The original plan was to develop jointly a single jet engine for the civilian aircraft market, but it grew into a much more elaborate collaboration. Thanks to voluntary efforts on the part of key managers early in the project, spontaneous contributions of key information (without the caution that typically attends such exchanges), and other trusting acts on the part of both firms, the partnership expanded to include the entire product line for non-military jet engines for the two companies. Doz points to a 'self-reinforcing cycle of heightened efficiency expectations, strengthened institutional commitments, deeper interpersonal trust, joint sense-making, and greater flexibility and adaptability' as the key ingredients in this very successful collaboration. Studies of this type would seem to be prototypes for stakeholder theory work on what makes firm–stakeholder relationships pay off for the firm and the stakeholder group involved.

Uzzi (1997) also has much to contribute to the study of good stakeholder management. His study of the garment trade in New York City is instructive for a number of reasons. First, firms in the supply chain – suppliers, designers, manufacturers and customers are the main players – worked very closely to bring fashions of appropriate style, quality, and price to the market with surprising speed. Relationships among the various firms and their stakeholders – often other firms – featured 'trust, fine-grained information transfer, and joint problem-solving arrangements' (Uzzi, 1997: 43). These features, in turn, allowed firms access to rapid decision-making and 'privileged and difficult-to-price resources' that heightened their competitiveness (Uzzi, 1997: 43). In addition, the cognitive effort needed to make key decisions was reduced significantly.

A study by Browning, Beyer and Shetler, (1995) might also prove instructive. SEMATECH, a consortium created by the semiconductor industry's top corporations in an effort to develop new manufacturing technology, was the subject of their inquiry. These authors attributed the success of SEMATECH to a radical transformation in the developmental environment. In the beginning, this environment featured separate agendas for each of the participants, attempts at coordination among (near) strangers, and an organizational structure seemingly inappropriate to the task at hand. By the end, the consortium had become what the authors called a 'moral community in which individuals and firms made contributions to the industry without regard for immediate and specific payback' (Browning, Beyer and Shetler, 1995). The free flow of critical information and the ability to coordinate activities within the consortium certainly contributed to its very substantial success.

Some strategy scholars have gone beyond the conclusion that trust can be an important driver of performance in strategic alliances, examining both: (1) how trust develops; and (2) organizational and alliance features that affect the trust–performance link. For example, Gulati (1995) explored the value of repeated instances of alliances between two firms and found that 'familiarity' significantly reduces the need for equity linkages between the partners. Interfirm trust often takes time to develop, and repeated alliances are a good means of assuring that a firm has chosen a trustworthy partner. This strategy literature is also beginning to move beyond simply discovering the financial benefits and identifying drivers of such efficiencies in alliance-type arrangements. International alliances, of course, present some unique problems with respect to forming firm–stakeholder relationships, largely because cultural differences may make communication and other trust building activities more difficult. One set of scholars (Lyles et al. 1999), concluded that trust among partners in international ventures is too costly and too risky and can seriously harm alliance performance. While noting this apparent anomaly, a recent paper by Robson, Katsikeas and Bello (2008) attempts to isolate reasons for this problem, and finds that trust-based international alliances grow stronger when the alliance drops in size. Presumably, it is easier to govern a relationship through trust when there are fewer partners that must be assumed (or discovered to be) trustworthy. The similarity of the partners and fair distribution of the benefits and burdens required by the alliance were found to be key elements in the development of partnerships based on trust.

Knowledge Sharing

We live in what has been called a 'knowledge economy', an economy in which the production, possession and use of knowledge is often of great value to corporations. It follows that knowledge can be a significant source of differential performance among companies. But knowledge, as a corporate asset, has some features that make its use and transfer risky. First, once intellectual property is revealed to another party, there is a substantial risk that it will be appropriated by that party and used, perhaps in a slightly modified form, for that party's own purposes. Second, the value of knowledge often cannot be known until it is combined with other assets/ capabilities to create value. Therefore, negotiations over its potential value can be difficult because of radically different valuations by the negotiating parties. Third, some knowledge is tacit and cannot be easily or readily transferred because it cannot be easily described or circumscribed. All of these features of knowledge as a corporate asset make dealing with knowledge in firm–stakeholder relationships quite difficult. Yet, it would seem that effective use and transfer of knowledge between a company and its stakeholders – customers and suppliers would be the relevant stakeholders here – holds the key to substantial economic benefits for the firm (and the stakeholder) in question.

Indeed, Dyer and Chu (2003), in the study of automobile manufacturers and their suppliers described above, found – in addition to the substantially reduced transactions costs noted above – far superior information sharing, further adding to the performance benefits that they attribute to trust. In a study exploring Toyota's vaunted production network, Dyer and Nobeoka (2000) found that, by creating a strong network identity among the company and its suppliers, Toyota has solved a number of problems associated with knowledge transfer within a network. Critical to Toyota's success in this area of corporate operations is the fact that knowledge related to the production process is considered to be the property *of the network*, not the company or any of the individual suppliers. In essence, knowledge need not be *transferred* at all within the network because it is already jointly owned. Protecting the value of intellectual property, for example, is in the interest of all parties, and the risks associated with appropriation are reduced considerably.

Firm–Employee Relationships

A great deal of research has been done on how to motivate employees. It is almost a corporate cliché that 'employees are our most important asset'. Scholars attempting to develop theories of 'good stakeholder management' should certainly examine this extensive literature carefully. However, one paper indicates what stakeholder theorists should be looking for and merits special attention. Mele (2003) raises the issue of 'organizational humanizing cultures' and suggests that they might be capable of generating social capital for corporations. The important features of organizational humanizing cultures are several, but two stand out as potentially significant for the building of social capital. These cultures must: (1) recognize the person and his/her dignity, rights, uniqueness and capacity for personal growth; and (2) inspire management for the common good rather than particular interests, among other things. Only through a careful examination of the actual workings of the relationships between firms and their employees can stakeholder scholars determine which, if any, characteristics of these relationships actually help the firm build social capital and, ultimately, perform better than it otherwise would.

Generic Firm–Stakeholder Relationships

Some studies outside the normal stakeholder theory literature address the firm–stakeholder relationship from a more general perspective. An example is the work of Child and Mollering (2003). These scholars employ the Chinese context to examine the role of 'active trust development' in the creation of trust between firms and their stakeholders. Importantly, they distinguish between trust that results from 'contextual confidence' in social institutions to protect transactors and trust that is unique to the trustor–trustee dyad. China represents an excellent context for such a study because its institutions are clearly limited in their ability to, for example, enforce contracts. Given these limitations, the importance of active trust development is much more pronounced than it is in countries with more fully developed institutions. Once again, insights from papers of this type present valuable sources of information to those wishing to link good stakeholder management to improved financial performance.

Although they base their empirical work in the relationships between client firms and the outside contractors that do R&D work for them, the conclusions of Carson et al. (2003) could be extended to other firm–stakeholder relationships. These scholars address the problem of misplaced trust, focusing on its costs and risks. More specifically, they argue that the ability of exchange partners to 'read' each other – that is, the ability to process trust-relevant information about the firm's partners – can substantially reduce the incidence of broken trust and identify four factors that can affect this ability. Since being victimized by opportunistic partners can be devastating to a firm's profitability, the value of this research should be readily apparent to Business and Society scholars exploring the link between good stakeholder management and firm financial performance.

WHAT IS TO BE DONE?

In this chapter, I have argued that the continuing quest among SIM scholars to link CSP to FP, in its current form, has run its course. Freeman's 1984 book represented an opportunity to redirect CSP–FP research along more coherent theoretical lines. Some of this reorientation has been effective. However, if they are to make more profound and more lasting discoveries, SIM scholars must now look more deeply into firm–stakeholder relations. Unfortunately, the next steps in this quest will be more difficult than the earlier ones were. Scholars can no longer simply tap the information in a readily available database to conduct their empirical work. The KLD indicators, no matter how useful they may be to investors seeking socially responsible investments or how useful they have been to past research, are not up to the task of moving us forward from this point.

Researchers must now take a careful look at what Freeman (1984) called the transactional elements of firm–stakeholder relationships, which he regarded as the key to 'high stakeholder management capability'. This reorientation will involve new types of research strategies that examine the nature of firm–stakeholder relations themselves. The new orientation will require the gathering of much more information-rich data that reveals details about how firms actually interact with their stakeholders, exactly what Freeman (1984) admonished us to do over 25 years ago. Data gathering will involve surveys, interviews with key managers, actual observation of corporate operations or even participant/observer studies, as done by Robert Jackall some 20 years ago in his study of organizational ethics (Jackall, 1989).

What sorts of information should we be looking for in these research efforts? One preliminary answer is that a scholar who is trying to parse the elements of organizational success should not be looking for anything in particular. It is almost axiomatic that one tends to find what one is looking for. Human psychological processes being what they are, information that runs counter to, or irrelevant to, a preconceived notion of what the researcher expects to find tends to get filtered out in the data-gathering process. The issues behind this axiom have been well aired in the context of the debate over political power in democratic societies between pluralists and elite theorists (also called social stratificationists) in political science and sociology. The pluralists hewed to a form of empirical purism, a purism that claimed that if you cannot observe a phenomenon, it cannot be presumed to exist. Elite theorists, on the other hand, argued that much power is exerted in unobservable 'behind the scenes' acts that set the agenda, and hence controlled, the range of acceptable political decisions (for example, Bacharach and Baratz, 1962).

The collection of data through surveys obviously must start with some notion of what the researcher is looking for, but in other cases – for example, interviews, observation – a *tabula rasa* approach might yield some interesting and important data. With respect to surveys, stakeholder scholars should look to prior studies for clues about the forms that superior operations might take. Improved coordination and reduced transaction costs, improved use of knowledge, improved negotiations outcome, and improved stakeholder motivation would certainly be areas that should be highlighted. In addition, stakeholder researchers should seek to identify what features of a firm's relationships with its stakeholders drive superior operations. Based on prior research, an obvious place to start is the existence of mutual trust. Or, perhaps fair treatment of stakeholders alone is enough to elicit greater motivation, reduced tendencies to act in an opportunistic manner, less adversarial bargaining techniques and/or improved knowledge flows in firm–stakeholder relationships. Of course, other drivers of relational efficiency may emerge as well.

In summary, if stakeholder theory advocates intend to make real advances in discovering what constitutes 'good stakeholder management', they will first have to abandon the 'policies and actions' perspective present in so many studies to date and virtually mandated by the use of KLD indicators. They will then have to adopt some data collection techniques – for example, surveys, interviews and observation – that have been used sparingly in the past. Ideally, studies that take these forms and that are done in a number of research settings, could, taken collectively and through a process sometimes called grounded theory building, yield a more general theory of good stakeholder management. That is, stakeholder theorists could synthesize the findings of numerous individual research projects to create a more general theory. In the process, one facet – a more refined view of what constitutes 'high stakeholder management capability' – of Freeman's (1984) multifaceted stakeholder approach to strategic management could finally be realized.

ACKNOWLEDGMENTS

This paper is based on a presentation made in honor of the Silver Anniversary of the publication of R. Edward Freeman's 1984 book, *Strategic Management: A Stakeholder Approach,* at the 2009 annual meeting of the Academy of Management in Chicago, IL. It draws some material from a manuscript co-authored with Professor Will Felps, Rotterdam School of Management, Erasmus University, Rotterdam, Netherlands.

REFERENCES

Arino, A., de la Torre, J. and Ring, P.S. 2001. Relational quality: managing trust in corporate alliances. *California Management Review*, **44**(1): 109–33.

Bacharach, P. and Baratz, M.S. 1962. Two faces of power. *American Political Science Review*, **56**(4): 947–52.

Browning, L.D., Beyer, J.M. and Shetler, J.C. 1995. Building cooperation in a competitive industry. *Academy of Management Journal*, **38**(1): 113–51.

Carson, S.J., Madhok, A., Varman, R. and John, G. 2003. Information processing moderators of the effectiveness of trust-based governance in interfirm R&D collaboration. *Organization Science*, **14**(1): 45–56.

Child, J. and Mollering, G. 2003. Contextual confidence and active trust development in the Chinese business environment. *Organization Science*, **14**(1): 69–80.

Doz, Y.L. 1996. The evolution of cooperation in strategic alliances: initial conditions or learning processes. *Strategic Management Journal*, **17**: 55–83.

Dyer, J.H. 1997. Effective interfirm collaboration: how firms minimize transaction costs and maximize transaction value. *Strategic Management Journal*, **18**(7): 535–56.

Dyer, J. and Chu, W. 2003. The role of trustworthiness in reducing transaction costs and improving performance: empirical evidence from the United States, Japan, and Korea. *Organization Science*, **14**(1): 57–68.

Dyer, J.H. and Nobeoka, K. 2000. Creating and managing a high-performance knowledge-sharing network: the Toyota case. *Strategic Management Journal*, **21**(3): 345–67.

Dyer, J.H. and Singh, H. 1998. The relational view: cooperative strategy and sources of interorganizational competitive advantage. *Academy of Management Review*, **23**(4): 660–79.

Freeman, R.E. 1984. *Strategic Management: A Stakeholder Approach*. Marshfield, MA: Pitman.

Freeman, R.E. 2009. Comment made at a session devoted to the 25th anniversary of the publication of his book, *Strategic Management: A Stakeholder Approach*, at the 2009 Meeting of the Academy of Management in Chicago, IL.

Griffin, J. and Mahon, J.F. 1997. The corporate social performance and corporate financial performance debate: twenty-five years of incomparable results. *Business and Society*, **39**(3): 254–303.

Gulati, R. 1995. Does familiarity breed trust? The implications of repeated ties for contractual choice in alliances. *Academy of Management Journal*, **38**(1): 85–112.

Heide, J.B. and John, G. 1992. Do norms matter in marketing relationships? *Journal of Marketing*, **56**: 32–44.

Hillman, A.J. and Keim, G.D. 2001. Shareholder value, stakeholder management, and social issues: what's the bottom line? *Strategic Management Journal*, **22**(2): 125–39.

Jackall, R. 1989. *Moral Mazes: The World of Corporate Managers*. Oxford, UK: Oxford University Press.

Klein, B., Crawford, R.G. and Alchian, A.A. 1978. Vertical integration, appropriable rents, and the competitive contracting process. *Journal of Law and Economics*, **21**: 297–326.

Lyles, M.A., Sulaiman, M., Barden, J.Q. and Kechik, A. 1999. Factors affecting joint venture performance: a study of Malaysian joint ventures. *Journal of Asian Business*, **15**(2): 1–20.

Mele, D. 2003. Organizational humanizing cultures: do they generate social capital? *Journal of Business Ethics*, **45**(1): 3–14.

Morgan, R.M. and Hunt, S.D. 1994. The commitment–trust theory of relationship marketing. *Journal of Marketing*, **58**: 20–38.

Orlitsky, M., Schmidt, F.L. and Rynes, S.L. 2003. Corporate social and financial performance: a meta-analysis. *Organization Studies*, **24**(3): 403–41.

Robson, M.J., Katsikeas, C.S. and Bello, D.C. 2008. Drivers and performance outcomes of trust in international strategic alliances: the role of organizational complexity. *Organization Science*, **19**(4): 647–65.

Ullmann, A. 1985. Data in search of a theory: a critical examination of the relationship among social performance, social disclosure, and economic performance. *Academy of Management Review*, **10**: 540–77.

Uzzi, B. 1997. Social structure and competition in interfirm networks: the paradox of embeddedness. *Administrative Science Quarterly*, **42**: 35–67.

Williamson, O.E. 1985. *The Economic Institutions of Capitalism*. New York: Free Press.

Zaheer, A., McEvily, B. and Perrone, V. 1998. Does trust matter? Exploring the effects of interorganizational and interpersonal trust on performance. *Organization Science*, **9**(2): 141–59.

APPENDIX 2.1   KLD INDICATORS

(adapted from Hillman and Keim, 2001)

Community Relations

(used by Hillman and Keim as a stakeholder management (SM) variable)

Concerns

- Fines or civil penalties paid
- Involvement in major litigation or controversies relating to a community in which the company operates
- Strained relations with a community in which the company operates due to a recent plant closing or general breach of agreements with the community

Strengths

- Consistent charitable donations of over 1.5 percent of pretax earnings or other demonstrations of generous giving in recent years
- A reputation for innovative giving, such as support for nonprofit agencies promoting self-sufficiency among the economically disadvantaged
- Support of education through a long-term commitment to improve programs at the primary or secondary level
- Prominent recent supporter of job training programs
- Prominent participant in public/private initiatives that support housing initiatives for the economically disadvantaged

Employee Relations

(Hillman and Keim, 2001 – SM variable)

Concerns

- Poor relations with its unions relative to others in its industry
- Recent lay-offs of more than 15 percent of employees in 1 year or 25 percent of employees in 2 years
- Paid significant fines or penalties over employee safety or has been involved in major safety controversies
- Substantially underfunded pension plan or an inadequate benefits plan

Strengths

- Strong union relations relative to others in its industry
- A long-term policy of company-wide cash profit sharing
- A substantial sense of worker involvement/ownership, sharing of financial information with employees or employee participation in management decision making
- Offers employees strong retirement benefits, or other innovative benefits, relative to others in its industry

Diversity Issues

(Hillman and Keim, 2001 – SM variable)

Concern

- Paid substantial fines or penalties or been involved in major controversies related to its affirmative action record

Strengths

- Company CEO is a woman or member of a minority group
- Notable progress in the promotion of women and minorities, particularly to line positions
- Women and/or minorities hold board seats in the company
- Outstanding benefit programs addressing work/family concerns
- A strong and consistent record of support for women and minority-owned businesses (purchasing from or investing in)
- Innovative hiring initiatives or other human resource programs directed at employment of the disabled

Product Issues

(Hillman and Keim, 2001 – SM variable)

Concerns

- Faces major recent product safety controversies
- Faces a major marketing controversy or has paid fines or penalties related to advertising practices, consumer fraud or government contracting practices

Strengths

- Long-standing company-wide quality program judged to be among the best in the industry
- An industry leader in research and development, as evidenced by expenditure as a percentage of sales, effective new product development or unusual inventiveness
- Part of the company's basic mission is provision of products or services for the economically disadvantaged

Environment Issues

(Hillman and Keim, 2001 – SM variable)

Concerns

- Liabilities for hazardous waste sites exceed US$30 million or has significant involvement in more than 30 federal Superfund sites
- Recently paid significant fines or penalties, has a pattern or regulatory problems, or has been involved in major controversies involving environmental degradation
- Emissions are among the highest legal emissions of toxic chemicals in the United States
- Among the top producers of ozone-depleting chemicals
- Legal emissions of toxic chemicals into the air and water are among the highest of the companies followed by KLD
- One of the largest producers of agricultural chemicals

Strengths

- Policies to reduce emissions through elimination of toxic chemicals
- A substantial user of recycled materials
- The company's environmentally sensitive property, plant and equipment is [sic] among the most superior environmentally
- Derives substantial revenues from developing, using or marketing fuels with environmental advantages, or has undertaken notable energy conservation projects
- Derives substantial revenues from alternative fuels including natural gas, wind power, and solar energy

Non-US Issues

(used by Hillman and Keim, 2001 as a social issue participation (SIP) variable)

Concerns

- Operations in Burma
- Operations in Mexico – Controversial especially related to employees or the environment

Strength

- A substantial, innovative charitable giving program outside of the United States

Other

(Hillman and Keim, 2001 – SM variable)

Concerns

- Notably high levels of compensation to top management or board
- Involved in tax disputes
- Owns a substantial portion of a company with social concerns

Strengths

- Notably low compensation for top management or board
- Owns a substantial part of a company with social strengths

Exclusionary screens

- Alcohol/tobacco/gambling
- Military weapons contracting or supplies to Department of Defense
- Nuclear power electrical utility
- Designs or constructs nuclear energy plants or uranium

3.   Freeman: win–win and the common good

Edwin M. Hartman

Among the terms that define the Ed Freeman tradition, some of the most significant, in addition to *stakeholder*, are *win–win*, *conversation*, *pragmatist* (sometimes modified by *raving*), *separation thesis* and *values*. A subtext in Freeman's thought is baseball. I shall address all of these, with *stakeholder* at the center, but I shall suggest some Aristotelian views that Freeman should find congenial. At least they afford an opportunity to continue the conversation.

Since there are many possible theories about stakeholders, I am content to make some general and useful observations about them. Freeman, Harrison and Wicks (2007) offer two such observations. I agree with both of them, under an interpretation that may involve a little friendly extrapolation. The first is that a certain kind of win–win situation is an essential aim of managing with stakeholders in mind. The second is that values are essential as well. Put the two together and we can say that one can and should create an ongoing win–win situation with stakeholders through conversations that get at common values.

According to the standard view of things, a firm marshals its resources and, in particular, its managers and employees to defeat its competitors in the market and thus make profits for its stockholders. Where do stakeholders come in? Some critics have interpreted the stakeholder approach as claiming that an organization has an affirmative moral obligation to some or all stakeholders. Even the Milton Friedman (1970) view of corporate responsibility can accommodate the presence of stakeholders: they are to be dealt with in whatever way the firm's profitable operation requires. They may offer obstacles, support and challenges of various sorts. Firms should regard dealing with stakeholders as a means to corporate success. That view is consistent with exploitative treatment of stakeholders; but since an organization might have difficulty in getting away with that sort of thing for very long, a Friedmanite could advocate treating stakeholders honestly.

This chapter explores a notion that lies somewhere between Friedman and serve-all-the-stakeholders. I argue, following Freeman, that a firm ought to seek win–win situations with stakeholders where that is feasible. This makes good sense from the point of view of the stockholders, and it has something to do with fairness as well.[1] The point is not just that the results of most transactions will provide some benefit for both parties, as is typical in competitive markets. I shall argue that where relations with stakeholders have the characteristics of the prisoner's dilemma or the commons, as is often the case, standard negotiation is not always the best way to get the parties to win–win. But not all stakeholder relationships can be win–win. Sometimes a trade-off is the best possible option, and in those cases there is not always a handy principle that tells one how to trade.

I claim that the prisoner's dilemma and the tragedy of the commons model some stakeholder relationships, and that in these cases good stakeholder management is a matter of avoiding the dilemma or the tragedy. Then I consider the claim, made by the Canadian political philosopher Charles Blattberg (2000), that relationships between contesting parties should be addressed through *conversation*, a process in which the parties reach an accord by coming to adopt common values rather than agreeing to disagree and then compromising. We might think that this view works better as a theory about citizens than about stakeholders, but I shall argue that it does apply to stakeholders, including even competitors. Stakeholders should be able to agree on the value of competing honestly on the basis of excellence. Businesspeople should be excellent competitors in a sense that I shall explain. That is what brings out the productive best in capitalism.

We might want to have a coherent set of principles that describe the best possible stakeholder relations in all possible circumstances, but there are no such principles. Pragmatists know that that is the way it often is in moral philosophy, though principles are not useless. Our consideration of how to deal with stakeholders leads us to contemplate good character, and the pride and satisfaction to which good character is entitled. I shall argue that a virtue-based approach can add value to stakeholder theory.

It may seem odd to say that business is about finding some common goods and converging on values. Surely competitors and employees and other stakeholders are not all in the same boat, not united as fellow citizens ought to be. I do not minimize differences among stakeholder classes; in particular, I recognize the centrality of competition. But stakeholders can and should unite behind a conception of honest competition, and a conception of what an excellent businessperson, a real pro, looks like.

We begin by considering an important class of stakeholders.

PROBLEMS ABOUT DEALING WITH SUPPLIERS

Supply chain management is about managing relations with direct and indirect suppliers, who are stakeholders of a challenging sort. Its purpose is to ensure an adequate and uninterrupted supply of quality goods and services at good prices. This is a non-trivial task because markets are imperfect. A perfect market would determine the price of the item and other terms on which the supplier sells to the company. In that imaginary situation, each party gains from the transaction, and there is no fighting over the division of any surplus. In the real world there are transaction costs, as Coase (1937) famously claimed. Finding the best deal is costly for both parties. Negotiating is never cost-free, and the resultant contract may be risky for one or both parties. For example, it will usually entail a bet on future prices. The contract will not likely cover all contingencies; as a result, enforcing it or getting relief may be costly. The parties may have different interpretations of the contract; hence more negotiation and more expense. And if one of the parties proves unable to afford to meet the terms of the contract, perhaps as a result of unexpected events, what do we do? If information is asymmetric and the parties know it, the party with less information will be wary and may try to drive too hard a bargain to reduce the risk.

There are particular problems in cases of so-called asset specificity, in which an investment to support a particular transaction has much more value there than elsewhere. For example, the supplier may offer a technology that is of great value to a certain customer but not to anyone else. The customer, in turn, may alter some manufacturing process to take advantage of the technology. Both parties will see in this joint investment an opportunity for leverage but at the same time some serious risk, and haggling may be intense. Or, in the absence of trust, there may be no deal at all.

On the Coase view, the customer sometimes has reason to save on transaction costs by no longer buying from the supplier but instead making whatever the supplier has been selling, typically by acquisition. The very reason for having firms, according to Coase, is that going into the market for everything you need – materials, labor, managers, lawyers and so forth – would be prohibitively clumsy and expensive. Maybe hiring longshoremen or buying bananas on a daily basis would work; hiring scientists or buying large machinery that way would not.

Not every make-or-buy decision will be to buy, for at least two reasons. First, managing what you have bought creates problems of its own. I am about to argue that dealing with your own employees involves some of the very problems associated with dealing with suppliers. Second – and here is a point crucial to this essay – there are other ways to reduce transaction costs.[2]

PROBLEMS OF MANAGEMENT

Acquiring the supplier sometimes does reduce uncertainties and risks. For the acquiring company to manage what it acquires is not a trivial matter, however. The task is to give employees some reason to contribute to the success of the organization. (In the following paragraphs, I shall use the term *employees* to apply to collections as well as individuals.) One difficulty in doing this in some organizations is that the logic of the commons is at work.[3] Employees and management, whatever their distinct interests, share an interest in the organization's prosperity, at least in the sense that they will be better off if the organization does better, other things being equal. What contributes to organizational effectiveness – typically including employees' and managers' cooperative effort – serves employees' and managers' interests as well as those of stockholders. In some organizations an employee can contribute less than his/her share of the work while still getting his/her full share of the earnings of the company. Where that is true, an employee who is rational in the sense most familiar to economists will reason this way: I want to maximize my compensation and at the same time minimize the amount of work I do. I shall therefore be as unproductive as I can get away with being. But if every employee reasons and acts that way, the organization will be less effective. Since by hypothesis all gain from greater organizational effectiveness, everyone will be worse off as a consequence.

One possible solution is to prevent people from being unproductive in much the same way as regulation prevents pollution. But the kind of supervision that might accomplish this is difficult in most of today's complex organizations, which must deal with a turbulent and fluid environment. Jobs cannot be broken down into tasks done on the basis of an identifiable individual's effort and skill. The stream of unexpected problems may require that groups be put together quickly as different talents become temporarily necessary, or as different people happen to be available. Effectiveness requires teamwork, in which the individual's contribution is not always easily evaluated.[4] We can say much the same about individual incentive compensation, which is the equivalent of privatizing the commons, as each employee is to be paid according to what s/he contributes. Teamwork aside, some jobs demand competence that the manager cannot readily assess.

Both of these standard ways of preserving the commons amount to

.....ing contracts with employees. Employment contracts are sometimes necessary, but they have some of the same flaws as those between suppliers and customers. Negotiating and enforcing them can be expensive. They do not cover all contingencies. They are subject to interpretation and much negotiation after the fact. It is not always clear what to do when one party simply cannot meet the terms of the contract. And there is the problem of evaluating employee contributions.[5]

One possible way to make sure that people in the organizations do not act selfishly and damage the commons and thus themselves as well is to increase *social capital* – in particular, to get employees to care about one another's interests and the success of the organization, as many Japanese companies have allegedly done with good results.[6] Being proud of the company, not wanting to let the team down, not wanting to look bad to fellow employees – these are attitudes characteristic of a productive corporate culture. Freeman, Harrison and Wicks (2007, especially Chapter 4) argue that many successful organizations are driven by shared values. Managers and employees buy into what the company stands for, and think that it provides good reason for doing the work that they do. If this understanding leads people to do effective work for the company even when their doing it is not immediately necessary or sufficient for their being compensated, then all employees will benefit economically as well as in other ways.

Attitudes like this are not unheard of. Many people who would be better off as free riders are not inclined to ride free, but instead are willing to contribute to the cause if and only if others do their fair share as well. They do not want to be slackers, but they will not be suckers, either; so they need to know that others are pulling their weight. In this respect people are not narrowly rational *homines economici*. But an employee cannot always know whether others are pulling their weight, for some of the same reasons that management cannot; so preserving the commons requires the individual to trust the others, and to earn the trust of the others. Trust is essential to the effectiveness of the organization; it is self-fulfilling; it involves some risk; it is not easy to establish. Even between two individuals, it will take time for the strategy of defection – to put it in the terms of the prisoner's dilemma – to die out. It will take even longer for the players' regard for each other's interests, or for the shared values of the organization, to become a reason for them to cooperate.

So transaction costs may complicate life inside organizations too. I argue now that there are ways other than acquisition to reduce supply chain uncertainty and otherwise keep transaction costs to a minimum. These other ways have something to do with seeing common interests.

WAYS OF DEALING WITH SUPPLIERS

Sometimes, as I have noted, a contract between supplier and customer will be inadequate. A long-term contract will sometimes lock the customer in at an unexpectedly high price, and sometimes force the supplier under contract to sell at a loss. A contract that provides for such contingencies is difficult and expensive to negotiate, and the parties may not think of every contingency. The best thing for the parties may be to agree to the contract on the understanding that they will revisit it if things change radically. This sort of agreement requires a high level of trust: each side must believe that the other will permit some slack even if doing so is purely voluntary. There are no rules that tell how much slack one party should give the other, or how often it should be given. Whether I cut you some slack depends on whether I think you will cut me some slack, and that depends on whether you think I will cut you some slack, and that depends . . .

The parties are in a prisoner's dilemma, and need to find a win–win outcome. If I trust you to cut me some slack when appropriate and therefore cut you some slack, you are then better off, at least in the short run, if you do not cut me any slack when the situation is reversed; and vice versa. If we do not trust each other and never cut each other any slack, neither of us will exploit the other, but we will both be paying some high opportunity costs. The best possible situation, collectively, is that we trust each other and are trustworthy, and hence give each other slack as appropriate. Here as elsewhere in business, particularly in the case of asset specificity, it is important to trust but difficult to verify.[7]

I am more likely to trust you if you have established a reputation as trustworthy. I can infer your trustworthiness from your treatment of me and from your treatment of others. In repeat games, the habitual defector's reputation will cause others to stay away, or to play hardball if compelled to play. A bad reputation is costly, and the virtue of honesty has some payoff. Still, there are no guarantees.

The problem of imperfect information can be addressed through some mutual disclosure. There are no rules, however, for determining exactly how transparent a party should be, or what it is appropriate to reveal. That will vary from one situation to another; perhaps more transparency is called for in certain businesses. A customer with oligopsony power over a supplier – Wal-Mart comes to mind – will often demand and get a full accounting of the supplier's costs and other matters. In a dependable win–win relationship each party should at least be satisfied with the information that the other discloses.

Trust may be the result of a kind of loyalty. Each party may want the other to be successful, and may therefore be disinclined to withhold information or undertake strategies that would undermine the other party. A company will care about the success of a supplier if, as is sometimes the case, the supplier's failure would damage the company's supply chain. One less supplier is not a good thing, particularly if it is a supplier that one knows better than one knows the others. And a supplier will not likely want to lose a good customer. One good outcome of this relationship of mutual caring is that neither side needs to worry as much about whether the other will end the relationship because there is another supplier or customer who makes an offer that is better by a penny a unit. Perhaps all the wining and dining that goes on between customers and suppliers has the good purpose of making them care about each other, though one might wish that the buyers would occasionally pick up the tab. This kind of connection increases social capital.[8] Everyone involved has something to gain from a good supply chain.

Here, as elsewhere, there are no codifiable rules to guide us in deciding how loyal to be to a supplier or purchaser, as any virtue ethicist would expect. We can be too close, as certain relationships sometimes found in Asia demonstrate, or we can be too far. The situation, not being rule-bound, requires that those involved in it have what Aristotle calls practical wisdom (*phronesis*), the cardinal virtue of good character. One would expect a pragmatist like Freeman to agree. The case also shows the futility of the separation thesis. In deciding what we owe our suppliers, we are making an ethical decision and a business decision.

VALUES IN THE SUPPLY CHAIN: WAL-MART[9]

Wal-Mart is one of the examples that Freeman, Harrison and Wicks (2007) discuss. The firm has always had a distinct mission: to deliver quality goods at low prices, principally to price-sensitive customers. It is able to do so though superior supply chain management, which allows it to get low prices from its suppliers. Wal-Mart has something close to monopsony power over many of its suppliers, but it makes a lot of money for them because it offers them high-volume purchases. In that rather narrow sense it is a win–win situation. The outcome is also win–win with respect to customers: Wal-Mart is able to take advantage of its outstanding supply chain management to offer low prices.

It does not do so by cutting its suppliers any slack. If a supplier discovers that a contract is not working out as expected, it is up to the supplier to deal with the problem or cease to be a supplier. Precisely because there are such great advantages to being a Wal-Mart supplier, there are usually others waiting to replace any link in the supply chain that would otherwise be missing. To maintain their positions, suppliers often become more efficient themselves, sometimes under the direct guidance of Wal-Mart, which is not shy about offering what some consider intrusive assistance.

One way to increase efficiency is to send jobs overseas, and Wal-Mart continues to be accused of permitting some overseas suppliers to violate its stated labor policies (see, for example, the website of the International Labor Rights Forum, 2009). Wal-Mart managers could deny responsibility for conditions that their suppliers, not they, inflict on these workers. But they gain from what the suppliers do, and in many cases they have the power to stop or alleviate any suffering gratuitously imposed; so it is hard to show that they bear no responsibility for it. And, as Adam Smith himself would no doubt ask, why would any normal person, possessed of a measure of human sympathy, want to be an enabler of cruel suppliers? In any case, the widespread belief that they are complicit can put their brand at risk.[10]

Wal-Mart may be in a position to improve matters in that area without great financial loss. To begin with, some sweatshop operators need to understand that abusing workers and ignoring health and safety problems is a false economy. If retailers do need to help pay for humane standards in sweatshop operation, they can all raise their prices very slightly so that the suppliers are not harmed financially and no retailer suffers a competitive disadvantage. In creating a win–win situation like this, a widespread concern for the welfare of the workers will help.

Whether Wal-Mart shares this concern is in doubt. Domestically it has not always treated its workforce well.[11] Wal-Mart not only pays low wages and offers modest benefits, but has apparently condoned gender discrimination. In 2008 the company settled 63 lawsuits alleging illegal wages discrimination against women (see Greenhouse and Rosenbloom, 2008.) Wal-Mart's opposition to unions is implacable: the company has spent many millions of dollars in preventing employees from organizing. Here too there has been some skirting of the law.

There have also been complaints that Wal-Mart is shutting down Main Streets: small businesses, many of them owned by families well known in the community, cannot compete on price. There is a clash of values here. If we think of social capital in a way that highlights connections with small-town institutions like the mom and pop store, Wal-Mart harms communities. But if Wal-Mart can save shoppers money and reduce the time they spend shopping, it may enhance their quality of life, including their social life.

No matter how hard stakeholders strive to find win–win situations, satisfying everyone is neither possible nor morally obligatory. Wal-Mart has no trouble finding eager vendors, qualified workers and good customers, because it adds value to them all, in accordance with its mission. At the very least, it adds mutual value in the way in which a free market does. In some areas it does more than that. But to do so requires lower costs, and that is not compatible with paying high prices for goods and high wages for unskilled labor or holding local inefficient businesses harmless.

Wal-Mart's corporate mission benefits its two most important stakeholders. It solves a prisoner's dilemma problem with its suppliers – though not in a truly cooperative way – whom it does not permit to wine and dine its buyers, and it shares its savings with its customers. Wal-Mart has responded to criticism by listening as well as advocating, and by making substantive adjustments as necessary. It has taken initiatives with respect to the environment, with the prospect of cost savings, and has demanded the same of its suppliers – another win–win. Wal-Mart cannot please everyone, however, and some employees and unions are among those who are seriously displeased.

Some critics argue that Costco is ethically superior to Wal-Mart because Costco pays its employees much better while still offering its customers low prices. It is worth noting to begin with that Costco is a membership store. Costco economizes on choice: the customer has a narrower range of brands to choose from. Most Costco stores do not accept food stamps, or the cards that have now replaced the old stamps. It is hard to see any economic basis for this policy. Perhaps the idea is that Costco does not wish to cater to food stamps people – not our sort, you know. But that is speculation.

It may be that Wal-Mart and Costco just have different customer bases. Wal-Mart attracts working-class people, particularly in areas of the United States in which unions are viewed with some suspicion. Costco is more successful in bringing in upper-middle-class liberals, who support unions and may even avoid Wal-Mart on principle. Because the two corporations have different priorities in accommodating customers, they have different priorities for other stakeholders as well. A different mission and different values will do that. Rational arguments about values are surely possible, but it may not be possible to come to the rational conclusion that Wal-Mart's values are better than those of Costco or vice versa.

Neither Wal-Mart nor Costco can eliminate trade-offs in the supply chain. Lower prices create challenges for suppliers and raise questions about labor practices. Lower prices also undercut local merchants, and reduce one set of indices of social capital while increasing another. Not everything can be maximized. Both have extraordinary market power, and can get most of the surplus in any deal with a supplier. Their suppliers, in turn, can offer sweatshop workers a subsistence wage. The suppliers and the sweatshop workers do win something, but the latter especially do not win very much.

In at least one area, however, Costco comes closer to win–win: Costco pays its employees much better than does Wal-Mart. One result is higher labor costs, but not so much higher as one might suppose: Costco has about one-fifth the turnover that Wal-Mart has, and turnover entails training costs and costs associated with inexperience. Lichtenstein (2009: 247) cites estimates that Wal-Mart could pay at the level of Costco and unionized retailers if it raised its prices 2.2 percent.

In another way Costco makes up some of the difference. We can infer from its turnover figures that Costco has loyal employees, who will be much more likely than are their Wal-Mart counterparts to care about the success of the company as a whole. This is an important point, which we have touched on and will consider further in discussing the commons.

It is not clear that these savings make up for the cost of higher wages, but they surely help. Wall Street would prefer that Costco pay lower wages and generate higher profits,[12] but James Sinegal, its chief executive, appears to believe that the stockholders are receiving a fair return. He himself has made a fortune in Costco stock. Given the fairness of the return and the savings achieved by low employee turnover and high loyalty, Costco is not offering a zero-sum game, though there is still some trading off.

A true believer in Friedman might argue that Costco management has a moral responsibility to favor the stockholders over the employees in this case. Freeman would disagree, and so do I. This raises an obvious question: what is the right balance – assuming *balance* is a useful term here – of stockholder versus employee rights or interests? We cannot give a wholly satisfactory answer, though some have weighed in confidently. For example John Tierney, not widely known as an advocate for needy people, has argued that improving Wal-Mart employees' lot amounted to 'tak[ing] money out of the pockets of the poor' (Lichtenstein, 2009: 247). We can say that a certain level of generosity to the employees is inappropriate because it will endanger the company, and at the other extreme that subsistence wages are at best morally problematic. In the absence of perfect competition, we cannot say that employees ought to be paid as they would be in perfect competition; so the mere fact that there are applicants who would work for very low wages does not in itself justify paying very low wages. But there is no formula for deciding how to manage the trade-off between employees and stockholders. Over time a corporation will at least sometimes get the stockholders that buy into what the corporate mission says about the entitlements of the stockholders, but even then it does not follow that the mission is right.

There are stakeholder relations beyond the supply chain, but the problems arise elsewhere too. A relationship can be better than zero-sum but still not fair. Being a free rider is not the only way to exploit a stakeholder.

Is there some way to determine what is fair? Can we develop relationships that go even beyond win–win?

A BOLD SUGGESTION

I want to explore a bold suggestion that Charles Blattberg (2000) makes. In his view we arrive at fair political and commercial arrangements through *conversation*. In that respect his position has something in common with that of Phillips (2003), who invokes Habermas on communicative action. I invoke Aristotle, the greatest pragmatist of them all.[13] But although it makes sense to undertake a dialectical search for a solution to an issue or a principle for solving issues, I claim that the useful principles on which we can reach consensus are narrow, and that in any case they are not enough in the end to give us clear solutions to practical problems. What stakeholder-oriented management requires is a certain sort of character. It needs a real pro.

Blattberg has a radical view of how to create win–win relationships. He puts forward the remarkable idea that we do not need to accept trade-offs or compromises or irreconcilable values. He contemplates stakeholders coming to agreement about values. Even if I cannot entirely justify Blattberg's bold claims, I believe that they point towards some useful ways of thinking about stakeholders.

Blattberg argues for what he calls the *patriotic* approach to governance and dispute resolution. His proximate target is pluralism,[14] advocated by Rawls and many other liberals: they are satisfied with our living together in peaceful democracy because we are willing to ignore certain essentially private ideological differences and be governed according to that subset of principles that we do or should hold in common. Patriotism involves a concern for and agreement about a certain conception of the common good. Citizens – including firms and their stakeholders – can do more than accommodate their differing values through compromise and negotiation: they can arrive at broad agreements about what is good and what to do.[15]

People get to a consensus on moral issues through conversation, which in Blattberg's conception is a little like Aristotelian dialectic, which is supposed to align our intuitive moral judgments with principles that account for them. Rawls's reflective equilibrium is a successor concept; Habermas's communicative action is similar as well. The presupposition seems to be that we do hold certain fundamental views in common, and that these can be surfaced. Blattberg claims that one's goods ought to fit together into a coherent whole – so coherent a whole, in fact, that to change one of them entails changes in the others.

Blattberg is optimistic about the possibility of bringing about genuine accord between and among people through conversation as opposed to negotiation. The latter recognizes abiding differences of opinion concerning what is good, and accepts tradeoffs and compromises. In the best possible situation, two or more parties have a conversation about what is the right thing to do, with each side bringing along its ideas about ethics. A wholly successful conversation is one in which all participants come to share not only a view of what is good in this situation but also a whole coherent set of values, which presumably will answer other ethical questions that they may have. In the end, if all goes well, we reach a shared conception of the common good. So if we apply Blattberg's notion, a supplier and a buyer should be able to get beyond what is minimally acceptable to both parties and arrive at an agreement that both justifiably think best, on the basis of a very broad agreement about goods.

The kind of detachment characteristic of some liberal approaches is not desirable. What patriotism requires is the engagement of one's values in the conversation, not abstraction from it. Both sides should care a lot about what happens, and they will indeed care if conversation leads them to an agreement that is consistent with their values. The goal is not 'solidarity among strangers', but something like Aristotle's conception of friendship, according to which what is good for one's friend is good for oneself.

Blattberg invokes Aristotelian *phronesis*, or practical wisdom: there are no principles, Rawlsian or otherwise, that give the conversants guidance on how to get to the best outcome. Available principles, being thin, abstract from some of the most important features of the situation.[16]

One's first reaction may be incredulity. To begin with, as Socrates and others have shown with devastating effect, most people just do not have a coherent body of values. Some incoherence may be the result of an adjustment of one's values,[17] but our values do not usually evolve from one coherent set to another. In any case, as many social psychologists tell us, our deliberations about morality, politics and other matters tend to issue in self-serving rationalizations. What reason do we have to believe that we can have the right kind of conversation and reach the right kind of agreement with fellow citizens and with suppliers as well as other stakeholders? The suggestion seems utopian.

Of course getting the right answer to any serious moral question will be difficult to impossible, and getting broad agreement to that answer is another hard task. So why should we not try to reach whatever agreements we can, particularly if we are satisfied with agreements of limited scope? Perhaps Blattberg's suggestion that we move beyond mere negotiation and try to find some genuinely ethical answers offers us some useful guidance in thinking about stakeholders.

To begin with, as I have argued, we know enough about the prisoner's dilemma to work our way around the dominant consequences of short-term selfish rationality. It requires some trust and some concern for the welfare of the other party, but those can be cultivated. More important, the typical customer is also a supplier. Managers ought to be able to see the supplier–customer relationship from both sides and think of ways of managing it that are productive as well as fair to both sides. Being both a supplier and a customer may help one arrive at a coherent conception of what the one owes the other.[18]

We can broaden the point. Every organization, having stakeholders, is itself a stakeholder to many other organizations, and ought to be able to manage its stakeholder relations with that fact in mind. Even oil company executives prefer to breathe clean air; even factory owners prefer to drink clean water. Even members of the Sierra Club benefit from a productive economy and can understand that others do as well.

All stakeholders should therefore consider all their positions in relation to one another. If you are a customer, I need not ask you to put yourself in your supplier's shoes: I can simply remind you that you are a supplier and that you have certain views about how you ought to be treated in that role. You can have a useful conversation with yourself about how customers and suppliers should treat each other, and your dual position will give that conversation some insight and some objectivity, though no detachment.

Blattberg advocates something like friendship among fellow citizens, and by extension stakeholders. This seems on its face a fresh leap into implausibility. The friend, Aristotle says, is another self; so I want what is best for my friend. But should a customer really want what is best for a supplier? Yes, in this sense: the relationship that works best in the long run for both supplier and customer is one that solves the prisoner's dilemma by developing a relationship of trust and, as necessary, flexibility. As Blattberg suggests, and Freeman (not to mention Aristotle) would probably agree, we cannot formulate rules that tell my supplier or me exactly how trusting and flexible to be, when to give up on having a win–win conversation, or when to sever the relationship. But both parties must seriously explore the options and their likely consequences with a view to developing a mutually beneficial relationship. The supplier may not really be my friend, and I do not help my supplier succeed because I am a nice guy. But I do see how we are in this together, and how we need to work towards our common benefit.

Most important, I should see how my justification for treating this supplier as I do must apply also to how my customers will treat me. An honest person will argue in exactly the same way when s/he is a customer as when s/he is a supplier. S/he may well contemplate being on the other end of the relationship, as s/he sometimes is. Sometimes we say that it takes an effort of moral imagination to see a situation from the point of view of the other party. No doubt a successful conversation will often require that kind of moral imagination. In this case, though, it is easier to see things from the other's point of view because one is oneself a supplier as well as a customer. The point can be generalized, as I claimed earlier: any organization that has stakeholders is itself a stakeholder.[19]

There are cases in which an organization squeezes its suppliers but loudly objects when it is squeezed by its customers. What is wrong with that, from a moral point of view, is not so much that it is nasty to squeeze suppliers, but that it is unprincipled and hypocritical to demand that the rules be changed when you are the supplier. It is not clear that one must always be nice to one's stakeholders. What is clear is that one has no right to treatment not afforded to one's stakeholders just because one believes it would enrich one's stockholders. One's counterpart presumably has stockholders too. Even a hard-nosed businessperson will understand such ethical limits to what one should do for one's stockholders.

Those limits are set, and other questions about stakeholders should be addressed, by reference to a wider common good. I have in mind, though perhaps Blattberg does not, something stronger than mere consensus on what is good, though still no mysterious collective entity. I make the claim, plausible I hope, that in some cases aiming at the good of the firm or community is a good thing from the point of view of the individual.

From Friedman to the most fervent advocate of corporate social responsibility, it is agreed that free market business produces many goods. Many successful businesspeople will happily acknowledge that they are strong competitors and that they are working for their stockholders primarily. But they will also acknowledge that they are doing so within a system that in the long run benefits nearly everyone. In the words of Yeats: 'Those that I fight I do not hate.' Competitors are competitors, not enemies. Sometimes you cooperate with your stakeholder for the common good; sometimes you compete with your stakeholder for the common good. You do not ask yourself what you are going to do today for the common good, but if what you do fails to contribute in some way to the common good, that is a problem. This is less than Blattberg would have us agree on, but it is something important.[20]

We can get at this common good by asking the question, what is the point of business? Most would say that business ought to be an engine of general prosperity, though they would also agree that managers should not make every decision with an eye to increasing general prosperity. I want to explicate this notion by arguing that business has some of the characteristics of a sport. There is much to be said for competition among resourceful and intelligent people all of whom want to do their best in providing something primarily to customers but to others as well. One can take justifiable pride in competing successfully on the basis of the quality and price of the goods and services one offers to the market, where quality in particular may be an elusive notion that only superior insight can fully grasp. One does not have reason to be proud of winning by lying or breaking the law.

BASEBALL AND THE COMMON GOOD

If Friedman were right, baseball players ought to take it as their mission to make profits for the consortium of owners of the team. But they do not, and there is no reason why they should. We say that a player is good because he contributes to the team's winning games. The same is true of people in the front office. One might object that this is just because winning is profitable. Not so. The Chicago Cubs organization makes a lot of money from attendance at Wrigley Field and from television, but the Cubs are not considered successful, because they have not won a World Series since 1908.[21]

What counts as corporate success? Who decides? In the case of a baseball team, profit and the owners are not obviously the right answers. Nor are they right in the case of a publicly held corporation of doctors. There is a serious question about values here. Blattberg envisages convergence on values through conversation. In the spirit of his claim, we can consider a common good to which all stakeholders have reason to contribute because it is productive for all contributing stakeholders. But suppose I object that I as an individual player have reason only to contribute to my own good. If I do say that, I am exposing myself to the strong possibility of a lose–lose situation.

But beyond looking for win–win situations, does it follow that we have or should seek a consensus on the nature and priority of all goods? What vision of the common good unites Wal-Mart and Costco? They could probably never agree on their obligations to stakeholders, but they – and we and others – may well be able to agree on an important common good: a good business system. They might agree that they should be contributing to a business system that is a value-creating engine that encourages and rewards managers who prosper by competing hard to create excellent products and services. They might agree that profit is a significant but imperfect indicator of value. They surely ought to agree that, whatever the immediate motivations of the individual players, the whole thing is supposed to produce value. Market fundamentalists agree to that; Friedman defends it partly on that basis. For what if it proved to be the case that the pursuit of profit actually had strongly antisocial consequences? Even Ayn Rand would not recommend it.

If stakeholders can agree on a certain kind of business community as a common good, they can generate some useful, though not immutable, principles for competitors. One is that competition should be based on quality and price primarily. Another is that certain market failures should be eliminated insofar as possible. Another is a principle of fairness: competition and other stakeholder relations should be fair in the sense that one should not be a defector while demanding that one's stakeholders be cooperators. But the real action-guiding work is done not by principles from Kant or Mill but by those that emerge over time through experience. By trial and error and observation of others, and most of all by serious, engaged conversation with stakeholders, businesspeople learn how to achieve win–win situations, how to arrive at a consensus on values, when to abandon the search for consensus and turn to negotiation, and when to walk away. The overarching guide is a notion of a productive business system.

THE REAL PRO

Excellence in any practice[22] requires some abstract and concrete knowledge, but a kind of skill as well. It also requires character of a certain sort. The parties need to be honest, fair-minded, patient but not too patient (a nice example of an Aristotelian mean), trustworthy, competent and well-informed. This is what Aristotle calls excellence (sometimes translated as virtue). In some fields we use the expression 'real pro' – someone who achieves success by doing things right. As we are talking about practices, what is right about what the real pro does cannot be reduced to principles. The real pro's excellences or virtues include a determination to play the game the right way. The key to dealing with stakeholder issues is to have a real pro in charge.

How would someone like that deal with suppliers, for example? I have already mentioned the importance of trust and trustworthiness, flexibility and other virtues that create a mutually productive relationship. The customer and the supplier should converse about how to make their relationship work well for both parties, cut transaction costs, reduce surprises and the problems that they create, increase product quality, and in these and other ways create value and contribute to the economy. Their conversation would not raise the question, 'How do we contribute to the well-being of society as a whole?' It would be about how to create and maintain a productive relationship. The relationship depends on trusting and trustworthy people understanding that they are in this together and that they are going to do things right. It is not easy. The hardest thing is to frame situations in ways that are engaged but not self-serving. But no one ever said that good character was easy, or that most businesspeople are real pros.

Carlton Fisk, the highly professional catcher for the Red Sox and the White Sox, understood excellence as well as any player. He once saw the flashy Deion Sanders fail to run out a pop-up and shouted at Sanders to 'play the game right', or suffer physical violence from Fisk. Fisk always played hard, and his aggressive play sometimes led to fights with opponents. But he would have said that trying to win and even sometimes fighting showed that he and the players on opposing teams shared an appropriate respect for the game. It is significant that some other players who were equally aggressive disliked Fisk. But if ballplayers had extended conversations about how to play, most of them would probably agree that Fisk did it right, and that he was right to confront Sanders as he did, even though by doing so he might have helped strengthen Sanders's team, at that time the Yankees, whom Fisk loved to beat. No doubt Fisk would say that players who took steroids also showed no respect for the game.

Professional athletes compete hard, and they admire others who do the same. They know that they are partners as well as competitors in their game. The purpose of the game is to entertain the spectators, but ballplayers are not supposed to stand at the plate or on the mound or in their defensive positions and think about how they are going to entertain the fans or make money for their owners. But sometimes, even in the heat of battle, they think about the integrity of the game and what they owe it.[23]

It is the task of philosophers to encourage and deepen the conversation. The result may be consensus, or sometimes just understanding, which is at least better than mindless hostility. It is appropriate to expect the conversation within the organization to lead to a consensus on some important values. Those who cannot accept the values should consider going elsewhere. Values will more likely differ from one organization to another. So Wal-Mart and Costco may just have different constituencies and different values, including different rankings of stakeholders. But if Wal-Mart and Costco were to converse about what they consider important, they might both learn something about each other's values and their own. That would be a good outcome even if they could not agree on all values, though we would expect them to agree on the importance of a good business community.

We do not expect competitors to make particular decisions in the light of the common good, even if in the long run they contribute to it. Think of the justice system. Its ultimate goal is justice – the punishment of the guilty rather than the innocent. But in a trial the defense and the prosecution make the best case they can against and for guilt, and the truth is supposed to emerge. A pragmatist might say that trial by jury is the closest we can get to justice. Similarly, we might say that the best and fairest possible outcome will emerge from a perfectly competitive market. But even if there were any such thing as perfect competition, not even a pragmatist would have reason to believe that it would satisfy our demands with respect to utility and fairness.[24]

Blattberg advocates patriotism. Surely we do not have quite the same responsibility to competitors or fellow employees that we do to fellow citizens. Yet with some care – the kind we associate with pragmatism – we can apply his lessons to both. In particular, it is important to be able to converse with stakeholders external and internal, and to find values that are held in common. We may negotiate with them sometimes, and sometimes have conversations that lead to deeper reconciliation. Practical wisdom requires that our conversation aims to get both the facts and the ethics right. And if the separation thesis is wrong, as both Aristotle and Freeman would agree it is, you cannot get either of them entirely right without getting the other one right.

Blattberg's vision can probably seldom be achieved, though conversation towards reconciliation improves understanding, and that is something. It will also solve the prisoner's dilemma in some cases. The conversations that clarify and deepen our values will often not lead to consensus on all matters, but they may lead to mutual respect and respect for the game. But nothing in Blattberg's vision tells us how to determine fairness in a particular case. There is no algorithm that helps Wal-Mart decide how to treat its suppliers or labor unions. That is a point in favor of virtue ethics generally.[25] Pragmatists will differ from Blattberg, and Aristotle as well, in their belief that the conversation never ends. New facts, new insights, new intuitions will keep us talking.

Even if Blattberg is too optimistic, there is something to be said for moving in the direction that he suggests. I may believe that I have my values and you have yours, that I need not accept or even fully understand your values but should instead try to get the best deal I can by negotiation. My objective is to get the best price I can, though I am aware that the better my price is, the worse yours is. Your price is your problem. If we move in the direction of the patriotic position, you and I may consider the possibility that in some ways we are in this together. In two ways we are. First, in some cases we may be locked in a prisoner's dilemma game and want to avoid double defection. Second, we are both players in the great game of business, and we should want to play the game the right way.

The game of business has some of the characteristics of the commons.

We strengthen the commons insofar as the stakeholders care about one another's interests as Adam Smith believed they could and usually did. They do not need to be friends. What they need, above all, is to respect the game and play it right. That is a value that stakeholders should hold in common: the sort of competition for which the real pros, the Carlton Fisks of the world, demand the respect of all who participate. This sort of rivalry will lead to prosperity.

A PESSIMISTIC NOTE

Things do not always work this way. It is hard to see the senior managers of Wal-Mart as real pros in the sense I have in mind. They do not think they need to find true common ground with their suppliers because they need not, and there is little advantage in doing so. They essentially control them. Nor do they need to worry very much about whether a supplier is succeeding, because there is nearly always another one available if the supplier fails. Much the same is true of employees: there are always people eager to take a job at Wal-Mart. The example of Costco suggests, though it does not prove, that Wal-Mart could do better by its employees and recoup some of the additional cost through the kind of loyalty that helps preserve the internal commons, but Wal-Mart does not choose to do so.[26] That Costco does pay more may be largely a result of its locations being in tougher labor markets as much as its view of the interests of the employees as opposed to the stockholders.

There is good reason to believe that a more competitive labor market would improve the employees' lot, and that stronger competition for suppliers' goods would raise their prices. As things are, the genuinely strong competition for shoppers' dollars combined with oligopsony with respect to suppliers puts the latter in a difficult position, though in most cases a profitable one.

What would a real pro do about this? The answer is not obvious. It is possible to be demanding of suppliers but not unreasonable, so long as suppliers are making significant profits from the arrangement. We can imagine that a real pro would treat employees well and expect their loyalty in return, as Costco seems to do. But why should the trade-off between employees and stockholders be tilted more towards the former than in the Wal-Mart case? Undue generosity to the employees and neglect of the stockholders will harm the company and therefore in due course the employees themselves.

The real pro might go even further, and take the view that a good company contributes to the economy by not only providing goods and services at reasonable prices but also contributing to the development of a strong middle class. Is this the sort of thing that corporations ought to think about? It could be part of the mission of a successful corporation, so long as it does not create a competitive disadvantage. And if Collins and Porras (2004) are right, a corporate mission that involves contributing to prosperity will often create a competitive advantage.

So we find ourselves saying that the absence of a competitive market for suppliers' goods causes problems, and at the same time we find ourselves saying that a highly competitive retail market can cause problems as well. This is not a conclusion designed to gladden ideologues.

We must also say that, while businesspeople may take professional satisfaction in selling good products and services at fair prices, there will be arguments about what counts as professional and about how reliably professionalism guarantees a good outcome for all stakeholders. But as anyone who knows anything about virtue ethics will tell you, we cannot expect to find a formula that sets out just what a real pro will do, for virtues are not reducible to dispositions to act on principles. Perhaps we can say at least that over time real pros, whose experience helps them assess opportunities wisely, will develop tools and mindsets that help them navigate among stakeholders in ways that do justice to legitimate claims and contribute to the kind of widespread prosperity that is the pride of capitalism.

A FINAL OPTIMISTIC WORD ON CHARACTER

Being a real pro, or more generally a person of good character, typically leads to win–win situations, but there is more to it than just mutual advantage. I have argued that an organization in which management gives employees good reason to be loyal creates a sense of identification with the organization and its mission helps preserve the commons and benefit everyone. There is one more thing to be said for such an organization: it is the home of what we might follow MacIntyre and arguably Aristotle in calling the virtuous *practice*: managers and employees are involved in a 'coherent and complex form of socially established cooperative human activity,'[27] or more than one such activity.

Insofar as the organization makes other stakeholders partners in cooperative practices, it increases the virtuous circle. This will not be possible with all stakeholders. It may, though, be possible with others in one's supply chain when circumstances are favorable. But where it can be done there is good reason, from the point of view of both virtues and good outcomes, to do it.

Most successful businesspeople, especially the real pros, enjoy what they do because it teaches and exercises some virtues that, as Aristotle rightly says, in action make for happiness of a particularly deep sort: intelligence (emotional and rational), courage, sensitivity, cooperativeness, empathy, respect for excellence, patience and, when appropriate, impatience, honesty. Contrary to what MacIntyre seems to believe, both fair competition and fair cooperation can teach these business virtues. At its best this is a good game, a good life.

ACKNOWLEDGMENT

Thanks to Rob Phillips for several useful suggestions.

NOTES

1. So my account will agree in some important respects with that of Phillips (2003), who claims that fairness requires not being a free rider.
2. When Coase offered his view, supply chains were long and inefficient, and supply chain management was pretty much an unknown discipline.
3. I discuss this point in more detail in Hartman (1996), especially Chapter 3.
4. Alchian and Demsetz (1972) address this difficulty, though not in exactly these terms.
5. Jensen and Meckling (1976) famously address the 'agency problem' and argue that the key is to write contracts that align managers' and stockholders' interest. It seemed like a good idea at the time.
6. I define social capital as a set of connections that encourage collective action that is mutually beneficial in that it leads to win–win situations and preservation of the commons. Social capital typically generates capital of other sorts, including economic. The most influential recent treatment of the notion is that of Putnam (2000).
7. The problem of asset specificity arises within firms. A typical joint investment inside the organization would be employee training that is specific to a particular job. If the employee resigns or is fired, both parties stand to lose.
8. There is a literature on social capital in supply chains. See for example Lawson, Tyler and Cousins (2008).
9. The literature on Wal-Mart and Costco is vast. I have relied particularly on Greenhouse (2009), Moreton (2009) and Lichtenstein (2009).
10. See Phillips and Caldwell (2005) on responsibility for what goes on far away in the supply chain.
11. See Lichtenstein (2009) for an account that is critical but not heavy-handed.
12. Costco has a higher price/earnings ratio than does Wal-Mart, but that may reflect investors' expectations about Wal-Mart's greater future growth. It appears that those expectations are being disappointed.
13. There is controversy over the precise status of dialectic in Aristotle's ethics.
14. He also criticizes deliberative democracy, which also aims at the common good but has, he claims, too weak and pessimistic a view about the possibilities of conversation.
15. Blattberg is claiming something like Aristotle's doctrine of the unity of the virtues, as he acknowledges. He also notes some similarities to Aristotle in advocating a certain social solidarity.
16. Rosenzweig (2007) advocates something like a virtue-based notion of strategy, since he believes that we cannot find strategic principles that guarantee anything.

17. So Phillips has suggested to me.
18. It is possible for me to know what I owe and not much care: I might make demands on my suppliers that I would never let my customers make on me. But the probable loss of social capital might be expensive.
19. Here I believe I am in accord with Patricia Werhane's views as expressed in her contribution to this volume.
20. Blattberg might fairly reply that agreement on values is the best way to produce social capital.
21. In fact their defeat of the New York Giants and their consequent victory in the 1908 Series came as the result of a dubious decision based on a previously unenforced rule.
22. On practices, especially in business, see MacIntyre (1985), Moore (2002, 2005a, 2005b, 2008, 2009) and Wallace (2009). MacIntyre and Moore, virtue ethicists, argue that excellence in practices is what ethics is about. But MacIntyre believes that the institutions of business undermine virtuous practices, and Moore disagrees, rightly in my view.
23. Manfred von Richthofen, the Red Baron, the most lethal of all German fighter pilots in the Great War, killed as many as 80 British pilots before being killed himself. His body, borne to the grave by allied pallbearers of his rank, was buried amid wreaths in a military ceremony as his enemies' guns fired a salute.
24. Of course one might claim that utility is a matter of getting what you choose and that justice is a relationship between the value of your input and that of your output. Such claims require actual argument.
25. Taking something seriously that cannot be measured goes against the grain of many who study organizations. Not all, however, Rosenzweig (2007) seems to have a healthy skepticism about taking what can be measured seriously because it can be measured.
26 Wal-Mart tries to unite its people in loyalty to certain Christian principles, which turn out to benefit management a lot more than labor. See Moreton (2009).
27. Cf. note 17. See MacIntyre (1985: 187; quoted in Moore, 2009), 43. MacIntyre argues that there cannot be virtuous practices in firms; Moore argues, effectively in my view, that there can be and ought to be.

BIBLIOGRAPHY

Alchian, A.A. and H. Demsetz 1972. Production, information costs, and economic organization. *American Economic Review*, **62**: 777–95.

Aristotle 1894. *Ethica Nicomachea*. Edited by I. Bywater. Oxford: Clarendon Press.

Aristotle 1985. *Nicomachean Ethics*. Translated by T.H. Irwin. Indianapolis: Hackett Publishing Company.

Blattberg, C. 2000. *From Pluralist to Patriotic Politics: Putting Practice First.* New York: Oxford University Press.

Coase, R.H. 1937. The nature of the firm. *Economica*, **4**: 386–405.

Collins, J. and Porras, J.I. 2004. *Built to Last.* New York: HarperBusiness.

Freeman, R.E. 1994. The politics of stakeholder theory: some future directions. *Business Ethics Quarterly,* **4**: 409–21.

Freeman, R.E., Harrison, J.S. and Wicks, A.C. 2007. *Managing for Stakeholders: Survival, Reputation, and Success.* New Haven, CT: Yale University Press.

Friedman, M. 1970. The social responsibility of business is to increase its profits. *New York Times Magazine*, 13 September.

Greenhouse, S. 2009. *The Big Squeeze: Tough Times for the American Worker.* New York: Anchor Books.

Greenhouse, S. and Rosenbloom, S. 2008. Wal-Mart settles 63 lawsuits over wages. *New York Times,* 23 December.

Hartman, E.M. 1996. *Organizational Ethics and the Good Life.* New York: Oxford University Press.

International Labor Rights Forum 2009. Wal-Mart campaign. Available online: http://www.laborrights.org/creating-a-sweatfree-world/wal-mart-campaign, accessed 16 January, 2011.

Jensen, M.C. and Meckling, W.H. 1976. The theory of the firm: managerial behavior, agency costs, and ownership structure. *Journal of Financial Economics,* **3**: 305–60.

Lawson, B., Tyler, B.B. and Cousins, P.D. 2008. Antecedents and consequences of social capital on buyer performance improvement. *Journal of Operations Management,* **26**: 446–60.

Lichtenstein, N. 2009. *The Retail Revolution: How Wal-Mart Created a Brave New World of Business.* New York: Metropolitan Books, Henry Holt and Company.

MacIntyre, A. 1985. *After Virtue.* 2nd edition. Notre Dame: University of Notre Dame Press.

Moore, G. 2002. On the implications of the practice–institution distinction: MacIntyre and the application of modern virtue ethics to business. *Business Ethics Quarterly,* **12**: 19–32.

Moore, G. 2005a. Corporate character: modern virtue ethics and the virtuous corporation. *Business Ethics Quarterly,* **15**: 659–85.

Moore, G. 2005b. Humanizing business: a modern virtue ethics approach. *Business Ethics Quarterly,* **15**: 237–55.

Moore, G. 2008. Re-imagining the morality of management: a modern virtue ethics approach. *Business Ethics Quarterly,* **18**: 483–511.

Moore, G. 2009. Virtue ethics and business organizations. In J.D. Smith (ed.), *Normative Theory and Business Ethics.* New York: Rowman and Littlefield, pp. 35–59.

Moreton, B. 2009. *To Serve God and Wal-Mart: The Making of Christian Free Enterprise.* Cambridge, MA: Harvard University Press.

Phillips, R.A. 2003. *Stakeholder Theory and Organizational Ethics.* San Francisco, CA: Barrett-Koehler Publishers.

Phillips, R.A. and Caldwell, C.B. 2005. Value chain responsibility: a farewell to arm's length. *Business and Society Review,* **110**: 345–70.

Putnam, R.H. 2000. *Bowling Alone: The Collapse and Revival of American Community.* New York: Simon and Schuster.

Rawls, J. 1971. *A Theory of Justice.* Cambridge, MA: Harvard University Press.

Rosenzweig, P. 2007. *The Halo Effect . . . and the Eight Other Business Delusions that Deceive Managers.* New York: Free Press.

Wallace, J.D. 2009. *Norms and Practices.* Ithaca, NY: Cornell University Press.

Walzer, M. 1994. *Thick and Thin: Moral Argument at Home and Abroad.* Notre Dame, IN: University of Notre Dame Press.

Yeats, W.B. 1919. An Irish Airman Foresees his Death. In *The Wild Swans at Coole and other Poems.* New York: MacMillan Company.

4. Stakeholder theory in strategic management: a retrospective

Jeffrey S. Harrison

This chapter will provide a description of the personal journey of the author who, as a newly graduated Ph.D. in strategic management in 1985, embraced stakeholder theory. Perhaps one of the interesting aspects of this narrative is that the field of strategic management itself was in its infancy at the time of my graduation. So I have 'grown up' in the strategy field while simultaneously observing and to some extent participating in the development of what we now call stakeholder theory. Over the past two and a half decades I have frequently found myself frustrated by my strategy colleagues' lack of understanding of the stakeholder concept and their inability to comprehend its potential to address many of the most important problems in the strategy field. My own attempts to remedy this situation while continuing to do mainstream strategy research are described herein.[1] Of course, in recent years the stakeholder concept has begun to gain greater acceptance in the strategy field. At the end of the chapter, I will describe some potentially fruitful applications of the stakeholder concept in strategic management research.

A DISCIPLINE IS BORN

The birth of the academic field now known as strategic management probably occurred at a conference at the University of Pittsburgh in May 1977. This is not to say that scholars were not already exploring related ideas and theories, but to keep with the birth analogy, these early activities are better described as the gestation period in which the baby was forming. The conference organizers, Dan Schendel and Charles Hofer, commissioned 14 research papers to describe and define the field of strategic management, examine research methods and provide direction for future research (Schendel and Hofer, 1979). Participants also included panelists, moderators, discussants, practitioners and a few additional members of the Business Policy and Planning division of the Academy of Management. A model that looked very much like a stakeholder map (Newman, 1979)

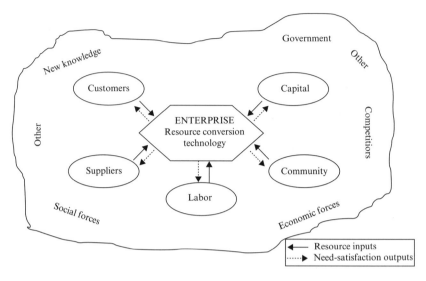

Source: Newman (1979: 45).

Figure 4.1   *Generalized contributor group interaction between the firm and its environment*

crept into the conference as a commentary to a paper presented by Igor Ansoff on the changing shape of the strategic problem (see Figure 4.1).

Porter published the first of his now-classic books in 1980, and by the mid-1980s both the proceedings of the Pittsburgh conference and Porter's work were among a few standard texts for doctoral students in the growing field of strategic management. I remember at the time that scholars in our newly emerging discipline were obsessed with gaining acceptance from other business disciplines as a credible academic field. The field itself had emerged, in part, from a need for practical guidance in making high-level corporate decisions, and much of the literature had a practical focus (even Porter's work). Since the strategy field did not have much in the way of its own theory to build upon, it was not surprising that many scholars were building on theory that was largely economics based (Chandler, 1962; Rumelt, 1974; Williamson, 1975; Jensen and Meckling, 1976; Pfeffer and Salancik, 1978; Porter, 1985).[2] Early scholars also applied empirical research methods from other disciplines, especially finance and organizational behavior. Financial performance became (and still is) the most important dependent variable in the field.

Consistent with the economics foundation, the widely accepted theories and prescriptions in strategic management at the time tended to be amoral. This probably was more of a practical consideration rather than an intentional oversight. Moral considerations are an added dimension that slow down and complicate the research process. It is much easier to assume they do not exist. To fill the void, a group of scholars with interest in the moral dimensions of management was forming a separate interest group at the Academy of Management. This allowed the two camps, Business Policy and Business and Society (now called Social Issues in Management), to pursue their own agendas without much cross-fertilization of ideas.

A STAKEHOLDER APPROACH TO STRATEGIC MANAGEMENT

I graduated in 1985 and read *Strategic Management: A Stakeholder Approach* (Freeman, 1984) shortly thereafter. The book transformed my thinking about strategic management, which had an impact on my teaching and research. To me, a stakeholder-based perspective of strategic management was completely intuitive. After all, managing stakeholders is precisely what managers do and stakeholders are the obvious building blocks of a competitive firm. I could not understand why many of my colleagues in strategic management did not recognize the potential of the stakeholder perspective in explaining competitive performance. In addition, I was drawn to the stakeholder approach because of its moral appeal.

The practicality of a stakeholder approach to strategic management made it very appealing to me as a teaching tool, yet it was not represented in any of the mainstream strategy textbooks of the time, so in the early 1990s I began talking to publishers about writing a book with stakeholder theory as the foundation. Since my experience was in corporate-level strategy, I sought a co-author who could complement me by providing more of a micro-view of the field. Caron St. John, who was trained in operations management, agreed to work with me on the project by managing all the cases and writing the implementation chapters. This left me eight chapters to write, covering internal and external analysis, strategic direction (missions, visions and purpose), business-level strategy, corporate-level strategy, and strategic control and restructuring.

My approach to writing my eight chapters was to start with a basic stakeholder foundation and then build on it the other topics and ideas that were important in the strategic management field at the time. For instance, the external analysis chapter was built on a foundation of external stakeholder analysis. Stakeholders with which a firm has reciprocal influence based on regular transactions were treated as part of the operating environment, while other stakeholders were a part of the firm's broad environment. Porter's (1985) Five Forces became a part of the operating environment: suppliers, customers, and three types of competitors (existing, substitute and potential). Consistent with stakeholder theory, the chapter also advocated both evaluating and managing relationships with stakeholders. Stakeholder management included strategies for communication and formation of various types of alliances. The internal analysis chapter viewed employees, managers, directors and owners as internal stakeholders. And, of course, the strategic direction chapter included a heavy dose of ethics and enterprise strategy.

To our delight, the first edition (Harrison and St. John, 1994) was widely adopted across most of the 50 US states. Equally satisfying, the adoption list included many of the best universities. However, between the first and second edition two things happened. First, and most important, a competing textbook based on the resource-based perspective was launched by the same publisher. Second, our publisher was acquired just before the second edition came out. There was a lot of confusion in the company at the time, and the sales representatives were focusing on the other textbook. At one point, a few months after our second edition came out, a publisher's representative actually tried to sell me the competing book. When I mentioned that I was an author for his company and that our second edition had come out recently he was really surprised. So it was not unexpected that the second edition did not sell particularly well. Nevertheless, I was very happy to observe that most of the strategic management texts at the time immediately or eventually added the stakeholder perspective. This outcome was consistent with my original purpose for writing the book.

Also satisfying during this period was a publication that grew out of some theory Caron and I developed as we wrote the book (Harrison and St. John, 1996). The paper suggests that firms should partner with (as opposed to monitor) stakeholders that have a large impact on the environmental uncertainty they face. It also helps to define which stakeholders are likely to have that sort of impact, based on the power they possess.

A PERIOD OF MISCONCEPTIONS

As I alluded to previously, the resource-based view of the firm was sweeping the strategy field in the early 1990s (Barney, 1991). There was so much interest in the resource-based perspective that it was difficult for me to engage other strategy scholars in meaningful discussions about the stakeholder approach. In addition, misconceptions regarding the stakeholder perspective were so ingrained at the time (Phillips, Freeman and Wicks,

2003) that stakeholder theory was all but ignored in the mainstream strategic management literature. This is manifest by the fact that not one article with the word 'stakeholder' in the title was published in *Strategic Management Journal* during the 1990s.

Later in the decade the relational view (Dyer and Singh, 1998; Gulati and Singh, 1998), now sometimes referred to as network strategy (Hitt, 2005), was introduced. In spite of strong conceptual similarities between the relational view and stakeholder theory, these scholars did not cite Freeman (1984), nor did they acknowledging the growing literature on stakeholder theory in the management literature (Hill and Jones, 1992; Donaldson and Preston, 1995; Jones, 1995; Greenley and Foxall, 1997; Mitchell, Agle and Wood, 1997). This was very frustrating to me and, I assume, to other strategy scholars who were advocates of a stakeholder perspective.

Discussions with colleagues drew me to the conclusion that most strategic management scholars genuinely did not understand stakeholder theory in the 1990s. Most of them envisioned it as a purely ethical theory with little strategic value. Misconceptions such as a belief that stakeholder theory requires that all stakeholders be given equal priority in strategic decisions led them to determine that the theory is impractical. The fact that members of the Social Issues in Management Division in the Academy of Management wholeheartedly embraced stakeholder theory did not really help the battle for acceptance of stakeholder theory in strategic management. Instead, it reinforced the perception that the theory is only about social responsibility. Also reinforcing this perception were publications in management journals that made use of stakeholder theory under the label of social responsibility (that is, Turban and Greening, 1996; Waddock and Graves, 1997; see also Elms et al. in the current volume). Nevertheless, a growing group of strategy scholars were friendly to stakeholder theory because they thought of it as a public relations tool that could help build a firm's reputation. Since the resource-based view suggests that hard-to-imitate resources are valuable to competitive advantage, and reputation is hard to imitate (Fombrun and Shanley, 1990), these strategists began to see value in the stakeholder approach as a means to gaining a better reputation. Also, some scholars became interested in the influence of stakeholders on organizational strategy and the distribution of value (Rowley, 1997; Coff, 1999; Frooman, 1999).

A SPECIAL ISSUE

By the late 1990s, there were enough management scholars examining the stakeholder approach to warrant special issues in management journals. I was serving on the editorial board of the *Academy of Management Journal* at the time, and the editor Anne Tsui was very supportive of a special issue on a stakeholder theme. Ed Freeman and I had become friends as he generously allowed Caron and I to use his material in our textbook. When I contacted Ed, he was excited about the prospect of co-editing a special issue on stakeholder theory. Firm performance was included in the call for papers because it is the primary dependent variable of interest to strategy scholars. We added the concept of social responsibility to the call to increase interest and ensure an adequate number of submissions. I realized then, as I do now, that this addition also served to reinforce the perception among strategy scholars that stakeholder theory is about social responsibility. However, the decision represented a tradeoff and we wanted to ensure the success of the issue as much as possible. The final topic of the research forum was 'Stakeholders, Social Responsibility and Performance'.

To our delight, we received 49 submissions, which led to a strong issue (Harrison and Freeman, 1999). Among the outstanding papers we had the good fortune to receive were several studies that focused on important stakeholder questions. One was an empirical test of the stakeholder salience model developed by Mitchell, Agle and Wood (1997). Agle, Mitchell and Sonnenfeld (1999) collected primary data from CEOs and discovered that particular stakeholder attributes increase their salience to managers. Another fascinating paper examined the motives behind a firm's attempts to address the interests of their stakeholders (Berman et al., 1999). The authors discovered support for the instrumental view that firms advance stakeholder interests because they believe that doing so can enhance firm performance and not because of a moral commitment to those stakeholders.

The four other papers in the special issue also deserve mention. Luoma and Goodstein (1999) investigated factors that influence the proportion of board seats filled by nonshareholding stakeholders. Ogden and Watson (1999) examined the attempts of UK water companies to balance the interests of customers and shareholders, and discovered that shareholders were able to compensate for short-term losses associated with customer satisfaction possibly because of the anticipated positive longer-term effects of the firm actions that created the losses. In another paper, Weaver, Treviño and Cochran (1999) examined the influence of external pressure and top management commitment on the nature of ethics programs within firms. Finally, Johnson and Greening (1999) tested the effects of institutional influences and other governance factors on corporate social performance. These last two papers were focused more on social responsibility in the way the term is traditionally used.

AN EXPLANATION FOR COMPETITIVE PERFORMANCE

Somewhere around the time of the special issue, I began putting on paper my own thoughts regarding the relationship between the way a firm manages its stakeholders and competitive performance. As one would expect from a strategist, my approach was very practical and instrumental, and strongly influenced by the work of Tom Jones (1995). In my mind, the positive relationship between treating a broad group of stakeholders well and high firm performance was obvious – my goal was to help explain why the relationship exists in terms that a strategist could appreciate. Consistent with some of the work I did with Caron (Harrison and St. John, 1994, 1996), I began to examine what it is about particular types of relationships that can enhance firm performance. Others had already provided some excellent ideas on this issue, but they had not yet achieved the level of acceptance in the strategy field that I thought they deserved. I built on their ideas, and a paper cycled through several meetings and countless peer reviews. At the University of Richmond, I was able to convince two outstanding co-authors, Doug Bosse and Robert Phillips, to join me.

To date, two papers have come out of our collaboration, both published in *Strategic Management Journal*. The first of these papers provides a social justice foundation upon which the second paper builds (Bosse, Phillips and Harrison, 2009). The core idea of paper one is that the widely held assumption that economic actors are self-interested is bounded by norms of fairness. Reciprocity stemming from distributional, procedural and interactional justice may allow some firms to enjoy competitive benefits that other firms do not enjoy. Building from the foundation created in the first paper, Harrison, Bosse and Phillips (2010) define firms that 'manage for stakeholders' as those that allocate more resources to satisfying the needs and demands of their important stakeholders than what is needed to ensure their continued participation in the value-adding processes of the firm. In this context, resources include time, information, attention and respect, as well as tangible allocations of value. Stakeholders of firms that exhibit this sort of social justice are more likely to share nuanced information about their utility functions. This knowledge can be used by firms to allocate resources more efficiently, to innovate and to deal better with changes in the environment. The paper also integrates resource-based theory. It explains that the competitive advantages coming from knowledge about stakeholder utility functions are sustainable because they are associated with causal ambiguity and path dependence.

A SURGE OF INTEREST

The first ten years of this century have been satisfying in terms of spreading the word about the stakeholder perspective. Corporate scandals and an increasing awareness of the value of ethical business practices have encouraged strategy scholars to give more attention to stakeholder theory. Several stakeholder-oriented works published in top journals seem to be recognized more widely by strategists than previous publications (that is, Hillman and Keim, 2001; Walsh, 2005; Jones, Felps and Bigley, 2007). In addition, some new and very convincing empirical evidence has added support to previous work that demonstrates a positive relationship between managing for stakeholders and high firm performance (Sisodia, Wolfe and Sheth, 2007; Choi and Wang, 2009).

Also helpful in advancing the stakeholder perspective are several highly talented scholars that have joined the movement.[3] In addition, supporters of the stakeholder perspective have been appointed to positions in which they are helping to decide which papers will get published in the top research journals. In terms of publication volume, only ten papers have been published in *Strategic Management Journal* with the word 'stakeholder' in their title and all of those have been published since 2001. If we use a more generous criterion of having 'stakeholder' anywhere in the abstract, 27 papers have been published in the journal, with two of them in the 1980s, four in the 1990s and 21 since 2001.

Because so much excellent work related to the stakeholder concept has been published, Ed Freeman, Andy Wicks and I formed a partnership to write two books. The first, *Managing for Stakeholders: Survival, Reputation and Success* (2007), is an update to Freeman (1984). The second book is a comprehensive examination of the work that has been done on the subject across all disciplines, including strategic management, marketing, finance, management, accounting, law, health care, public administration, environmental policy, business ethics and corporate social responsibility. The book also includes some introductory material that places stakeholder theory in its appropriate theoretical context, a treatise on stakeholder theory and capitalism, and suggestions for future research directions. Bidhan Parmar and Simone de Colle joined us in the effort. The extent of reach of stakeholder theory into such a wide variety of disciplines was astounding to each of us (Freeman et al., 2010).

Of course, there is much work still to be done, and the stakeholder approach seems well suited to many of the issues strategic management scholars and practitioners are attempting to address. The 'Great Recession' and its causes, combined with a general moral meltdown in business, have caused many to rethink the efficacy of current models upon which much of business is conducted. One set of questions that would appear to have great value deals with the influence of various approaches to managing stakeholders on firms' longevity (or sustainability), risk and risk propensity, governance structures, relationships with regulators or ability to adapt to rapid, hostile environmental changes.

Strategic management researchers may also benefit from research on how value creation can be measured. The field of strategic management is focused primarily on financial performance as a dependent variable. However, financial returns merely scratch the surface of the value a firm creates (or destroys) through its actions. A multi-stakeholder perspective has the potential to broaden the field's definition of performance. For instance, rather than focusing exclusively on financial outcomes from firm actions such as mergers, alliances or international diversification, researchers could examine other outcomes that are important to employees, suppliers, communities or customers. With a broader perspective on value creation, tradeoffs associated with firm actions can be better addressed.

Another fruitful avenue for research may be the integration of stakeholder theory with other popular theories in strategic management, such as the resource-based perspective. The resource-based perspective and stakeholder theory seem to be more complementary than competing (Freeman et al., 2010; Harrison, Bosse and Phillips, 2010). Also, as mentioned previously, there are some obvious parallels between network theory and stakeholder theory. Because it is such a broad-based perspective, stakeholder theory joined with any other theory may have the potential to provide a better explanation of firm performance, broadly defined.

In addition, stakeholder theory is also applicable to strategic management from an ethical perspective. At its core, strategic management is about people making decisions that influence people. There are ethical implications associated with every phase of the strategic management process, from collecting information about the internal and external environment, to the processes through which information is evaluated and decisions made, to the manner in which decisions are communicated, implemented and evaluated. My impression is that both practitioners and scholars in the strategy arena are interested in ways to join ethics and efficacy. Stakeholder theory is well suited to this task.

A SIMPLE AND COMPELLING TOPIC

From my perspective, stakeholder theory is both a simple and a compelling topic and one that has the potential to transform thinking in the field of strategic management just as it transformed my own thinking. I am glad to be a part of the movement and grateful to be included in such a bright group of scholars. I continue to believe that stakeholder theory eventually will come to be accepted as a theoretical underpinning for strategic management in much the same way as industrial organization economics, resource-based theory, agency theory or transactions costs economics.

As I conclude, I ask the forgiveness of readers for taking such a personal (self-promoting) approach to the topic. However, I think there may be value to readers in understanding the struggle for acceptance of the stakeholder concept in the field of strategic management, especially since it is likely to become even more important in the field in the future. My entrance into strategic management coincided with the publication of Freeman (1984). Consequently, in some ways my own personal struggle to get the theory accepted by my colleagues is similar to the path the stakeholder concept has taken in strategic management. I have always been grateful to the trailblazers, most of whom I have cited herein, for the energy and talent they have brought to the fight.

NOTES

1. This is probably a reasonable time to acknowledge the rather obvious fact that this narrative is written from my perspective and thus contains my own biases.
2. This retrospective is not intended to be a review of the strategic management literature nor is it a detailed review of the stakeholder concept in the field of strategic management (which can be found in Chapter 4 of Freeman et al., 2010). Consequently, the citations found in this chapter are merely representative of those that influenced the thinking of the author.
3. I am not going to name them here because I do not want to offend anyone by leaving them off the list.

REFERENCES

Agle, B.R., Mitchell, R.K. and Sonnenfeld, J.A. 1999. Who matters to CEOs? An investigation of stakeholder attributes and salience, corporate performance, and CEO values. *Academy of Management Journal*, **42**: 507–25.

Barney, J.B. 1991. Firm resources and sustained competitive advantage. *Journal of Management*, **17**: 99–120.

Berman, S.L., Wicks, A.C., Kotha, S. and Jones, T.M. 1999. Does stakeholder orientation matter? The relationship between stakeholder management models and firm financial performance. *Academy of Management Journal*, **42**: 488–506.

Bosse, D.A., Phillips, R.A. and Harrison, J.S. 2009. Stakeholders, reciprocity and firm performance. *Strategic Management Journal*, **30**: 447–56.

Chandler, A.D. 1962. *Strategy and Structure: Chapters in the History of the American Industrial Enterprise*. Cambridge, MA: MIT Press.

Choi, J. and Wang, H. 2009. Stakeholder relations and the persistence of corporate financial performance. *Strategic Management Journal*, **30**: 895–907.

Coff, R.W. 1999. When competitive advantage doesn't lead to performance: the resource-based view and stakeholder bargaining power. *Organization Science*, **10**(2): 119–33.

Donaldson, T. and Preston, L.E. 1995. The stakeholder theory of the corporation: concepts, evidence, and implications. *Academy of Management Review*, **20**: 65–91.

Dyer, J.H. and Singh, H. 1998. The relational view: cooperative strategy and sources of interorganizational competitive advantage. *Academy of Management Review*, **23**: 660–79.

Fombrun, C. and Shanley, M. 1990. What's in a name? Reputation building and corporate strategy. *Academy of Management Journal*, **33**: 233–58.

Freeman, R.E. 1984. *Strategic Management: A Stakeholder Approach*. Boston, MA: Pitman.

Freeman, R.E., Harrison, J. and Wicks, A.C. 2007. *Managing for Stakeholders: Survival, Reputation, and Success*. New Haven, CT: Yale University Press.

Freeman, R.E., Harrison, J.S., Wicks, A.C., Parmar, B. and de Colle, S. 2010. *Stakeholder Theory: The State of the Art*. New York: Cambridge University Press.

Frooman, J. 1999. Stakeholder influence strategies. *Academy of Management Review*, **24**: 191–205.

Greenley, G.E. and Foxall, G.R. 1997. Multiple stakeholder orientation in UK companies and the implications for company performance. *Journal of Management Studies*, **34**: 259–84.

Gulati, R. and Singh, J.H. 1998. The architecture of cooperation: managing coordination costs and appropriation concerns in strategic alliances. *Administrative Science Quarterly*, **43**: 781–814.

Harrison, J.S. and Freeman, R.E. 1999. Stakeholders, social responsibility and performance: empirical evidence and theoretical perspectives. *Academy of Management Journal*, **42**: 479–85.

Harrison, J.S. and St. John, C.H. 1994. *Strategic Management of Organizations and Stakeholders*. St. Paul, MN: West Publishing.

Harrison, J.S. and St. John, C.H. 1996. Managing and partnering with external stakeholders. *Academy of Management Executive*, **10**(2): 46–60.

Harrison, J.S., Bosse, D.A. and Phillips, R.A. 2010. Managing for stakeholders, stakeholder utility functions and competitive advantage. *Strategic Management Journal*, **31**: 58–74.

Hill, C.W.L. and Jones, T.M. 1992. Stakeholder-agency theory. *Journal of Management Studies*, **29**: 131–54.

Hillman, A.J. and Keim, G.D. 2001. Shareholder value, stakeholder management, and social issues: what's the bottom line? *Strategic Management Journal*, **22**: 125–39.

Hitt, M.A. 2005. Spotlight on strategic management. *Business Horizons*, **48**: 371–77.

Jensen, M. and Meckling, W. 1976. Theory of the firm: managerial behavior, agency costs and capital structure. *Journal of Financial Economics*, **3**: 305–60.

Johnson, R.A. and Greening, D.W. 1999. The effects of corporate governance and institutional ownership types on corporate social performance. *Academy of Management Journal*, **42**: 564–76.

Jones, T.M. 1995. Instrumental stakeholder theory: a synthesis of ethics and economics. *Academy of Management Review*, **20**: 404–37.

Jones, T.M., Felps, W. and Bigley, G.A. 2007. Ethical theory and stakeholder-related decisions: the role of stakeholder culture. *Academy of Management Review*, **32**: 137–55.

Luoma, P. and Goodstein, J. 1999. Stakeholders and corporate boards: institutional influences on board composition and structure. *Academy of Management Journal*, **42**: 553–63.

Mitchell, R., Agle, B.R. and Wood, D.J. 1997. Toward a theory of stakeholder identification and salience: defining the principles of who and what really counts. *Academy of Management Review*, **22**: 853–86.

Newman, W.H. 1979. Commentary. In D.E. Schendel and C.W. Hofer (eds), *Strategic Management: A New View of Business Policy and Planning*. Boston, MA: Little, Brown and Company, pp. 44–7.

Ogden, S. and Watson, R. 1999. Corporate performance and stakeholder management: balancing shareholder and customer interests in the UK privatized water industry. *Academy of Management Journal*, **42**: 526–36.

Pfeffer, J. and Salancik, G.R. 1978. *The External Control of Organizations: A Resource Dependence Perspective*. New York: Harper and Row.

Phillips, R.A., Freeman, R.E. and Wicks, A.C. 2003. What stakeholder theory is not. *Business Ethics Quarterly*, **13**: 479–502.

Porter, M. 1980. *Competitive Strategy: Techniques for Analyzing Industries and Competitors*. New York: The Free Press.

Porter, M. 1985. *Competitive Advantage: Creating and Sustaining Superior Performance*. New York: The Free Press.

Rowley, T.J. 1997. Moving beyond dyadic ties: a network theory of stakeholder influences. *Academy of Management Review*, **22**: 887–910.

Rumelt, R.P. 1974. *Strategy, Structure and Economic Performance*. Boston, MA: Harvard Business School Press.

Schendel, D.E. and Hofer, C.W. 1979. *Strategic Management: A New View of Business Policy and Planning*. Boston, MA: Little, Brown and Company.

Sisodia, R., Wolfe, D.B. and Sheth, J. 2007. *Firms of Endearment: How World-Class Companies Profit from Passion and Purpose*. Upper Saddle River, NJ: Wharton School Publishing.

Turban, D.B. and Greening, D.W. 1996. Corporate social performance and organizational attractiveness to prospective employees. *Academy of Management Journal*, **40**: 658–72.

Waddock, S. and Graves, S.B. 1997. The corporate social performance–financial performance link. *Strategic Management Journal*, **18**: 303–19.

Walsh, J.P. 2005. Taking stock of stakeholder management. *Academy of Management Review*, **30**: 426–52.

Weaver, G.R., Treviño, L.K. and Cochran, P.L. 1999. Integrated and decoupled corporate social performance: management commitments, external pressures and corporate ethics practices. *Academy of Management Journal*, **42**: 539–52.

Williamson, O.E. 1975. *Markets and Hierarchies: Analysis and Antitrust Implications*. New York: The Free Press.

5. Globalization, mental models and decentering stakeholder approaches

Patricia H. Werhane

In the last 25 years, stakeholder theory has grown from Ed Freeman's embryonic idea spelled out in his 1984 book, *Strategic Management,* to a set of full-blown theses that have influenced both ethical theory and corporate practice. The term 'stakeholder' has become commonplace in the academic literature, in corporate boardrooms, in annual reports, and in the language of non-government organizations (NGOs). Freeman's original idea and its offspring have become central to the theory and practice of business, and we are profusely grateful for Freeman's seminal contribution. Yet, and this will be my argument in this chapter: in a diverse globalized 'flat' world with expanding economic opportunities and risks, we need to revisit and revise our mindsets about stakeholder analysis and corporate governance. Taking the lead from the final chapters of *Strategic Management,* I want to suggest that how one constructs a stakeholder graphic creates certain kinds of mental models, frames our perceptions and narrows our foci, thus affecting corporate governance issues, management behavior, and ethical decision making. Reframing those graphics enables companies and their managers to think more globally and systemically about corporate responsibility and corporate governance.

THE 'FLAT WORLD'

In a recent book, *The World is Flat,* Tom Friedman developed a set of persuasive arguments that '[g]lobalization has now shifted into warp drive' (Wright, 2005). That is, free enterprise has not only infiltrated most of the corners of the earth, but jobs, ideas, goods and services, like the internet, are now global. This is not simply that one's telephone, computer and flight information are outsourced to many other parts of the world or that a chat room is accessed by people from all parts of the globe. On a flight recently, I met a Dutch software expert who was heading for Argentina to write code for an Indian high-tech company that markets its products in over 50 countries in the world. An X-ray taken in a Chicago hospital is likely to be sent electronically to a physician in India to be read, analyzed and returned within 24 hours. Cell phones and electronic banking have infiltrated the poorest and most remote regions of the planet.

> The hardware in a Dell Inspiron 600m laptop comes from factories in the Philippines, Costa Rica, Malaysia, China, south Korea, Taiwan, Germany, Japan, Mexico, Thailand, Singapore, Indonesia, India and Israel; the software is designed in America and elsewhere. The corporations that own or operate these factories are based in the United States, China, Taiwan, Germany, South Korea, Japan, Ireland, Thailand, Israel and Great Britain. And Michael Dell [CEO of Dell] personally knows their CEOs. (Wright, 2005)

The now infamous BP oil platform Deepwater Horizon was originally constructed by a Korean manufacturer, Hyundai, for Transocean Corporation, a Swiss based company. The platform was leased to BP, a British firm, and Halliburton, an American company, installed the final sealing operation for the well (Krauss, 2010: A12). In Friedman's words,

> This is a triple convergence – of new players, on a new playing field, developing new processes and habits for horizontal collaboration. That, I believe, is the most important force shaping global economics and politics in the 21st century. . . . The scale of the global community soon is going to be able to participate in all sorts of discovery and innovation the world has simply never seen before. [In other words] the world [of the 21st century] is flat. (Friedman, 2005: 213)

This example is carefully crafted to focus on one set of globally integrated industries. It does not accurately reflect most of the 'on the ground' small local commerce existing in less developed countries. Nevertheless, if Friedman's conclusion is even partly accurate, for global organizations or multinational enterprises (MNEs), at least, there is no longer an 'over there' there. The global organization today is embedded in a complex adaptive set of global political, economic and cultural networks. What we once called 'externalities' are inescapably part of an interrelated networked global system in which businesses operate, and these former externalities must now be integrated into, not set aside from, corporate thinking. A company can no longer 'outsource' environmental degradation or dump waste in less developed countries (even with the permission of that country) without that action affecting the global environment and receiving media attention. That conclusion is widely understood and accepted today. 'Globalization' also means that one cannot outsource underpaid labor, product or service quality, issues of diversity, disregard for cultural or religious differences, or even corporate responsibilities to the communities in which they operate or from which they export. If, for example, the clothes we wear are made under subhuman labor conditions *as defined in the country of origin*, one cannot dismiss that as another country's problem. It is ours. Cultural differences are not merely opportunity costs even when one is operating in remote and poor regions. These differences have to do with human relationships, with cultural conflicts as well as consensus, and one cannot ignore them. This 'flat' world, then, requires us to rethink our mental models about corporate governance and corporate responsibility in this now complex networked global economy.

SOCIAL CONSTRUCTION, MINDSETS AND MENTAL MODELS

> Although the term is not always clearly defined, the term, 'mental model' or 'mindset' connotes the idea that human beings have mental representations, cognitive frames, or mental pictures of their experiences, [socially constructed] representations that model the stimuli or data with which they are interacting, and these are frameworks that set up parameters through which experience or a certain set of experiences, is organized or filtered. (Werhane, 2008: 463; see also Senge, 1990, Chapter 10; Gorman, 1992; Werhane, 1999)

Because of the variety and diversity of mental models, none is complete, and as Mark Johnson points out, 'there are multiple possible framings of any given situation [and as a result], [t]here are . . . different moral consequences depending on the way we frame the situation' (Johnson, 1993).

According to this analysis, all our experiences are socially constructed through the various learned mental models or mindsets, each of which is incomplete, thus representing a certain point of view. Sometimes these perspectives are distorted, narrow or single-framed. Some clash with other perspectives on what appear to be the same phenomena. And while mindsets are socially learned and thus volatile and changeable, sometimes a mental model of the world becomes so ingrained that it is difficult to grasp the world from another perspective or imagine that one's point of view is just that, a viewpoint among others. Indeed, because of the ingrained nature of mental models, we simply 'experience' rather than experience these as perspectival. It is often difficult to step back, to study what mindsets are at play, and attempt to understand the perspectives of what appear to be faulty points of view of others. We thus become trapped in one set of mental models that preclude our consideration of more complex or creative but different points of view.

For example, in the recent testimony before Congress by Goldman Sachs executives, it became clear that they just did not see what the issues were or why they had been called to account for their behavior. According to one commentator, 'Goldman executives believe they have a public-relations problem, not a substantive one' (McLean, 2010: 83). That was perhaps because their ingrained investment banking mentality might have prevented them from imagining that it might be problematic to a customer who had lost a great deal of money through Goldman investments in the subprime mortgage markets while Goldman was hedging against these portfolios (Beresford, 2009; McLean, 2010). This conclusion is reinforced by the CEO of Goldman's now audacious statement to the London *Sunday Times*, 'I'm doing "God's work"' (Beresford, 2009).

Mental models function on the organizational and systemic levels as well as in individual cognition, as the foregoing examples illustrate. These companies appear to be trapped in their vision of themselves and their roles in ways that preclude understanding that theirs is only one of a set of possible perspectives, each of which is important to take into account. Focusing here on MNEs, what I want to suggest is that a firm-centric depiction of stakeholder relationships is a form of entrapment that may not fully capture the networked complex world of global economies.

FIRM-CENTRIC STAKEHOLDER MODELS

Most stakeholder models, even those framed by complex graphics that take into account critical and fringe stakeholders, are depicted with the firm in the center. A 'traditional' stakeholder map (Figure 5.1) first proposed by Freeman some time ago (for example, Evan and Freeman, 1988: 102), places the corporation in the center of the graphic, and that remains so in the Freeman, Harrison and Wicks' 2007 more complex iteration (Figure 5.2). Our mental model of corporate governance and corporate responsibility is partly constructed from these graphics, because effective graphs create or revise our mindsets, thus our views of the firm, its stakeholders, and its responsibilities. As Yves Fassin notes, '[a] single graph or scheme can be worth more than a thousand words; visual representations can simplify and aggregate complex information into meaningful patterns and they make sense of information, impose structure and highlight objects' (Fassin, 2008: 879).

In a firm-centric graph, the focus is first on the company or its managers, only secondarily on its other stakeholders. This is despite arrows depicting interrelated accountability relationships, and despite, from a stakeholder theory perspective, the claim that all critical stakeholders, those who most affect or are affected by the company, have, or should have, equal claims to value-added (Freeman, 1984 [2010]). Nevertheless this attention to the center, the firm, created by the construction of the

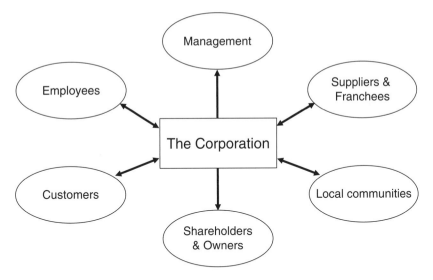

Source: Evan and Freeman (1988: 102)

Figure 5.1   A 'traditional' stakeholder map

graphic, I suggest, may have the effect of marginalizing other stakeholders even when that is not the deliberate intent. 'Stakeholders, not being in the center of the model, are externalized and become marginalized by default' (Stormer, 2003: 284).

Freeman himself states that '[o]rganizations are complex phenomena and to analyze them as "black boxes" with the organization in the middle of a complex world of external forces and pressures, does not do justice to the subtlety of the flavors of organizational life' (Freeman, 1984 [2010]: 216). Freeman then modifies his firm-centric model from the perspectives of managers or the CEO, placing various managers or the CEO in the center of the graphic (Figure 5.3). With this depiction the manager or CEO is better able to capture and capitalize on her or his responsibilities both to internal and external stakeholders. This is a worthwhile venture. However, it is still firm-centric, now focusing on those who manage the firm. Fassin (2008) suggests that one could manipulate the graphic further and place the Board of Directors at the hub. Such a move would draw Board attention to their stakeholder responsibilities that include, but are not exclusively, shareholder responsibilities, a broader set of responsibilities that are sometimes lost in boardrooms. But like the preceding moves, our attention is drawn to the firm, its managers and its board, so that the company is the center of attention.

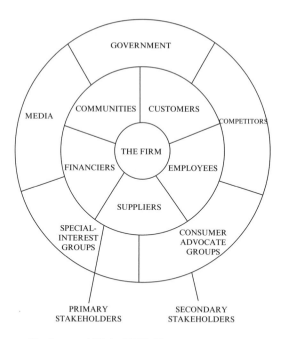

Source: Freeman, Harrison, and Wicks (2007: 51)

Figure 5.2   A more complex stakeholder model

Global companies have very complicated stakeholder maps as the Novartis example in Figure 5.4 illustrates. But in many (but not all) corporate graphics, the focus of attention is to the center of the graphic, and often, still, the firm remains in that center. When one's mental model of corporate governance and corporate responsibilities are framed with such a construction, how one thinks about corporate responsibility is different, say, than when that model is altered. Here the company is the agent for these relationships, not an embedded partner. This firm-centric depiction creates a mindset that may prevent companies and their managers from viewing the firm from the perspectives of others, their primary and secondary stakeholders, or from the context in which they operate, which may be culturally, politically or economically alien. Thus this sort of thinking may also preclude firms and even their stakeholders from taking into account perspectives that will affect their operations, particularly in diverse cultures.

For example, testifying about the BP oil spill in the Gulf of Mexico, BP blamed Transocean from whom they leased the rig, Transocean blamed

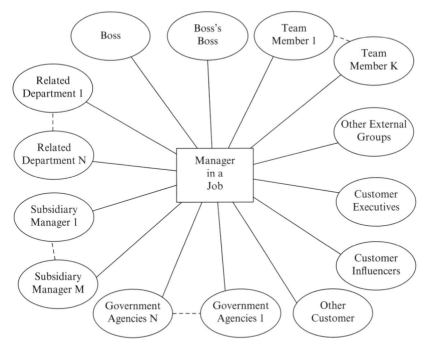

Source: Freeman (1984: 218)

Figure 5.3   'Internal stakeholders' in a managerial job

Haliburton who was in charge of performing the final sealing operation, Halliburton blamed Cameron International, who had installed a device designed to shut off the well, and Cameron blamed BP for the design, although the platform had actually been constructed by Hyundai. Not one of those executives imagined that it could have been at least partly their fault! They had engaged in a corporate mentality that precluded the possibility of making errors (Krauss, 2010: A12; Krauss and Rosenthal, 2010: A18).[1] In fact all these organizations have interrelated connections and responsibilities, a complex matrix of interactions that a decentered focus might have clarified (Figure 5.5).

DECENTERING STAKEHOLDER MODELS

There are a number of ways to deconstruct a firm-centric stake-holder model, each of which will affect our thinking about corporate

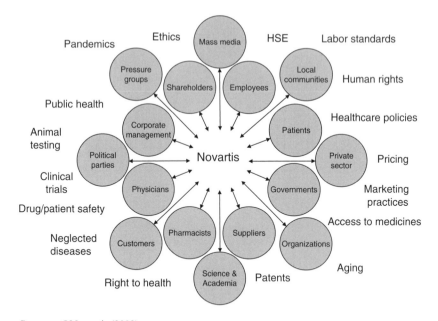

Figure 5.4   Companies operate in a challenging environment

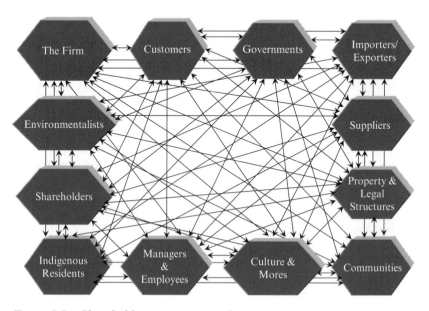

Figure 5.5   Shareholder systems networks

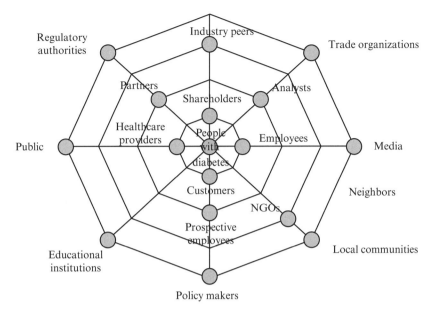

Source: Freeman, Harrison, and Wicks (2007: 97)

Figure 5.6   Stakeholders at Novo Nordisk

responsibility. I shall suggest four. First, one can replace the firm in the center with another stakeholder, as Freeman (1984: Chapter 3) illustrates, but that stakeholder need not be part of the firm. In Figure 5.6 from Novo Nordisk (Freeman, Harrison, and Wicks, 2007: 97) we find patients in the center, specifically patients with diabetes, thus prioritizing that set of patient-stakeholders for that company. This graphic redirects managerial mindsets to remind them that Novo Nordisk is in the business of alleviating disease, and that that is their primary mission and responsibility.

Another way to highlight and refocus attention is to place an actual picture of an individual stakeholder in the center. For example, in drawing attention to sweatshop workers employed in factories producing goods for export, one could put an actual picture of a worker in the center. Figure 5.7 depicts a 15 year-old Bangladeshi sweatshop worker, working at the Harvest Rich factory. She works 12–16 hours a day with two days off a month. Often she is not paid fully for her hours and the working conditions are horrendous even by Bangladeshi standards. She is expected to stamp a metal button on a pair of jeans every seven seconds. When her productivity decreases, she will either be transferred to an easier task or simply

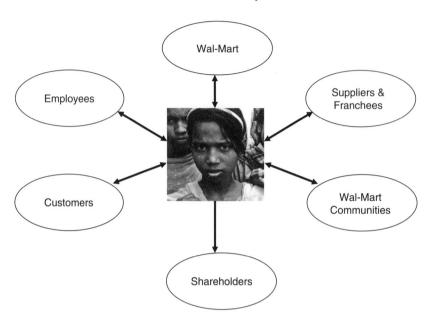

Figure 5.7   *'Names and faces' stakeholder approach*

replaced by another, faster, worker (National Labor Committee, 2006). By placing an individual person in the center of a stakeholder map we achieve two ends: drawing attention to a particular set of stakeholders, in this case these workers and their plight, and giving a 'name and face' to a very large group – there are probably close to two million sweatshop workers in Bangladesh alone. Freeman and John McVea have written on the importance of remembering that stakeholder groups represent real individual human beings (McVea and Freeman, 2005; see also Benhabib, 1992). This graphic reinforces that critical point, so easily lost when we speak, for instance, of two million workers as an anonymous collective. We then begin to identify with sweatshop workers and get some inkling of what this sort of work entails from their vantage points. As Freeman puts it, what he calls 'Stakeholder Behavior Explanation' 'asks the manager to put himself/herself in the stakeholder's place, and to try and emphasize with that stakeholder's position, that is, to try and feel what that stakeholder feels and see the world from that point of view' (Freeman, 1984[2010]: 133). That might have been a good exercise for Goldman executives to engage in. I would argue that decentering stakeholder graphics is essential to that process.

A manager of a large corporation will wonder how to give a name and face to its thousands of employees, and hundreds of thousands of shareholders and customers. Of course, that is impossible. But narratives about individual customers, employees, shareholders or even affected members of the community in question are effective ways to individualize groups of stakeholders, as we did with the Bangladeshi worker, and to begin to get a perspective on their mindsets. The recent American television program 'Undercover Boss' has been an effective way to bring to light employee perspectives and opinions to top management. While not every company wants to be on TV, the narrative approach of the program, 'getting into the shoes' of individual workers, can be emulated in other venues.

A third alteration in our thinking can be elicited by taking a systems approach to stakeholder theory. This is particularly useful for global companies. 'A truly systemic view considers how a set of individuals, institutions and processes operates in a system involving a complex network of interrelationships, an array of individual and institutional actors with conflicting interests and goals, and a number of feedback loops' (Wolf, 1999: 1632). A systems approach acknowledges that most of our practices and institutions are interconnected. Organizations are human systems, and 'every purposeful system is considered to have an environment and to be part of one or more larger systems. . . . A company can be taken as part of an industry and industry as part of an economy' (Ackoff, 1974: 55) and an economy as part of a larger global set of political economies. These organizations operate in a number of diverse environments or contexts, each of which has a particular character, but each of which shares some commonalities as part of a global system. It is the particularity of each setting and its functioning mental models that are important to capture.

For example, when Royal Dutch Shell first began drilling for oil in the Ogoni territories in Nigeria, working from a firm-centric viewpoint, it failed to take seriously the diverse setting in which it was drilling and the cultural impact of its exploration in that community. Thus Shell engendered mistrust among the Ogoni, and its alliance with the Nigerian military did little to mitigate that issue. After the Nigerian government hanged a well-known Ogoni protestor and activist, Ken Saro-Wiwa, Shell began to rethink their drilling activities in Nigeria and attempted to establish partnerships with the Ogoni (Newberry and Gladwin, 2002). As a 'lesson learned', Exxon Mobil, in partnership with the World Bank, has tried to think systemically in its drilling operations in Chad and the construction of its pipeline through Pygmy and Bantu territories in Cameroon. By working with indigenous people as partners, employing NGOs and social workers for that region, and engaging in public works projects, ExxonMobil and its partners have created more of a climate of collaboration (Useem, 2002).[2] None of these situations is perfect, but ExxonMobil has shown that one can create partnerships in settings alien to Western thinking and add value as well.

Global companies are mezzo-systems embedded in larger political, economic, legal and cultural systems. As purposeful systems they are examples of 'complex adaptive systems', a term used to describe open interactive systems that are able to change themselves and affect or are affected by changes in their interactions with other systems (Plsek, 2001). Figure 5.5 depicts this sort of configuration. What is characteristic of these types of systems is that all its subsystems and participants, for example, its stakeholders help to define that organization or system such that its characteristics and culture are altered, lost or at best, obscured, when the system is broken down into components. In studying global firms, if one is preoccupied with one set of stakeholders, for example, its employees, or its shareholders or customers, one obscures if not distorts the interconnections and interrelationships that characterize and affect that organization in its internal and, more importantly for this argument, its external multifaceted global relationships. In the case of the Deepwater Horizon platform tragedy, each company-participant seems to be preoccupied with defending itself against blame rather than depicting this as a collaborative venture with shared responsibilities.

Because a purposeful complex adaptive system consists of networks of relationships between individuals or groups of individuals, it affects and is affected by individuals, real people with names and faces. So how one conceives of a particular system, for example, a corporation, affects how it is perceived by and affects its stakeholders. One's mindset about the nature of firm–stakeholder relationships will define those relationships. Ignoring the embeddedness of a company within the global system of disparate cultures, organizations and political economies may skew how one frames these relationships, particularly when a firm is operating in a culture or context that is alien to its own cultural or political roots. Part of corporate moral responsibility is incurred by the particularity of its operations in diverse settings, and sometimes that particularity is lost in a firm-centric rather than systems oriented mental model of that responsibility. Thus a multiple-perspective approach is essential to take into account these sorts of responsibilities (Mitroff and Linstone, 1993; Emanuel, 2000; Werhane, 2008). Stormer suggests what she calls an 'inter-systems model', an even more complex model where 'business becomes one of many interacting systems . . . stakeholders become alternate systems which influence and are influenced by the activities of business, each having its own history, operating roles and rules of engagement that change over time' (Stormer, 2003: 285). To adequately encapsulate this idea graphically would involve creating a number of stakeholder maps about each firm. Some of the graphics in this chapter capture that idea. Alternately, Constance Kampf decenters the traditional stakeholder model by placing the firms within a

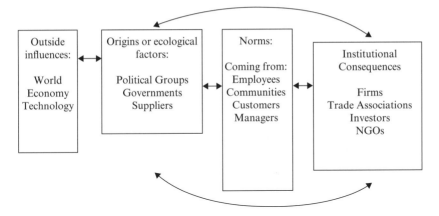

Source: Kampf (2007: 44)

Figure 5.8   A political approach to stakeholder analysis

political, cultural and global context (Figure 5.8). This is a challenging and worthwhile approach, but it fails to capture adequately the important relationships between *primary* stakeholders, for example, customers, employees, suppliers and shareholders, while placing emphasis on the external environment in which businesses operate.

While it is unlikely that a firm, particularly a global company, or its managers could take account of all the networks of relationships and systems in which they are involved, a systems approach forces companies to think more broadly and to consider issues and decisions from different perspectives. This is because each perspective usually 'reveals insights . . . that are not obtainable in principle from others' (Mitroff and Linstone, 1993: 98).

Freeman, however, at least in his 1984 book is wary of a systems approach. '[T]he general problem with the systems view [is] that there is not a starting point or entry point for how collaboration towards "the systems viewpoint," which is necessarily "God-like," is to proceed' (Freeman, 1984[2010]: 37). I would argue that the lack of a specific starting point such as the firm is the strength of a systems view. It forces the firm and its management to enter through the perspective of one or more disparate stakeholders, not necessarily the firm itself. It cannot be God-like or a purely disinterested 'view from nowhere' for the very simple reason is that a so-called 'God-like' viewpoint is itself socially constructed for a series of mental models. As Putnam and Rorty once put it, 'elements of what we call "language" or "mind" [our mindsets] penetrate so deeply into what we call "reality" that the very project of presenting ourselves as being mappers of something "language-independent" is fatally compromised from the start' (Putnam, 1990: 28; cited approvingly by Rorty, 1993: 443). A manager has to enter somewhere, from some viewpoint, and since neither the firm nor its managers are in the center of attention, s/he is often introduced, perhaps randomly, to another stakeholder mindset that may challenge his or her parochial attention. Then, if s/he can create a narrative about some of the individuals at that entry point, a more imaginative and broader perspective cannot help but develop (see Calton and Payne, 2003).

Global companies usually find themselves involved in a complex network of disparate stakeholders where they are not the center of attention. Pfizer Switzerland, for instance, depicts itself in that manner (Figure 5.9). In this graphic, the firm is one of a number of equal players, and this creates a more networked mental model of the global firm wherein the firm is an equal but not central stakeholder. A multiple perspectives approach is essential if, for example, a global corporation thinks of itself as a global company that affects and is affected by its suppliers and their employees *and* the various communities in which it contracts or operates. This method also helps to preclude a firm-centric Ptolemaic vision of itself as the center of what is importantly, an equally never a 'God-like' viewpoint.

Still, a multiple perspectives approach does not adequately take into account two important elements of corporate governance and corporate responsibility: First, one we mentioned earlier, stakeholders are individual human beings, thus must all be given 'names and faces' rather than homogenized as 'the others'. Second, in the present climate where companies are pressured to take on community, environmental and social responsibilities as well as creating economic value-added, companies need to position themselves from a perspective of the cultures in which they operate. Thus companies appear to have three sets of obligations: a set of corporate agent-centered reciprocal obligations to and with their primary and to a lesser extent their secondary stakeholders, including shareholders; another decentering individually focused set of obligations to these groups as individuals; and third, from a more disinterested perspective, to understand themselves as one of many interacting global players in very complex relationships (Goodpaster, 2010: 139–43)

A fourth kind of decentering depiction is useful when global companies form partnerships with NGOs and local officials in order to break down barriers of entry, cultural differences or local product distribution. For example, the Female Health Company (FHC), an over-the-counter publicly traded firm, distributes female condoms in 75 countries in the developing world. Because there are almost no paying customers for its products, and because the need includes a broad spectrum of countries

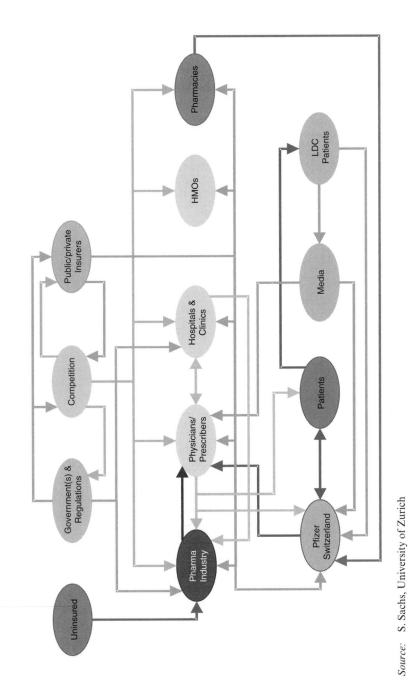

Source: S. Sachs, University of Zurich

Figure 5.9 A systems model

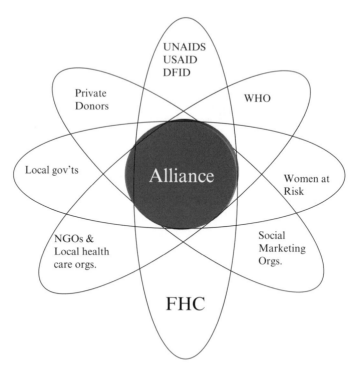

Source: Model Courtesy of Mary Ann Leeper, COO, Female Health Company

Figure 5.10   The FHC alliance model

and cultures, to be successful (and profitable) it has had to form alliances
with foundations and aid agencies for financial support, with NGOs and
local officials for distribution channels, and with social workers who
understand value differences in the countries and villages where this
product was to be distributed. FHC then redrew its stakeholder model
as an alliance model. The company realized that it did not merely have a
product. Rather, the company was engaged in a complex program where
the manufacture, education, funding and distribution, not the product or
the company, should be at the center of the alliance (Figure 5.10). And
notice that the possible victims of HIV have names and faces as well. In
2009, this company was listed as one of the 100 best small companies by
Fortune Magazine (Grant, 2009).

My argument, then, is that redrawing stakeholder maps is not merely
an exercise for academics. How these maps are drawn affects our mental
models – the ways companies, managers, and other internal and external

stakeholders think about themselves, their products and processes, their responsibility to their stakeholders and how they are perceived by outsiders in different contexts. The difference, if one uses a systems or alliance model, is the adaptation of multiple perspectives, trying to get at the mindset of each group of stakeholders from their points of view. A systems perspective or an alliance model brings into focus the responsibilities as well as rights of various stakeholders and communities from their perspectives, not merely from the firm's point of view. It takes seriously a multicultural global 'names and faces' approach.

ACKNOWLEDGMENTS

The theme for this chapter originally developed from a 2007 International Association of Business and Society presentation by Jerry Calton, Dominic Käeslin and Ruth Schmitt, titled, 'A de-centered stakeholder approach: towards a research agenda' (Calton, Käeslin and Schmitt, 2007). See also Stormer (2003), Kampf (2007), Calton, Payne and Waddock (2008) and Fassin (2008).

NOTES

1. In addition, everyone else is blaming the US Government Minerals Management Service, who allegedly gave BP permission to drill without the required permits (Krauss, 2010: A12; Krauss and Rosenthal, 2010: A18).
2. Unfortunately ExxonMobil and its other partner the World Bank have had to deal with Idriss Deby, the President of Chad who took the royalties targeted for roads, schools and health clinics, and invested in arms.

REFERENCES

Ackoff, R. 1974. *Redesigning the Future.* New York: John Wiley and Sons.
Benhabib, S. 1992. *Situating the Self.* New York: Routledge.
Beresford, P. 2009. I'm doing 'God's work.' Meet Mr. Goldman Sachs. *The Sunday Times,* 8 November, pp. 12–24.
Calton, J. and Payne, S. 2003. Coping with paradox: multi-stakeholder learning dialogue as a pluralist sense making process for addressing messy problems. *Business and Society*, **42**: 7–42.
Calton, J., Käeslin D. and Schmitt, R. 2007. A de-centered stakeholder approach: towards a research agenda. In B. Wempe (ed.), *Proceedings of the 18th Meeting of the International Association of Business and Society*, pp. 210–17.
Calton, J.M., Payne, S.L. and Waddock, S. 2008. Learning to teach ethics from the heart: a journey of discovery from the inside out. In D. Swanson and D. Fisher

(eds), *Advancing Business Ethics Education in the 21st Century*. Charlotte, NC: Information Age Publishing, pp. 147–66.

Emanuel, L. 2000. Ethics and the structures of health care. *Cambridge Quarterly*, **9**: 151–68.

Evan, W.M. and Freeman, R.E. 1988. A stakeholder theory of the modern corporation: Kantian capitalism. In T. Beauchamp and N. Bowie (eds), *Ethical Theory and Business,* 3rd edition. Englewood Cliffs, NJ: Prentice Hall, pp. 101–5.

Fassin, Y. 2008. Imperfections and shortcomings of the stakeholder model's graphical representation. *Journal of Business Ethics*, **80**: 879–88.

Freeman, R.E. 1984 [2010]. *Strategic Management: A Stakeholder Approach.* Cambridge, UK: Cambridge University Press.

Freeman, R.E., Harrison, J. and Wicks, A. 2007. *Managing for Stakeholders.* New Haven, CT: Yale University Press.

Friedman, T. 2005. *The World is Flat.* New York: Farrar, Straus and Giroux.

Goodpaster, K.E. 2010. Corporate responsibility and its constituents. In G. Brenkert and T. Beauchamp (eds), *Oxford Handbook of Business Ethics.* New York: Oxford University Press, pp. 126–57.

Gorman, M. 1992. *Simulating Science.* Bloomington, IN: Indiana University Press.

Grant, E.A. 2009. Reinventing the condom: for women. *CNNMoney.com*, 7 July, available at: www.cnnmoney.com, accessed 15 May 2010.

Johnson, M. 1993. *Moral Imagination.* Chicago, IL: University of Chicago Press.

Kampf, C. 2007. Corporate social responsibility: Wal-Mart, Maersk and the cultural bounds of representation in corporate web sites. *Corporate Communications*, **12**: 41–57.

Krauss, C. 2010. Senators offer bills to ban Pacific drilling and increase liability limits. *New York Times*, 14 May, A12.

Krauss, C. and Rosenthal, E. 2010. The price and who pays. *New York Times*, 13 May, A18.

McLean, B. 2010. The Bank Job. *Vanity Fair*, January, pp. 82–9, 123–8.

McVea, J. and Freeman, R.E. 2005. A names-and-faces approach to stakeholder management. *Journal of Management Inquiry*, **14**: 57–69.

Mitroff, I. and Linstone, H. 1993. *The Unbounded Mind.* New York: Oxford University Press.

National Labor Committee 2006. www.nlc.org, accessed 5 June 2009.

Newberry, W. and Gladwin, T.N. 2002. Shell and Nigerian oil. In T. Donaldson, P.H. Werhane and M. Cording (eds), *Ethical Issues in Business*, 7th edition. Upper Saddle River, NJ: Prentice-Hall Pearson, pp. 522–41.

Plsek, P. 2001. Redesigning health care with insights from the science of complex adaptive systems. *Crossing the Quality Chasm: A New Health System for the 21st Century.* Washington, DC: National Academy Press, pp. 310–33.

Putnam, H. 1990. *Realism with a Human Face.* Cambridge, MA: Harvard University Press.

Rorty, R. 1993. Putnam and the menace. *Journal of Philosophy*, **90**: 443–561.

Senge, P. 1990, *The Fifth Discipline.* New York: Doubleday.

Stormer, F. 2003. Making the shift: moving from 'ethics pays' to an inter-systems model of business. *Journal of Business Ethics*, **44**: 279–89.

Useem, J. 2002. Exxon's African adventure. *Fortune*, 15 April, pp. 102–14.

Werhane, P.H. 1999, *Moral Imagination and Management Decision-Making.* New York: Oxford University Press.

Werhane, P.H. 2008. Mental models, moral imagination and systems thinking in the age of globalization. *Journal of Business Ethics*, **78**: 463–74.

Wolf, S. 1999. Toward a systemic theory of informed consent in managed care. *Houston Law Review*, **35**: 1631–81.

Wright, R. 2005. Reading between the lines: the incredible shrinking planet. What liberals can learn from Tom Friedman's new book. Available at: http//www.slate.com/id/2116899, accessed 17 June 2008.

6. The inescapability of a minimal version of normative stakeholder theory

Thomas Donaldson

I want to critique concepts prominent in the debate between so-called stakeholder and non-stakeholder interpretations of the corporation. I hope to demonstrate the inconsistency of any view that stops fully short of normative stakeholder theory. My critique implies that any purely 'instrumental' or purely 'descriptive' stakeholder interpretation (Donaldson and Preston, 1995) of the corporation is conceptually impossible. Normative stakeholder theory – at least in a minimal form – is ineliminable when interpreting the modern corporation. As I shall show, the logic of the language used to inform the major, 'descriptive' views of the corporation, that is, agency theory (Jensen and Meckling, 1976; Fama and Jensen, 1983), new institutional economics (Williamson 1985, 1996a, 1996b) and even instrumental stakeholder theory (Jensen 2002), require on pain of inconsistency the attribution of moral rights to some non-owning stakeholders. Both descriptive and instrumental views of the corporation must posit moral property rights for shareowners; and this, in turn, commits them to normative conclusions about the attribution of moral rights to other stakeholders. Moreover, this attribution of moral rights to a variety of stakeholders entails moral responsibilities on the part of the corporation.[1]

In his famous article, 'The problem of social cost', Ronald Coase acknowledges limitations to non-normative approaches. He explains at the close of the article how even the economic concepts he has utilized are not fully sufficient for designing models of organizational governance. He asserts that 'problems of welfare economics must ultimately dissolve into a study of aesthetics and morals' (Coase, 1960). Few have noted this admission from the father of transaction cost economics, but if true – and there is no doubt that Coase held it to be true – this insight has ringing implications for the interpretation of the firm, and for stakeholder theory.

Let us review three basic aspects of stakeholder theory in order to discover where Coase's issues of 'morals and aesthetics' might lie. In an earlier article, Lee Preston and I classified stakeholder theories into three, *non-exclusive* forms, namely, (1) 'descriptive', (2) 'instrumental' and (3) 'normative' (Donaldson and Preston, 1995: 66). A 'descriptive' stakeholder theory posits a model that describes what a corporation is. Such a theory may be tested for descriptive accuracy and serve as a framework for testing any empirical claims relevant to the stakeholder concept. In contrast, an 'instrumental' stakeholder theory makes an important and specific claim about corporations whose managers happen to adopt a stakeholder philosophy of management, namely, that such corporations will, other things being equal, do better financially than those who do not (Donaldson and Preston, 1995: 67). The instrumental theory does not aspire to be the best descriptive picture of *all* corporations; rather, it merely claims that those corporations that happen to adopt a stakeholder philosophy will be more financially successful than others. Finally, the 'normative' stakeholder view claims nothing about either what *is* or *will be* in the future. Instead, it claims straightforwardly that corporations *ought* to adopt a stakeholder philosophy. The interests of all stakeholders from the vantage point of the corporation should possess *intrinsic value*. That is, the normative view holds that each group of stakeholders merits consideration for its own sake and not merely because of its ability to (instrumentally) further the interests of some other group, such as the shareowners. It does not follow that one group of stakeholders' interests might not be prioritized over others. One can even maintain a normative stakeholder view and demand that stockholders' interests trump those of employees, customers, and other stakeholders 99 percent of the time. The point of normative stakeholder theory is not about the relative weight of stakeholder interests, it is, rather, that the interests of all genuine stakeholders must have *some* intrinsic worth. These interests must be respected in a manner in which they are more than merely 'means' to the 'end' of serving shareholder interests.

It should be obvious that only the third, that is, 'normative' stakeholder theory, goes beyond empirical claims to reach the domain of the genuinely moral. It is the only theory of the three that embodies a genuine 'should'. Of course, instrumental stakeholder theory holds implications for how a manager should behave, but it is a conditional 'should'. The instrumental theory is relevant only on the condition that a manager wants to maximize financial success. The theory itself is a species of hypothetical empirical prediction, namely, 'If you adopt the stakeholder philosophy of management, then you will maximize firm profits'. Its advice comes in the form of what Kant called a 'hypothetical imperative'. It advises, 'If you (the manager) seek to maximize firm profits, then adopt the stakeholder philosophy of management'. An obvious irony, as Edwin M. Hartman points out in another chapter in this volume, 'Freeman: win–win and the common good', is that the stakeholder management philosophy can coexist happily alongside a stockholder-only interpretation of the function of the firm. In other words, an instrumental stakeholder theorist can assert that firms should do nothing other than maximize financial returns and also assert that managers should manage with an eye for the welfare of other stakeholders. This seemingly conflicting interpretation is analogous to the sometimes odd advice given to golfers with the tendency to slice their balls to the right: 'If you want to hit the ball straight down the middle, then aim to the left.' A now well-known version of instrumental stakeholder theory is espoused by Michael Jensen in his article, 'Value maximization, stakeholder theory, and the corporate objective function' (Jensen 2002), in which he argues that managers must attend to the interests of employees and customers but be measured only by the criterion of profit.[2]

Before continuing further, we must first draw a crucial distinction between ethics and law, and more specifically between moral rights and legal rights. Moral rights differ from legal rights because they are not enforced by government fines or punishments, that is, sanctions. Legal rights are by definition backed by sanctions, and although some moral rights have counterparts in formal law, it is unnecessary for their status. Maintaining the moral/legal distinction is important, and many moral rights should not have legal counterparts. For example, we rightly reject having a law that fines or punishes a lover who flagrantly lies to her beloved; but, of course, a *legal* entitlement to lie does not entail a *moral* right to lie. Lies are usually wrong on ethical grounds, even when permitted by law.

The first and most important phase of my argument may be framed as a simple syllogism:

1. Descriptive and instrumental theories of the for-profit corporation require reference to the moral right to property. (Major premise)
2. The right to property requires reference to the moral rights of stakeholders other than stockholders. (Minor premise)
   ∴ Descriptive and instrumental theories of the for-profit corporation require reference to the moral rights of stakeholders other than stockholders. (Conclusion)

The first premise is easily verified by noting that the very concept of the for-profit corporation is affixed to the moral right to own property. The corporation cannot be conceived except through the notion of joint ownership. When Marxist countries deny their citizens' moral rights to hold property and to own corporations and fail to establish a legal right to property, we condemn their legal failure on moral grounds. The right to property, indeed, is one of the central moral rights enshrined in the United Nations' *Universal Declaration of Human Rights.* Hence, what cannot be doubted is that corporations are entities owned by shareholders who possess rights in virtue of such ownership. What *can* be doubted is whether or not any other stakeholders have rights, either because of additional property rights or for some other reason. Agency theory and new institutional economic theory stress the property rights of shareholders and examine inefficiencies in transactions and arrangements affecting such rights. They express what has been called a 'shareholder primacy' model (Blair and Stout, 1999). But any descriptive *stakeholder* theory must grant that the corporation reflects in part the property rights of its owners. This underlying fact cannot be denied, for to do so would be to contemplate an entity that would not qualify as a 'corporation'. There could be no true corporation in a Marxist state that failed to recognize the right to property.

Instrumental theories are parasitic upon a property rights' interpretation of the corporation, and can coexist with a descriptive view of the corporation that is not a stakeholder one, for example, one that relies on 'agency theory', 'nexus of contracts' or the idea of a 'mechanism to reduce transactions costs'. But any such non-stakeholder, descriptive view of the corporation must at least presume that shareholders and their rights are part of the description of the for-profit corporation. Hence, any descriptive theory, whether or not a stakeholder one, must reference the moral right to property.

The second premise, that 'the right to property requires reference to the rights of stakeholders other than stockholders', has a more complex but equally solid justification. As the backdrop for our discussion, let us consider a generic, imaginary world much like ours in which people freely coordinate their activities in the form of jointly held stock corporations. People possess the right to own property and corporations are considered the property of shareowners. Shareowners agree to risk their money on the condition that the corporation attempts to maximize their financial welfare, and when managers fail to fulfill this fiduciary duty, they are subject to legal suits from aggrieved owners. Shareowners and managers and employees agree to produce collectively products and services, while customers, in turn, buy the products or services. The reciprocal responsibilities of employment contracts are not fully detailed (for purposes of efficiency) and corporations manage relationships with customers, stockholders and the general public in differing ways: sometimes they issue disclaimers, sometimes they do not; sometimes they warn employees before a layoff, sometimes they do not. In this world employees engage in legally binding agreements, formal or informal, in which they agree to work for specified remuneration and to be fired at will. Customers usually purchase products and services without signing formal or informal purchase agreements, but laws govern some aspects of purchasing. In short, this imagined world reflects many aspects of real corporations around the globe.

Note first that in this generic, imaginary world an employee, customer or shareowner interacting with the corporation through law or contract does not thereby waive his or her moral rights. As ethical theory has established, moral rights are held by humans solely because they are rational beings deserving of moral respect. Next, consider in this vein one of the most ingenious arguments from the history of ethical theory: The argument's conclusion is: *If any rights exist at all, then the right to personal freedom exists.* The argument is subtle, but powerful. Consider any right, such as the right to property. Just as any other right, the right to property turns out on closer inspection to be a complex entity, both entitling rights holders and restricting them. That is to say, a right entitles the right holder to the object of the right, but it entails responsibilities for non-rights holders. If your right to your house as property is meaningful, it imposes responsibilities on me not to enter your house without permission, not to burn it down, and not to retain its rent. This is an essential element of the meaning of the right to property. A right is, in Joel Fienberg's words, a 'justified claim or entitlement *to* something and *against* someone' (Feinberg, 1966). Any right constitutes a moral justification for limiting someone else's freedom in relation to the object of the right. Because of your right, I am not free to burn your house, retain its rent, and so on. But notice – and this is the subtle part – this consideration assumes that in the absence of the claim of your right to property I would have a right to behave freely as I want, and that in order to restrict my freedom with respect to your house, you must make a moral claim against me by asserting your right. Your moral claim against my freedom to use your house is precisely your moral 'right' to property. Hence, any right assumes implicitly that each of us starts with the more basic right to freedom, and that, in turn, rights are claims against this deeper, natural right. *If any rights exist at all, then the right to personal freedom exists.*

Thus, nobody in the real world of corporate jurisdictions that also displays the generic characteristics of our imaginary one, for example in the UK, Germany, Japan, Brazil or the US, waives his right to personal freedom when he transacts business with the corporation, whether he is an employee, a customer or a shareowner. This moral reality is sufficiently profound that even laws reflect it. If I sign a written contract that declares I will be your slave in return for a million dollars, it is null and void. It is meaningless, because I may not contract away something that I possess as a part of my self. My right to freedom is, in the words of the framers of the US Constitution, 'inalienable', that is to say, it cannot be separated from me. Other legal doctrines such as post-employment-restraint agreements or 'non-competes', reflect the same truth. Unlike other contracts, non-compete agreements in US courts are judged by a standard of 'reasonableness'. If I sign a contract that specifies that if I leave your employment, I will not work for a competing company for 15 years, it is not legally enforceable because it is an 'unreasonable' restriction on my future personal freedom. The time period is too long.

We have seen, then, that the existence of at least one additional moral right, namely the right to individual freedom, can be derived from the moral right to private property. But how about other moral rights? If a corporation must, morally speaking, respect its stakeholders' rights to property and rights to individual freedom, then must it also respect their right to life? Must the corporation also respect their right to privacy? To non-discrimination?

Henry Shue's now famous strategy for uncovering 'basic rights' helps answer the question. Shue's strategy is based on the logical implications of the concept of a 'right', where a right is understood as a justified demand that is socially guaranteed. The strategy is one of simple 'if, then' reasoning. If one has a right to something, and it happens to also be true that another thing is necessary for enjoying that something, then one also has a right to the other thing. The 'other thing' is not whatever would be useful in enjoying the right, but only what is indispensable to its enjoyment (Shue, 1980: 31). Using Shue's strategy we can ask: if corporate stakeholders have a right to personal property and individual freedom, then what other things are indispensable for the enjoyment of those rights?

Some indispensable things for the enjoyment of these two rights fall beyond the ability of the corporation to provide. For example, the enjoyment of the right to property entails the existence of a judicial system capable of protecting that right when abused. But some other things arguably fall within the corporation's ambit. These include the rights to physical security, non-deceptive communication and some degree of privacy. Consider the following examples:

- *Physical security*: Indispensible for an employee's enjoyment of the right to individual freedom is physical security. No employee or contractor could enjoy individual freedom in a context where a corporation allowed dangerous chemicals or unsafe, hazardous conditions to become a threat to his or her physical security.
- *Privacy:* Indispensible for an employee's enjoyment of the right to property is the privacy of personal information and materials

to which the corporation has access. For example, it would be a violation of an employee's right to property if the company failed to provide any safeguards from unwarranted searches and seizures while the employee was at work. And, similarly, certain kinds of private information about the employee held by the company, for example, healthcare records or confidential personal information, qualify as personal property of the employee, and require safeguarding by the company.

● *Non-deceptive communication:* Meaningful individual freedom is more than the absence of external restraints. Free choice requires knowledge of the options of choice and of the consequences of choosing various options. Companies that intentionally mislead employees have indirectly interfered with their employees' ability to choose freely. A company that lies to employees, saying that no layoffs will occur while knowing that they will has precluded the possibility of an employee's freely choosing other options. Consider the following example. A successful company lies to a small group of new employees hired for a new initiative, and tells them that the business prospects for the initiative are good and that their jobs are secure, when it knows that the venture is a high-risk gamble and that all the new employees will likely be laid off within a year. Even in the context of the legal employment-at-will doctrine in US law under which the company retains the legal right to fire the employees described above, the employees may be said to possess a moral right to be told the truth, and probably to be treated differently in the aftermath of the lie. (The employment-at-will doctrine permits firing for 'good reason', for 'bad reason' and even for reason that is 'morally wrong'.)

The same is true for customers and shareowners. As a shareowner, I have certain moral rights to the truth, for example, to a truthful account from managers of the corporation about the financial health of the corporation I own, regardless of legal requirements. Even if there were no investor protection laws, I have a moral right as a shareowner not to be given a duplicitous, Enron-style balance sheet. And even if there were no consumer protection laws, I have a right as a customer not to be sold a bottle labeled 'dandelion oil' that contains deadly belladonna.

At this point, we have arrived at a stage in our analysis that reveals that the corporation must, on pain of contradiction, be viewed through the normative lens of at least some kind of 'stakeholder' framework. In particular, the corporation must treat all those who transact business with it as moral rights holders. As moral rights holders, customers and employees, and not only owners, have legitimate moral claims, and these claims restrict the actions of the corporation. No agreement, including an agreement that specifies that the corporation is to be run entirely for the benefit of the shareowners, can conflict morally with these claims because they derive from the logically prior concept of a moral right and the analysis of two rights that cannot be expunged from the corporate agent, namely, the right to property and the right to individual freedom. No matter what contracts are signed and no matter what implicit contracts may exist, the corporation must not treat employees or stockowners simply as a resource, or customers simply as a means of revenue production. It must not, because these groups, in contrast to inanimate resources such as land or money, are made up of moral rights holders. They are stakeholders in this sense precisely because they are moral rights holders.

A caveat applies to the above conclusion. While moral rights such as property and freedom cannot be alienated from their bearers, they can be 'shaped' through mutual agreement, although only up to a point. For example, it is not a violation of one's freedom of movement to agree to punch a time clock in connection with the terms of one's employment. But at some point, as with most conditions of so-called 'indentured servitude' contracts, or with those of extraordinarily long, post-employment restraint contracts, even personal agreements are not allowed to shape the right to freedom. They are proscribed by the more fundamental moral right to freedom.

We also must be candid about the limits to the broader conclusions of the above argument. The argument has justified only a 'weak' normative stakeholder interpretation because it has demonstrated only that that the corporation and its agents must shoulder a narrow range of obligations to advance the interests of customers, employees or other stakeholders when making decisions. This conclusion, which may be called a 'Stage #1' stakeholder conclusion, is that the members of such constituencies are the objects of normative duties only in the indirect sense that they are moral rights holders. To reach a Stage #2 conclusion containing a more robust interpretation of the inevitability of the normative stakeholder model, more argument is required.

I cannot attempt here to settle the issue of whether Stage #2 can be reached. I believe it can be reached, but that doing so involves reference to a different form of argument, namely, one of social contract.[3] This is a lengthy and complicated task lying beyond the reach of this chapter. The principal point of my paper has been only to show that normative stakeholder theory is inescapable in its weaker, that is, Stage #1, form.

One caveat is important. The inevitability of a normative stakeholder interpretation of the modern corporation, while clearly entailing moral responsibilities for corporations, does not thereby entail legal responsibilities. The preceding argument maintains the critical distinction between ethics and law. Again, many moral responsibilities ought not to be enforced by law.

Normative stakeholder theory, we have seen, is *conceptually* inescapable when interpreting the modern corporation. It is inescapable simply because the right to property is ineliminable from the concept of the corporation. This very presumption of the right to property can be unpacked to reveal its deeper commitments: both to the right to individual freedom and to the correlative rights that property and freedom entail. It follows that the corporation must not regard employees or stockowners simply as resources, or customers simply as a means of revenue production. These groups, in contrast to inanimate resources such as land or money, are made up of moral rights holders. They are stakeholders precisely because they are moral rights holders.

And yet, in reaching this inescapable commitment to normative stakeholder theory, we acknowledge that it is a weak moral commitment, at least when laid against what many normative stakeholder theorists claim for their theory. In particular this weak commitment does not specify that any company has any obligation to advance the interests of stakeholders when making decisions – other, that is, than respecting their moral rights. As we have seen, in order to reach a more robust, Stage #2 commitment to normative stakeholder theory, a more extensive normative analysis of the corporation must be undertaken.

NOTES

1. My analysis here is an extension of an idea I sketched briefly in an earlier article with Lee Preston (Donaldson and Preston, 1995), in which I argued that the normative stakeholder model could be justified by analyzing the right to private property.
2. Jensen argues there that any other criteria are too malleable and exploitable for practical evaluation purposes.
3. The argument is similar to one I advanced many years ago in Chapter Three of *Corporations and Morality* (Donaldson 1982). When employees, managers, and owners cooperate in a 'productive organization' they are undertaking a specific kind of activity subject to specific, additional moral considerations. Their activity is subject to analysis in the form of a social contract. In the social contract with productive organizations, contractors in the state of nature quickly recognize that the productive organization's special advantage over the state of individual production lies in its productive contribution. The principal, although not the only, reason why members of society should want to have productive organizations rather than a state of nature is the enhanced contribution possible to them, considered both as consumers and participants (employees). The resulting net increase in productivity that flows from moving away from the state of individual production is beneficial to social contractors because it promises to enhance the welfare

of these two overlapping classes of stakeholders: those who participate in the productive process, i.e., employees, and those who consume its products or services, i.e., consumers. Hence, hypothetical contractors in a state of nature will demand that the obligations of productive organizations extend not only to consumers and employees, but to all others affected by that organization's activities.

REFERENCES

Blair, M.M. and Stout, L.A. 1999. Team production in business organizations: an introduction. *Journal of Corporation Law*, **24**(4): 743–50.

Coase, R.H. 1960. The problem of social cost. *Journal of Law and Economics*, **3**: 1–44.

Donaldson, T. 1982. *Corporations and Morality*. Englewood Cliffs, NJ: Prentice-Hall.

Donaldson, T. and Preston, L. 1995. The stakeholder theory of the corporation: concepts, evidence, and implications. *Academy of Management Review*, **20**(1): 65–91.

Fama, E.F. and Jensen, M.C. 1983. Agency problems and residual claims. *Journal of Law and Economics*, **26**(2): 327.

Feinberg, J. 1966. Duties, rights and claims, *American Philosophical Quarterly*, **3**: 137–44.

Jensen, M.C. 2002. Value maximization, stakeholder theory, and the corporate objective function. *Business Ethics Quarterly*, **12**(2): 235–47.

Jensen, M.C. and Meckling, W.H. 1976. Theory of the firm: managerial behavior, agency costs and ownership structure. *Journal of Financial Economics*, **3**(4): 305–60.

Shue, H. 1980. *Basic Rights: Subsistence, Affluence, and U.S. Foreign Policy*. Princeton, NJ: Princeton University Press.

Williamson, O.E. 1985. *The Economic Institutions of Capitalism: Firms, Markets, Relational Contracting*. New York: Free Press.

Williamson, O.E. 1996a. Economics and organization: a primer. *California Management Review*, **38**(2): 131–46.

Williamson, O.E. 1996b. *The Mechanisms of Governance*. New York: Oxford University Press.

7. Where is the theory in stakeholder theory? A meta-analysis of the pluralism in stakeholder theory

Andreas Georg Scherer and Moritz Patzer

In the 25 years since the publication of Freeman's book *Strategic Management: A Stakeholder Approach* in 1984, stakeholder theory has had a profound impact on our perception of the relation between the corporation and its social environment. Although originally intended as a textbook in Strategic Management (see Freeman 2004: 229), Freeman's publication has been widely recognized in fields such as Business and Society, Corporate Social Responsibility (CSR), and Business Ethics (see Freeman and McVea, 2001; Jones, Wicks and Freeman, 2002; Freeman, 2004; Walsh, 2005; Agle et al., 2008; Laplume, Sonpar and Litz, 2008).

Its core notion is that of a managerial approach that goes beyond a neoclassical shareholder-orientation and recognizes the strategic relevance of stakeholders in an increasingly complex world (for example, Freeman, 1994; Jones, Wicks and Freeman, 2002; critically, Jensen, 2002; Sundaram and Inkpen, 2004; Walsh, 2005). The inclusion of the latter, understood as 'any group or individual who is affected by or can affect the achievement of an organization's objectives' (Freeman, 1984: 46; see also Mitchell, Agle and Wood, 1997), has prepared the ground for a new understanding of the firm's social embeddedness. The work of Freeman and his colleagues has sparked enthusiastic calls for an integrative theory of the firm with stakeholder theory as a 'central paradigm for the business and society field' (Jones, 1995: 432; see also Donaldson and Preston, 1995; Wood and Jones, 1995; Harrison and Freeman, 1999). Likewise, it has been considered as a foothold in the 'Normative Revolution' in the understanding of markets and corporations (see Donaldson, 2008: 174; also Donaldson, 2002 and current volume). Phillips, Freeman and Wicks (2003: 481) emphasize the critical perspective as a special feature of stakeholder theory in comparison to other approaches to (strategic) management that lack this kind of explicit normative claim:

> Stakeholder theory is distinct because it addresses morals and values explicitly as a central feature of managing organizations. [. . .] The ends of cooperative activity and the means of achieving these ends are critically examined in stakeholder theory in a way that they are not in many theories of strategic management.

However, with the term 'stakeholder' becoming ubiquitous in organization and management literature (for example, Phillips, 2003; Phillips, Freeman and Wicks, 2003; Laplume, Sonpar and Litz, 2008), skeptical voices have lamented the state of the stakeholder approach as a theoretical concept. In their recent review of the stakeholder theory literature, Laplume, Sonpar and Litz (2008) point towards the growing critique which considers the approach to be undertheorized (for example, Stoney and Winstanley, 2001; Sundaram and Inkpen, 2004) and too broad (for example, Treviño and Weaver, 1999b; Phillips, Freeman and Wicks, 2003), as well as lacking in integration (for example, Donaldson and Preston, 1995; Donaldson, 1999; Gioia, 1999; Margolis and Walsh, 2003). Stoney and Winstanley summarize:

> Because of the myriad of interpretations, generalizations and definitions, the term stakeholding has become content free and can mean almost anything the author desires [. . .]
> Consequently, the confused and often shallow nature of the stakeholder debate has made it possible for academics, managers and politicians to embrace the term without having to explain the concept in theoretical or practical terms. (Stoney and Winstanley, 2001: 605 f.)

At the root of this pluralism of perspectives lie theoretical challenges, which are inherent to the field: the normative foundation of stakeholder theory, the appropriate role of the firm in society, the problem of stakeholder identification, stakeholder legitimacy and the evaluation of their claims, as well as the relevance of ethics, philosophy and the multitude of background theories, pose significant hurdles in the undertaking labeled 'stakeholder theory' (see Driver and Thompson, 2002; Jones, Wicks and Freeman, 2002; Post, Preston and Sachs, 2002; Phillips, 2003; Phillips, Freeman and Wicks, 2003). These issues have to be resolved otherwise a critical examination of the 'ends of cooperative activities and the means of achieving these ends' (Phillips, Freeman and Wicks, 2003: 481) is not possible. In addition, the underlying concept of 'theory' is unclear. While one finds research in stakeholder theory that has been developed in the tradition of the social sciences and their dominant positivist or natural science model of research, there are also works that have been heavily influenced by the philosophic thinking of the humanities and post-positivist methods (Wicks and Freeman, 1998). These paradigmatic differences imply various meanings of the concept of 'theory' and lead to incommensurable views on how the study of stakeholders and their relations to the firm should be conducted. Facing this pluralism of theories, Freeman (1999: 235) even prefers to speak of 'narrations' instead of theories. Further complications result from the fact that, despite the explicit mention of 'society', the business and society field in general (and stakeholder theory is not an exception) has reflected only rarely on the underlying competing concepts of 'society' discussed in political philosophy and social theory, such as liberal, libertarian, communitarian, republican and deliberative perspectives on democratic society (see Moon, Crane and Matten, 2005). As a result the link between the individual, the firm, and society remains highly contested (see Scherer and Palazzo, 2007; cf. Elms, Johnson-Cramer and Berman, in the current volume).

This pluralistic state of stakeholder theory has itself triggered heterogeneous meta-positions, ranging from a favoring of convergence (for example, Donaldson, 1999; Jones and Wicks, 1999a, 1999b), to the support of a moderate eclecticism (for example, Freeman, 1994, 1999; Treviño and Weaver, 1999a, 1999b), to authors who claim that an integration of the various positions is not possible (Gioia 1999). Yet the lack of meta-analytic endeavors since Donaldson and Preston's 1995 review of the academic stakeholder literature threatens to obstruct the capabilities of the respective stakeholder approaches to contribute to the fundamental questions of the field. Therefore, we would like to explore why there are so many perspectives and why and in what sense integration is possible (or impossible), or even at all desirable.

We suggest that the pluralism and heterogeneity of perspectives within stakeholder theory can be analyzed once the different research interests (Habermas, 1971) and paradigmatic assumptions (Burrell and Morgan, 1979) of the various perspectives are fully understood. It is therefore the aim of this chapter to suggest a meta-theoretical framework based on a paradigmatic systematization of different stakeholder approaches along their research interests and their underlying fundamental assumptions concerning ontology, epistemology, methodology and the concept of human nature. This would shed a light on the reason for and the contribution of the different answers to the field's questions. Lastly we try to point towards a possible way to bring together the different perspectives in a pragmatic manner, and to acknowledge their contributions despite the paradigmatic differences. At the same time we want to avoid the relativistic fallacies of many of the anti-positivist perspectives (cf. Wicks and Freeman 1998: 127) that emphasize the culture and history-bound roots of any scientific or philosophical endeavor and endorse pluralism as having a value of its own.

NORMATIVE, DESCRIPTIVE AND INSTRUMENTAL STAKEHOLDER THEORY: THE DONALDSON AND PRESTON TAXONOMY AND ITS CRITIQUE

The stakeholder theory can be, and has been, presented and used in a number of ways that are quite distinct and involve very different methodologies, types of evidence, and criteria of appraisal. (Donaldson and Preston, 1995: 70)

One of the most frequently cited taxonomies of stakeholder approaches is that of Donaldson and Preston (1995). Donaldson and Preston differentiate between three types of stakeholder theories, namely (1) descriptive/empirical ones, (2) instrumental representations and (3) normative conceptions.

(1) Descriptive/Empirical

In its *descriptive* form the theory describes the corporation as a nexus of heterogeneous interests that are ascribed an 'intrinsic value' (Donaldson and Preston 1995: 66). At the heart of these empirical attempts that try to depict observed reality lies the analysis of corporate characteristics and behaviors with respect to their social embeddedness. It is their goal to explain corporate behavior and to model the corporate decision process as an attempt to pursue corporate goals by addressing stakeholder expectations, or by involving stakeholder concerns in the respective decision processes.

(2) Instrumental

'*Instrumental* stakeholder theory proposes stakeholder-oriented answers as to how managers should meet specific objectives, which may or may not have ethical elements. For example, what should managers do to maximize profits, to maximize returns to shareholders, or to maximize total welfare?' (Hendry, 2001: 163). An instrumental understanding, therefore, tries to produce theories on the systematic relationships between stakeholder management and corporate performance. The latter is normally designed as economic performance and measured in terms of profitability, growth and so forth (see Donaldson and Preston, 1995: 67). The task is to identify cause-and-effect relationships that explain economic performance and to transform these theoretical insights into recipes for enhancing performance. As such, an instrumental approach is prescriptive; it justifies the stakeholder-perspective in contrast to the traditional shareholder-view with regard to long term monetary pay-offs (see also Harrison and St. John, 1996).

(3) Normative

Lastly, normative approaches are characterized by the authors as 'attempts to interpret the function of, and offer guidance about, the investor-owned corporation on the basis of some underlying moral or philosophical principles' (Donaldson and Preston, 1995: 72; see also Donaldson, current volume). Stakeholder orientation is therein justified not by potential pay-offs but by it being the 'right thing to do'. It proposes categorical answers to the problems of ethically sound management and its scope of responsibility.

Donaldson and Preston (1995) consider these three perspectives as mutually dependent, and understand them as inherent to stakeholder theory and, as such, also discernable in Freeman's early work. Still, their taxonomy has sparked controversy. Despite their acknowledgment of Donaldson and Preston's efforts to provide order and coherence, Freeman (1994, 1999, 2000) as well as Jones, Wicks and Freeman (2002) criticize this typology for two reasons: first for reinforcing the 'separation thesis' and second for the categories' 'lack of distinctiveness'.

Fairly straightforward, the 'separation thesis' stands for a conceptual differentiation between the ethical and the economic, with respective exponents campaigning either for the primacy of the normative or the primacy of the empirical approaches (for a detailed analysis of the separation thesis, see Sandberg, 2008, and the reactions to his paper by Harris and Freeman, 2008, and others). Freeman argues that authors like Donaldson and Preston (1995) or Mitchell, Agle and Wood (1997) promote the perception of a separation of business and morality in stakeholder theory (as well as in social science as a whole) that is detrimental for an adequate understanding of actual business practice (for example, Wicks and Freeman, 1998; Freeman, 1999, 2000: 172 f., 2004, 2008: 163; Harris and Freeman, 2008). We will expand upon this argument below.

The taxonomy has also been critiqued for the lack of distinctiveness of the three categories presented (see Jones and Wicks, 1999a; Jones, Wicks and Freeman, 2002; as well as Ulrich 2008: 421 f.). Since Donaldson and Preston see the three aspects 'nested within each other' (1995: 74) with the normative at the core of stakeholder theory, they explicitly advocate a primacy of the normative perspective. As a consequence stakeholder theory has to address the following questions: (1) How can moral norms and values that may deliver an anchor point for the descriptive and instrumental stakeholder view be justified? (2) How can the moral and the economic perspective be balanced under the conditions of economic competition? (3) How can the role of the individual and of the corporation in capitalist societies be defined? Furthermore, it remains unclear to what extent descriptive and instrumental approaches can be differentiated from each other, and how and in what sense the latter can be based on the former.

In our view, these questions pose challenges not just for Donaldson and Preston (1995) but for theorizing on stakeholder theory, in general, as they touch upon the fundamental premises of stakeholder theory, its purpose, methods and underlying philosophical assumptions about the concept of human nature, the concept of the firm and the concept of society. Obviously, there is no common paradigm, but instead a pluralism of partly contradicting views in stakeholder theory on how these fundamental issues may be addressed (see the various contributions to stakeholder theory in Phillips and Freeman, 2010, and the above-mentioned review articles). We cannot deliver a complete overview or an integration of all these diverse views here, and the problem of incommensurability may, finally, remain an obstacle for true integration (see Gioia, 1999, and below). Still, we would like to stress the advantages of a robust meta-analytical framework in order to understand theory pluralism and to assess the various contributions in the field of stakeholder theory. In this light we suggest a framework that is based on the differences in paradigmatic premises of heterogeneous fundamental perspectives instead of substantial differences (see also Freeman and Lorange, 1985).

POSITIVIST AND POST-POSITIVIST STAKEHOLDER THEORY: A META-ANALYTIC FRAMEWORK

In accordance with earlier suggestions made for organization theory (see Scherer, 1998, 2003), CSR (see Scherer and Palazzo, 2007) and most recently leadership ethics (see Patzer, 2010) we propose a conceptual distinction of contributions to stakeholder theory. At its roots lies the notion of *paradigms* as alternative approaches to the explanation of social phenomena that may provide a more distinct insight into the different existing research traditions in stakeholder theory. Basically, a paradigm provides the answer to the two fundamental questions of research: (1) What is the purpose of research? and (2) By what means and methodologies can this purpose be achieved? (see Scherer, 1999, 2003; Scherer and Patzer, 2008). These questions take into account research interests on the one hand and the variety of methods applied (methodology), the assumptions about the examined object (ontology) and the way to examine it (epistemology) that characterize modern science in its pursuit of 'truth' on the other (see Kuhn, 1962; Pfeffer, 1993; Weaver and Treviño, 1998; Scherer and Patzer, 2008). A widely recognized systematization of paradigms, here defined as the distinct ways of how researchers gain knowledge about social phenomena, is that of Gibson Burrell and Gareth Morgan (1979; see also Gioia and Pitre 1990; for alternative taxonomies see Astley and Van de Ven, 1983; as well as Hollis, 1994). They suggest that social science theories, in general, and organization theories, in particular, are based on a 'theory of society' and on a 'philosophy of science'. In the understanding of the authors both imply a dichotomous dimension.

The 'theory of society' dimension (Burrell and Morgan 1979) depicts the normative frame of a theory in terms of 'regulation' and 'radical change' of social systems. A 'sociology of regulation' represents research that examines why social entities persist and what the conditions for the preservation of the status quo are. By contrast, a 'sociology of radical change' addresses the change processes to which social entities are exposed. This work is decidedly normative, engaged in criticizing and improving the present status quo of social systems. In particular, it is concerned with the question of how individuals and social communities can be freed from the structural constraints that are repressing their development (see Burrell and Morgan, 1979; Steffy and Grimes, 1986; Scherer and Patzer, 2008; Scherer, 2009).

The 'philosophy of science' dimension (Burrell and Morgan, 1979) addresses fundamental questions with regard to ontology, epistemology, methodology and basic assumptions concerning human nature. *Ontology* is about the essential characteristics of the object of research. Here, Burrell and Morgan distinguish between two positions: realism and nominalism. In the realist perspective, the object of research and its structure (that is, its elements and the relationships between these elements) are predefined and given to the researcher. In the nominalist perspective, the object of research is not given or predefined but is constructed only by way of investigation. *Epistemology* deals with the question of how knowledge about the object of research can be acquired? Here, Burrell and Morgan contrast (what they call) the positivist methods of the natural sciences with the interpretive approach from the humanities. In the positivist perspective, 'the task of the researchers is to find reality rather than to create or interpret it' (Wicks and Freeman, 1998: 125). *Methodology* considers what particular methods can be applied. Here nomothetic methodologies such as experiments, systematic observation of large samples and empirical hypothesis testing that search for regularities and law-like relationships of observed social phenomena can be distinguished from idiosyncratic methods such as ethnography, hermeneutics, or grounded theory, that try to capture the history and culture specific singularities of a social occurrence. Finally, the assumptions about *human nature* will differ depending on whether humans are thought to be (largely) determined by the environment (determinism) or whether they can deliberately influence the

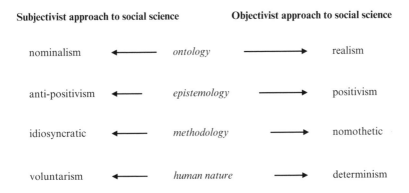

Source: Adapted from Burrell and Morgan (1979: 3, modified).

Figure 7.1   Subjectivist and objectivist approaches to the social sciences

environment (voluntarism) (see Phillips et al., current volume). Along these dichotomous sub-dimensions Burrell and Morgan (1979) distinguish 'subjective' and 'objective' approaches to the study of social phenomena (see Figure 7.1)

Both these dimensions, the purpose of research and the philosophy of science applied as a means can be combined and further substantiated by Jürgen Habermas' introduction of three cognitive research interests that have also been discussed in management research (see Stablein and Nord, 1985; Steffy and Grimes, 1986; Scherer, 2003, 2009; Willmott 2003). In his book *Knowledge and Human Interest*, Habermas (1971) distinguishes between technical, practical and emancipatory research interests. The pursuit of a *technical research interest* attempts to explain the social conditions for the preservation of a social order, seeking to expose the functional mechanisms used to stabilize the status quo of a social system. Many social scientists advocate a value-free science and do not want to develop prescriptive knowledge, but instead merely focus on the description of social phenomena by way of explanation. However, this perspective is criticized for its potential to deliver instrumental knowledge and social technologies for the preservation of the status of those actors who are in power (see the *Positivismusstreit* in German sociology where this problem has been discussed intensively, Adorno et al., 1976). A *practical research interest* focuses on an interpretation of the actions of individuals through the understanding of their subjective meanings. This hermeneutic approach conceives of reality as the result of a process of social construction. It aims to describe the actors' patterns of interpretation underlying their social actions and processes of social exchange (Evered and Louis, 1981; Steffy and Grimes, 1986). Here again, the primary focus of the researcher is on the description of social phenomena (by way of subjective understanding or *Verstehen* instead of objective explanation). Likewise, this perspective is affirmative to the social status quo as it does not address power imbalances or how dependency and domination influence the interpretations of the focal actors (Stablein and Nord 1985). As a result, the interpretations of the most powerful actors are not challenged and marginalized voices are often neglected in the interpretive analysis of social systems. By contrast, an *emancipatory research interest* focuses on the critical reflection of the social structures and processes and the power imbalances that make up and influence these structures and processes (see Habermas, 1971; Steffy and Grimes, 1986; Willmott, 2003; Scherer, 2009). Here the perspective is decidedly normative: situations of dependency and domination should be addressed and social change should be facilitated so that individuals are freed from marginalization or suppression and a more human, rational and just society can be developed. In Burrell and Morgan's (1979) framework, a 'sociology of regulation' pursues technical or practical research interests, while a 'sociology of radical change' emphasizes the emancipatory research interest. The various research interests are also apparent in the stakeholder and management theory literature, as can be seen from the brief summary in Table 7.1 (for more detailed analysis see Burrell and Morgan, 1979; Gioia and Pitre, 1990; Scherer, 2003, 2009; Willmott, 2003).

In accordance with these meta-analytical elaborations we suggest differentiating between positivist and post-positivist approaches to stakeholder theory. In our understanding, a *positivist research paradigm* stands for a perspective that pursues a technical research interest and approaches the social world through the use of the empirical methods of a naturalistic model of explanation, aiming 'to explain observable phenomena through general or statistical laws and situational conditions' (Scherer and Palazzo, 2007: 1098; see Donaldson, 1996; Hempel, 1998). It combines a technical research interest with positivist methods such as experiments, empirical hypothesis testing or economic modeling. It aims to explain observable social phenomena and to deliver objective knowledge about cause and effect relationships. This knowledge can be utilized to stabilize the status quo of social systems (and of those who are in power) by enhancing efficiency and by developing instruments for social control.

We argue, however, that positivist stakeholder theory approaches have at least two limitations. (1) They cannot sufficiently address the *normative issues* entangled with the engagement of business with society (Wicks and Freeman, 1998), such as the appropriate role of business in society or the

Table 7.1   Meta-analytic perspectives and research interests in the social sciences

Meta analytic perspective	Cognitive research interest	Purpose and focus	Method	Aim	Examples from management and stakeholder theory
Positivist research paradigm	Technical research interest	Explanation, prediction and control; Identification of cause and effect relationships	Empirical-analytical (e.g., empirical hypothesis testing, experiments; economic modeling)	Explaining observed phenomena; Enhancing efficiency; Developing instruments for social control	Contingency theory; Organizational economics theory; Instrumental stakeholder theory; Descriptive stakeholder theory (positivist variants)
Post-positivist research paradigm	Practical research interest	(Mutual) understanding; Interpretation of socially constructed reality	Historical-hermeneutic (e.g., ethnography, hermeneutics, grounded theory, thick description)	Interpreting (and understanding) social occurrences from the standpoint of the actors; Overcoming barriers of understanding	Interpretive theory; Identity theory; Organizational communication theory; Cultural theory; Descriptive stakeholder theory (interpretive variants)
	Emancipatory research interest	Critique of status quo of social systems; Identification of situations of dependency and domination	Critical and philosophical analysis (e.g., discourse analysis, dialectics, deconstruction, narrative analysis)	Social change; Development of a more humane, rational, and just society	Discourse theory; Postmodern theory; Critical stakeholder theory; Normative stakeholder theory

identification of stakeholder claims and the assessment of their justifica-
tions. Positivist approaches to social science naturalize social phenomena.
As a consequence they are unable to distinguish whether the observed regularities in the social world are the result of 'unchangeable laws of social
action' or whether they express situations of power and dependence that
are 'in principle subject to change' (Habermas, 1966: 294). (2) Positivist
approaches explore the social world only from an outside perspective and
only by focusing on observable phenomena that can be measured 'objectively' (Evered and Louis, 1981; Morris et al., 1999). The subjective perspective of the actors' values, intentions and interpretations is neglected.
However, if the normative issues need to be addressed, denaturalizing
the object of study and addressing the focal actors as subjects with their
own values, interests, interpretations, and world views is unavoidable.
Therefore, it is necessary for the researcher to change the perspective from
that of an observer to a participator (Scherer and Dowling, 1995) and
to communicate with the focal actors, to learn their values, interests and
interpretations, in order to view and interpret the social world from the
standpoint of the focal actors (Habermas, 1990).

   These issues can be better addressed within a *post-positivist paradigm.*
This stands on two pillars: an interpretive approach that follows a practical
research interest in order to capture the subjective interests and meanings
of the focal actors and a critical approach that follows an emancipatory
research interest in order to critically assess the interests and advanced
interpretations, to identify situations of dependency and domination, and
to develop a more humane, rational and just society.

   The interpretive approach advances a *practical research interest* and
is based on the assumption that social entities are not given as 'hard
facts' and cannot be investigated by observation from the outside only
(see Scherer and Patzer, 2008; Gioia and Pitre 1990). Rather they are
constructed and interpreted by the members of a social community.
Consequently, interpretivists do not see social phenomena as objective
entities, but rather as subjective meanings that emerge and evolve through
actions and communications (Evered and Louis 1981). The researcher
therefore does not adopt the role of an objective observer, as in the positivist paradigm, but takes a participative perspective in which he or she
tries to come to terms with the subjective meanings of the focal actors
(Habermas 1990). The investigator thus has to interpret the interpretation
of the actors ('double hermeneutics'). Though the positivist researcher
usually attempts to support his or her theories through large samples and
quantitative data, the interpretive researcher usually undertakes one or a
few case studies, in which theories are generated by conducting qualita-
tive in-depth interviews. The interpretive researcher collects data that are

relevant for the actors involved in the case and tries to understand them from the subjective point of view of the actors. In spite of all these methodological differences to positivism, the interpretive researcher shares the interest in the emergence and preservation of social order. Like the positivist, he or she does not deal with problems of social conflict and the legitimization of social change, unlike investigators working with an emancipatory interest and a critical view on social phenomena. Both the interpretive and the positivist researcher are oriented toward the status quo of a social order and not toward its criticism and possible change. Therefore, the interpretive perspective has to be combined with a *critical view* that delivers the normative vantage point for the critical analysis of social actions and institutions.

Researchers with a critical view pursue an emancipatory research interest and seek to free the members of a social community from paternalism, alienation, exploitation and suppression by criticizing and changing present social structures (see Scherer, 2009; Scherer and Patzer, 2008). This view assumes that existing structures in modern society are the result of social constructions that are mainly influenced by the subjective meanings of the most powerful actors. The aim of this perspective is criticism of the processes of power that are unfolding within the institutions of modern society as well as in everyday social life. Researchers with a critical perspective argue that the legitimacy of the interpretations of social constructs should be subject to examination, so that the illegitimate influence of power on meaning can be discovered. This perspective builds upon the methods of the interpretive paradigm (Steffy and Grimes, 1986). However, it goes one step further. While the interpretivists primarily try to explore how a certain social reality is constructed and what the subjective interpretations of the involved actors are, adherents of the critical perspective are concerned with the question of why social reality is constructed in this way and whose interests are served by this construction. The aim is to change social structures so that individuals are freed from situations of dependency and suppression, and can determine their own social life.

Both these approaches derive their methods from philosophy and the humanities rather than from the natural sciences, as is the case with the positivist paradigm. Combined together, their approach to theory is a normative one, concerned with the evaluation of the behavior of business action in terms of right or wrong (see Treviño and Weaver, 1994; Weaver and Treviño, 1994). As such, it represents a holistic perspective and combines practical and emancipatory research interests with the variety of post-positivist methods. Its pluralistic methodology can be integrated, however, by way of reasonable discourse and the acknowledgment of the 'good argument' only (Habermas, 1984). The assumption is that only by way of discourse can the claims of the various theoretical perspectives, the legitimacy of research goals, and the suitability of methods be assessed (see Scherer, 1998; Scherer and Steinmann, 1999).

Such a differentiation helps in understanding the category distinctiveness between instrumental, descriptive and normative approaches that is considered a problem of the Donaldson and Preston taxonomy. Yet, as both strands, positivistic and post-positivistic, differ in language, assumptions and theory on the basis of historically separated development of respective research traditions, they appear incompatible, implying paradigmatic incommensurability (Scherer, 1998; Scherer and Steinmann, 1999). Therefore, the question of the value added by such a meta-analytic taxonomy remains. We address this with regard to the field's recurring discussion of the separation fallacy.

THEORETICAL PLURALISM AND PRACTICAL UNITY: TAKING ANOTHER LOOK AT THE SEPARATION THESIS

As sketched above, the separation fallacy refers to the distinction between the discourse of business from the discourse of ethics (see Freeman, 1994, 1999; Wicks and Freeman, 1998; and more recently Freeman, 2008; Noland and Phillips, 2010). Freeman and others have repeatedly excavated the underlying assumptions that have led to this distinction and have, according to them, been incorporated in typologies like that of Donaldson and Preston.

First, they argue that the distinction between the 'normative' and 'descriptive' has no equivalent in business practice and therefore is only meaningful if it relies on itself (for example, Freeman, 1999; Jones, Wicks and Freeman, 2002; Harris and Freeman, 2008). Freeman considers this as the field's inheritance from continuing efforts to pit (normative) stakeholder theory against (descriptive/instrumental) shareholder theory. Yet, instead of making stakeholder theory the new battle-standard in a 'Normative Revolution' (Donaldson, 2008), he considers the efforts to be 'integrative' (Freeman, 2008), (finally) apprehending the nature of business practice 'that could never be devoid of morality' (Jones, Wicks and Freeman, 2002: 26; see also Freeman 1994). Consequently, exponents of this opinion argue that the continued separation between the philosophical and business discourses have a detrimental effect on comprehensive theory building.

A second aspect that is reappearing in this context is the critique of ethics' inability to assess instrumental theory. The latter is concerned with the link of means to ends. Freeman therefore argues that the normative foundations of stakeholder theory should be derived from an ethical theory that bases the moral evaluation of an action on its outcomes, hence he proposes consequential/teleological ethics. He tends to reject alternative foundations, namely deontological or Kantian ethics that rely on 'a separate normative realm, unrelated logically to the actual world we live in' (see Freeman, 1999: 235 f.; also, Noland and Phillips, 2010).

Both these proposals to rethink stakeholder theory, regardless of some Kantian (Evan and Freeman, 1983) and Rawlsian (Freeman, 1994) experiments, seem to originate in a deep pragmatist conviction held by Freeman and his co-authors (see Wicks and Freeman, 1998; Freeman, 1999, 2008): 'It is time to get on with it, and get on with it in the pragmatist vein' (Freeman, 1994: 419).

This is a contestable notion. We concur that the idea of theoretical conversion or even unity is highly problematic in the light of the indicated paradigmatic incommensurability. We have argued elsewhere that only the acknowledgment of the pragmatic turn, hence using problems of the actual practice as the starting point for theory-building, may indicate a way to overcome the problem of incommensurability (see Scherer and Dowling 1995; Scherer, 1998, 1999; Scherer and Steinmann, 1999). Yet we contest that the pragmatic turn implies a consequential ethics or the relativistic notion of stakeholder theory as 'a genre of stories about how we could live' (Freeman, 1994: 413). In order to avoid the view that all narratives are integrative and equally valid, Freeman calls for 'a conversation that encourages . . . divergent views, but one that quickly throws out those views that are not useful, not simple, and that do not show us how it is possible to live better' (Freeman, 1999: 235 f.).

The consequentialist approach, however, is limited because the consequences of the divergent theoretical views never speak for themselves but have to be interpreted and assessed as to whether they help us 'to live better' (Freeman). This can be done only by way of *discourse* where the pros and cons of the various views are assessed by way of argumentation (Scherer, 1998; Scherer and Steinmann, 1999). Freeman seems to be open to accepting such a perspective when he advocates a 'conversion' of the divergent views. However, he does not elaborate on the important status of discourse and communicative reason in the justification of stakeholder theory and business and society, in general, but instead emphasizes the importance of consequences. Therefore, in our view, the consequentialist notion of stakeholder theory is limited with regard to its potential to (1) contribute to the development of a non-relativistic conception of business and society and (2) to learn from the methodological pluralism and the inconsistency that is characteristic for modern social science research.

The former becomes relevant with regard to the problems of the foundation of democratic society and the role of business in society that is central to theorizing on the relationship between the firm and its stakeholders, yet cannot be sufficiently addressed from the pragmatist position suggested by Freeman. How can the principles and institutions of modern democratic society be justified? Can these institutions be derived from some universal normative principles? Or are these just the result of a social learning process, a social construction that is historically and culturally contingent? If the former is the case, how can these principles be justified objectively? If the latter is the case, how can the prevailing cultural relativism be avoided? In his seminal paper 'Solidarity or objectivity?', Rorty acknowledges this limitation of pragmatism. He tends to argue for a communicative construction of the normative foundations of society that is not universal but represents the best available knowledge we have in our culture and in our time:

> The pragmatists' justification of toleration, free inquiry, and the quest for undistorted communication can only take the form of a comparison between societies which exemplify these habits and those which do not, leading up to the suggestion that nobody who has experienced both would prefer the latter. (Rorty, 1990: 29)

Interestingly, Rorty does not just point to the consequences of these principles, but also emphasizes the role of undistorted communication for the well-being of society. Therefore, we would like to suggest exploring and developing a *communicative approach* to business and society further as this may be helpful to address both the limitations of a positivist approach and the limitations of a consequentialist or pragmatist approach. In their call for a modern philosophical foundation of stakeholder theory, Freeman et al. have not taken modern deontological theory into account, namely the discourse ethics of Jürgen Habermas (for example, Habermas, 1993) and Karl-Otto Apel (for example, Apel, 1980) as well as the closely related political concept of deliberative democracy (for example Habermas, 1996) which try to address the normative foundations of modern society (see also Scherer, 2009; Scherer and Patzer, 2011).

These arguments centre on the idea of a *procedural concept of communicative rationality* that permeates moral discourse and political deliberation, thereby retaining the notion of a justifiable concept of communicative reason as a basis for the foundation of the institutions of democracy and law in modern society (Habermas, 1996). These concepts have recently been introduced into CSR-theory by Scherer and Palazzo in order to address the operations of business firms in a global environment where there is often a lack of democratic control and an absence of the rule of law. In particular, Scherer and Palazzo analyze the political behavior of business firms and non-state actors such as NGOs in global governance processes, and develop a concept of 'political CSR' that helps to re-embed the political activities of multinational corporations in processes of democratic legitimization and control (see Scherer and Palazzo, 2007; see also Palazzo and Scherer, 2006; Scherer and Palazzo, 2008, 2011).

This perspective on the role of business in society reconstructs its normative core not from theoretical principles, but from the actual practice of argumentation, acknowledging the insights of the linguistic-pragmatic turn (Habermas, 2003; Scherer and Patzer, 2011). Thereby it does not depend on a detached normative realm or universal ethical principles and, in spite of differing accounts (Noland and Phillips, 2010), combines rational and moral ends (see Habermas, 1981: 141–51, especially 150; Habermas 1984: 571–606, especially 588). In conclusion, modern deontological ethics suggest a different frame of reference for stakeholder theory, taking into account the critique of Kantian approaches (as being too monological) and postmodern approaches (as being too relativistic) and providing answers to questions that cannot be sufficiently addressed from a pragmatist point of view.

Freeman and his co-authors highlight the unity of practice and criticize the narrow-mindedness of existing business and society literature with regard to its normative foundations and instrumental implications. This argument appears to be qualified. Still, practical problems spark a variety of research interests that are addressed by researchers with a variety of epistemological–methodological frameworks, all claiming to produce valuable insights (Burrell and Morgan, 1979; Gioia and Pitre, 1990; Weaver and Gioia, 1994). However, any researcher will follow a particular research interest and apply a particular method. This selectivity can be understood as a methodological bracketing, highlighting special aspects of management practice that are of interest to the respective scholar. As it remains unclear how the existing and 'useful' methodological pluralism can be unified or transcended in an overarching pragmatist framework, we feel that stakeholder theory is better imagined as an evolving, mutually informing network of methods with its respective discourses that address different aspects of actual problems in management practice. Freeman appears to be receptive to such a view when he suggests that one speak of 'narratives' instead of stakeholder theories (Freeman, 1999).

DEALING WITH THE PLURALISM IN STAKEHOLDER THEORY

For the student of stakeholder theory, the question now is which of the discussed perspectives are acceptable and which should be rejected (see

Scherer, 2003). Obviously, the problem is how to find a reasonable orientation in this pluralism of stakeholder narratives and meta-perspectives. In organization theory, this problem of theory pluralism has been addressed quite intensively and there are various opinions on how to answer that question (for an overview, see Scherer, 1995, 1998; Scherer and Steinmann, 1999). One position postulates that in comparison to more mature disciplines such as, for example, economics or the natural sciences, theory pluralism in a certain field indicates a premature stage in theory development, but a premature stage that can be overcome (Pfeffer, 1993). Therefore, many stakeholder theories based on different research interests and various methodologies must be produced and subjected to systematical empirical tests. The theories that pass this test can be considered to be 'corroborated' and contribute to the available body of knowledge. Here the pluralism of theories is considered as an intermediate state, which is necessary and can be overcome with the help of a universal empirical test-procedure adopted from the natural sciences (Popper 1959, 1969; Albert, 1985). This view is supported by the positivist paradigm, which is, however, as we have seen, only one possible type of knowledge creation, incompatible with the post-positivist perspectives (for example, interpretivism, critical theory, postmodernism).

A different point of view sees both the pluralism of theories *and* the pluralism of paradigms as necessary for pointing out the ambiguous character of organizational phenomena. As Gareth Morgan has repeatedly remarked, 'organizations are many things at once' (Morgan, 1986: 339). According to this perspective, the pluralism *should not* be overcome in order to gain more 'comprehensive' insights and not to overlook any important aspect (Gioia and Pitre, 1990). This point of view is supported by authors who believe that there is no objective criterion available for comparing the different theoretical and paradigmatic perspectives (Burrell and Morgan, 1979; Jackson and Carter, 1991). These authors base their argument on the problem of 'incommensurability', which says that there are no objective criteria that allow for a comparison between radically different theoretical perspectives (for a critical overview, see Scherer, 1995, 1998; Scherer and Dowling, 1995; Scherer and Steinmann, 1999). If those authors are right in their point of view, however, a critical reflection on stakeholder and management theories must be abandoned, as one theoretical perspective is as good as any other.

However, we do not think that this can and should be the last word (see Scherer and Steinmann, 1999; Scherer, 2003). To overcome this problem, one must take a pragmatic approach and conceive of 'doing research' as *action*. Based on this idea, the researcher intentionally follows his or her research interest. The selection of a research question and appropriate methods can be considered as a way to pursue one's research interest. According to one's research goal one can determine – by way of discourse – whether a particular method is more or less appropriate to reach one's objection. This is, however, only the technical dimension of research. Moreover, one can also open up the normative dimension and critically consider – by way of discourse – whether a research goal is legitimate or not. To do so, however, one must abandon the value-free thesis, but one must also make researchers accountable for what they do.

CONCLUSION

What does this imply for the use of meta-frameworks and the threat of the separation fallacy? With their call for a pragmatist consequential foundation Freeman and his co-authors suggest a specific normative frame for stakeholder theory wherein instrumental theory-building may take place. Yet, in the light of the characteristics of the practical problems as well as modern, pragmatic deontological ethics this frame remains contestable. Stakeholder theory therefore remains a field of intertwined discourses, each applying its methodological bracketing with regard to practical problems. It appears helpful to approach the resulting pluralisms through an understanding for paradigmatic differences. Herein our suggested meta-framework helps to systemize different approaches and informs researchers about the benefits and limitations of their respective applied methods. This is not meant to cement the discourses' separation but should rather foster an open dialogue between the heterogeneous research endeavors. The call for more useful and simple views (Freeman, 1999: 235 f.) should not necessarily mean that the pluralism of approaches be cast aside in favor of a 'unified pragmatist approach'. Rather, we should attempt to achieve practical unity there where it may be helpful to reach mutual understandings, or to benefit from collaborative research projects.

REFERENCES

Adorno, T.W., Albert, H., Dahrendorf, R., Habermas, J., Pilot, H. and Popper, K. 1976. *The Positivist Dispute in German Sociology*. London: Heineman.
Agle, B.R., Donaldson, T., Freeman, R.E., Jensen, M.C., Mitchell, R.K. and Wood, D.J. 2008. Dialogue: toward superior stakeholder theory. *Business Ethics Quarterly*, **18**, 153–90.
Albert, H. 1985. *Treatise on Critical Reason*. Princeton, NJ: Princeton University Press.

Apel, K.-O. 1980. *Towards a Transformation of Philosophy*. London: Routledge and Kegan Paul.

Astley, W.G. and Van de Ven, A.H. 1983. Critical perspectives and debates in organization theory. *Administrative Science Quarterly*, **28**: 245–73.

Burrell, G. and Morgan, G. 1979. *Sociological Paradigms and Organisational Analysis*. London: Heineman.

Donaldson, L. 1996. *For Positivist Organization Theory. Proving the Hard Core*. London: Sage.

Donaldson, T. 1999. Making stakeholder theory whole. *Academy of Management Review*, **24**: 237–41.

Donaldson, T. 2002. The stakeholder revolution and the Clarkson principles. *Business Ethics Quarterly*, **12**: 107–11.

Donaldson, T. 2008. Two stories. In B.R. Agle, T. Donaldson, R.E. Freeman, M.C. Jensen, R.K. Mitchell and D.J. Wood (contributors), Dialogue: toward superior stakeholder theory. *Business Ethics Quarterly*, **18**: 172–6.

Donaldson, T. and Preston, L.E. 1995. The stakeholder theory of the corporation: concepts, evidence, and implications. *Academy of Management Review*, **20**: 65–91.

Driver, C. and Thompson, G. 2002. Corporate governance and democracy: the stakeholder debate revisited. *Journal of Management and Governance*, **6**: 111–30.

Evan, W.M. and Freeman, R.E. 1983. A stakeholder theory of the modern corporation: Kantian capitalism. Reprinted in T.L. Beauchamp and N.E. Bowie (eds), *Ethical Theory and Business*, Englewood Cliffs, NJ: Prentice-Hall, pp. 75–93.

Evered, R. and Louis, M.R. 1981. Alternative perspectives in the organizational sciences. 'Inquiry from the inside' and 'inquiry from the outside'. *Academy of Management Review*, **6**: 385–95.

Freeman, R.E. 1984. *Strategic Management: A Stakeholder Approach*. Boston, MA: Pitman.

Freeman, R.E. 1994. The politics of stakeholder theory: some future directions. *Business Ethics Quarterly*, **4**: 409–421.

Freeman, R.E. 1999. Divergent stakeholder theory. *Academy of Management Review*, **24**(2): 233–6.

Freeman, R.E. 2000. Business ethics at the millennium. *Business Ethics Quarterly*, **10**: 169–80.

Freeman, R.E. 2004. The stakeholder approach revisited. *Zeitschrift für Wirtschafts- und Unternehmensethik*, **5**: 228–41.

Freeman, R.E. 2008. Ending the so-called 'Friedman–Freeman' debate. In B.R. Agle, T. Donaldson, R.E. Freeman, M.C. Jensen, R.K. Mitchell and D. Wood (contributors), Dialogue: toward superior stakeholder theory. *Business Ethics Quarterly*, **18**(2): 153–90.

Freeman, R.E. and Lorange, P. 1985. Theory building in strategic management. *Advances in Strategic Management*, **3**: 9–38.

Freeman, R.E. and McVea, J. 2001. A stakeholder approach to strategic management. In M.A. Hitt, R.E. Freeman and J.S. Harrison (eds), *The Blackwell Handbook of Strategic Management*. Oxford, UK: Blackwell Publishers Ltd., pp. 189–207.

Gioia, D.A. 1999. Practicability, paradigms and problems in stakeholder theory. *Academy of Management Review*, **24**: 228–32.

Gioia, D.A. and Pitre, E. 1990. Multiparadigm perspectives on theory building. *Academy of Management Review*, **15**: 584–602.

Habermas, J. 1966. Knowledge and interest. *Inquiry*, **9**: 285–300.

Habermas, J. 1971. *Knowledge and Human Interests*. Boston, MA: Beacon Press.

Habermas, J. 1981. *Theorie des kommunikativen Handelns. Band 2. Zur Kritik der funktionalistischen Vernunft*. Frankfurt am Main: Suhrkamp.

Habermas, J. 1984. *Vorstudien und Ergänzungen zur Theorie des kommunikativen Handelns*. Frankfurt am Main: Suhrkamp.

Habermas, J. 1990. Reconstruction and interpretation in the social sciences. In J. Habermas (ed.), *Moral Consciousness and Communicative Action*. Cambridge, MA: MIT Press.

Habermas, J. 1993. Remarks on discourse ethics. In J. Habermas (ed.), *Justification and Application*. Cambridge, MA: MIT Press, pp. 19–111.

Habermas, J. 1996. *Between Facts and Norms: Contributions to a Discourse Theory of Law and Democracy*. Cambridge, MA: MIT Press.

Habermas, J. 2003. *Truth and Justification*. Cambridge, MA: MIT Press.

Harris, J.D. and Freeman, R.E. 2008. The impossibility of the separation thesis. A response to Joakim Sandberg. *Business Ethics Quarterly*, **18**: 541–8.

Harrison, J.S. and Freeman, R.E. 1999. Stakeholders, social responsibility, and performance: empirical evidence and theoretical perspectives. *Academy of Management Journal*, **42**: 479–85.

Harrison, J.S. and St. John, C.H. 1996. Managing and partnering with external stakeholders. *Academy of Management Executive*, **10**: 46–60.

Hempel, C.G. 1998. Studies in the logic of explanation. In E.D. Klemke, R. Hollinger, D. Rudge and A.D. Kline (eds), *Introductory Readings in the Philosophy of Science*. Amherst, NY: Prometheus Books, pp. 206–24.

Hendry, J. 2001. Missing the target: normative stakeholder theory and the corporate governance debate. *Business Ethics Quarterly*, **11**: 159–76.

Hollis, M. 1994. *The Philosophy of Social Science: An Introduction*. Cambridge, UK: Cambridge University Press.

Jackson, N. and Carter, P. 1991. In defence of paradigm incommensurability. *Organization Studies*, **12**: 109–27.

Jensen, M.C. 2002. Value maximization, stakeholder theory, and the corporate objective function. *Business Ethics Quarterly*, **12**: 235–56.

Jones, T.M. 1995. Instrumental stakeholder theory: a synthesis of ethics and economics. *Academy of Management Review*, **20**: 404–37.

Jones, T.M. and Wicks, A.C. 1999a. Convergent stakeholder theory. *Academy of Management Review*, **24**: 206–21.

Jones, T.M. and Wicks, A.C. 1999b. Letter to AMR regarding 'convergent stakeholder theory'. *Academy of Management Review*, **24**: 621–3.

Jones, T.M., Wicks, A.C. and Freeman, R.E. 2002. Stakeholder theory: the state of the art. In N.E. Bowie (ed.), *The Blackwell Guide to Business Ethics*. Malden, MA: Blackwell Publishing, pp. 19–37.

Kuhn, T.S. 1962. *The Structure of Scientific Revolutions*, Chicago, IL: University of Chicago Press.

Laplume, A.O., Sonpar, K. and Litz, R.A. 2008. Stakeholder theory: reviewing a theory that moves us. *Journal of Management*, **34**: 1152–89.

Margolis, J.D. and Walsh, J.P. 2003. Misery loves companies: rethinking social initiatives by business. *Administrative Science Quarterly*, **48**: 268–305.

Mitchell, R.K., Agle, B.R. and Wood, D.J. 1997. Toward a theory of stakeholder identification and salience: defining the principle of who and what really counts. *Academy of Management Review*, **22**: 853–86.

Moon, J., Crane, A. and Matten, D. 2005. Can corporations be citizens? Corporate citizenship as a metaphor for business participation in society. *Business Ethics Quarterly*, **15**: 429–54.

Morgan, G. 1986. *Images of Organization*. Newbury Park, CA: Sage.

Morris, M.W., Leung, K., Ames, D. and Lickel, B. 1999. Views from inside and outside: integrating emic and etic insights about culture and justice management. *Academy of Management Review*, **24**: 781–96.

Noland, R. and Phillips, R. 2010. Stakeholder engagement, discourse ethics and strategy. *International Journal of Management Reviews*, **12**: 39–49.

Palazzo, G. and Scherer, A.G. 2006. Corporate legitimacy as deliberation: a communicative framework. *Journal of Business Ethics*, **66**: 71–88.

Patzer, M. 2010. *Führung und ihre Verantwortung unter den Bedingungen der Globalisierung. Ein Beitrag zu einer Neufassung vor dem Hintergrund einer republikanischen Theorie der Multinationalen Unternehmung*. Berlin: Patzer-Verlag.

Pfeffer, J. 1993. Barriers to the advance of organizational science: paradigm development as a dependent variable. *Academy of Management Review*, **18**: 599–620.

Phillips, R. 2003. *Stakeholder Theory and Organizational Ethics*. San Francisco, CA: Barett-Koehler.

Phillips, R. and Freeman, R.E. (eds) 2010. *Stakeholders*. Cheltenham, UK and Northampton, MA, USA: Edward Elgar.

Phillips, R.A., Freeman, R.E. and Wicks, A.C. 2003. What stakeholder theory is not. *Business Ethics Quarterly*, **13**(4): 479–502.

Popper, K.R. 1959. *The Logic of Scientific Discovery*. London: Hutchinson.

Popper, K.R. 1969. *Conjectures and Refutations: The Growth of Scientific Knowledge*. London: Routledge.

Post, J.E., Preston, L.E. and Sachs, S. 2002. *Redefining the Corporation: Stakeholder Management and Organizational Wealth*. Stanford, CA: Stanford University Press.

Rorty, R. 1990. Solidarity or objectivity. In R. Rorty (ed.), *Objectivity, Relativism, and Truth. Philosophical Papers*. Cambridge, UK: Cambridge University Press, pp. 21–34.

Sandberg, J. 2008. Understanding the separation thesis. *Business Ethics Quarterly*, **18**: 213–32.

Scherer, A.G. 1995. *Pluralismus im Strategischen Management*. Wiesbaden: Gabler.

Scherer, A.G. 1998. Pluralism and incommensurability in strategic management and organization theory: a problem in search of a solution. *Organization*, **5**: 147–68.

Scherer, A.G. 1999. Kritik der Organisation oder Organisation der Kritik? Wissenschaftstheoretische Bemerkungen zum kritischen Umgang mit Organisationstheorien. In A. Kieser (ed.), *Organisationstheorien, Stuttgart: Kohlhammer*, pp. 1–37.

Scherer, A.G. 2003. Modes of explanation in organization theory. In H. Tsoukas and C. Knudsen (eds), *The Oxford Handbook of Organization Theory*. Oxford, UK: Oxford University Press, pp. 310–44.

Scherer, A.G. 2009. Critical theory and its contribution to the emergence of critical management studies. In M. Alvesson, H. Willmott and T. Bridgman (eds), *The Oxford Handbook of Critical Management Studies*, Oxford, UK: Oxford University Press, pp. 29–51.

Scherer, A.G. and Dowling, M.J. 1995. Towards a reconciliation of the theory pluralism in strategic management: incommensurability and the constructivist approach of the Erlangen School. *Advances in Strategic Management*, **12A**: 195–247.

Scherer, A.G. and Palazzo, G. 2007. Towards a political conception of corporate responsibility: business and society seen from a Habermasian perspective. *Academy of Management Review*, **32**: 1096–120.

Scherer, A.G. and Palazzo, G. 2008. Globalization and corporate social responsibility. In A. Crane, A. McWilliams, D. Matten, J . Moon and D. Siegel (eds), *The Oxford Handbook of Corporate Social Responsibility*. Oxford, UK: Oxford University Press, pp. 413–31.

Scherer, A.G. and Palazzo, G. 2011. The new political role of business in a globalized world: a review of a new perspective on CSR and its implications for the firm, governance, and democracy. *Journal of Management Studies*, **48**: doi: 10.1111/j.1467-6486.2010.00950.x.

Scherer, A.G. and Patzer, M. 2008. Paradigms. In S. Clegg and J.R. Bailey (eds), *International Encyclopedia of Organization Studies* (Vol. 4), London: Sage, pp. 1218–22.

Scherer, A.G. and Patzer, M. 2011. Beyond universalism and relativism: Habermas's contribution to discourse ethics and its implications for intercultural ethics and organizational theory. In H. Tsoukas and R. Chia (eds), *Philosophy and Organization Theory*. New York: Elsevier Press, pp. 155–80.

Scherer, A.G. and Steinmann, H. 1999. Some remarks on the problem of incommensurability in organization studies. *Organization Studies*, **20**: 519–44.

Stablein, R. and Nord, W. 1985. Radical and emancipatory interests in organizational symbolism: a review and evaluation. *Journal of Management*, **11**: 13–28.

Steffy, B.D. and Grimes, A.J. 1986. A critical theory of organization science. *Academy of Management Review*, **11**: 322–36.

Stoney, C. and Winstanley, D. 2001. Stakeholding: confusion or Utopia? Mapping the conceptual terrain. *Journal of Management Studies*, **38**: 603–26.

Sundaram, A.K. and Inkpen, A.C. 2004. The corporate objective revisited. *Organization Science*, **15**: 350–63.

Treviño, L.K. and Weaver, G.R. 1994. Business ETHICS/BUSINESS ethics: ONE FIELD OR TWO? *Business Ethics Quarterly*, **4**: 113–28.

Treviño, L.K. and Weaver, G.R. 1999a. Dialogue: Treviño and Weaver's reply to Jones and Wicks. *Academy of Management Review*, **24**: 623–4.

Treviño, L.K. and Weaver, G.R. 1999b. The stakeholder research tradition: converging theorists – not convergent theory. *Academy of Management Review*, **24**: 222–7.

Ulrich, P. 2008. *Integrative Economic Ethics: Foundations of a Civilized Market Economy*. Cambridge, UK: Cambridge University Press.

Walsh, J.P. 2005. Book review essay: taking stock of stakeholder management. *Academy of Management Review*, **30**: 426–52.

Weaver, G.R. and Gioia, D.A. 1994. Paradigms lost: incommensurability vs. structurationist inquiry. *Organization Studies*, **15**: 565–90.

Weaver, G.R. and Treviño, L.K. 1994. Normative and empirical business ethics: separation, marriage of convenience, or marriage of necessity. *Business Ethics Quarterly*, **4**: 129–43.

Weaver, G.R. and Treviño, L.K. 1998. Methodologies of business ethics research. In C.L. Cooper and C. Argyris (eds), *The Concise Blackwell Encyclopedia of Management*. Oxford, UK: Blackwell Publishing, pp. 412–15.

Wicks, A.C. and Freeman, R.E. 1998. Organization studies and the new pragmatism: positivism, anti-positivism, and the search for ethics. *Organization Science*, **9**: 123–40.

Willmott, H. 2003. Organization theory as a critical science? Forms of analysis and 'new organizational forms'. In H. Tsoukas and C. Knudsen (eds), *The Oxford Handbook of Organization Theory*. Oxford, UK: Oxford University Press, pp. 88–112.

Wood, D.J. and Jones, R.E. 1995. Stakeholder mismatching: a theoretical problem in empirical research on corporate social performance. *International Journal of Organization Analysis*, **3**: 229–67.

8. Stakeholder orientation, managerial discretion and nexus rents

Robert A. Phillips, Shawn L. Berman, Heather Elms and Michael E. Johnson-Cramer

A growing research tradition in management studies deals with how firms manage relationships with their various stakeholders. Among the features distinguishing this research tradition from other approaches is its claim to produce *managerial* theory. Explaining this notion, Donaldson and Preston (1995: 67) write: 'The stakeholder theory is managerial in the broad sense of that term. It does not simply describe existing situations or predict cause–effect relationships, it also recommends attitudes, structures, and practices that, taken together, constitute stakeholder management.'

In the pursuit of such a theory, stakeholder researchers have often accorded great importance to managerial decisions and actions as factors which shape firm–stakeholder relationships (for example, Freeman, 1984; Berman et al., 1999; Phillips, Freeman and Wicks, 2003; de Luque et al., 2008). When social scientists ask, 'What effects can a firm's treatment of its stakeholders have on its performance?' and ethicists ask, 'What moral obligations do firms have to treat their stakeholders in certain ways?' the uniting assumption is that managers (and by extension, their firms) have latitude to choose their course of action in managing these relationships.

However, this latitude is not without limits. A few stakeholder researchers have emphasized the role of external factors in influencing firm behavior toward stakeholders. They argue that, because firms exist and function within a constellation of constituencies with varying levels of power (Mitchell, Agle and Wood, 1997), their actions are necessarily constrained. The network structure of the actors surrounding a firm affects how it behaves toward them (Rowley, 1997), and the patterns of resource dependencies and group identities impact upon how and when stakeholder groups act to influence the behaviors of these firms (Pfeffer and Salancik, 1978; Frooman, 1999; Rowley and Moldoveanu, 2003). In this picture, managers have a lesser degree of latitude to choose their own course, as external constraints often trump managerial preferences and practices. This perspective raises serious questions for proponents of a managerial stakeholder theory. As social scientists, we cannot hope to explain the importance of stakeholder management as a factor affecting a firm's social or financial performance without acknowledging the external forces that condition this effect. As ethicists, we cannot reasonably hold firms accountable for mistreating stakeholders if we have no sense of the limits of their freedom to do otherwise. Any successful attempt to produce a genuinely managerial stakeholder theory rests on our ability to weigh the relative importance of managerial choice and external constraint in firm–stakeholder relationships. To date, however, the question of choice and constraint in stakeholder theory has been left implied at most – and more often ignored entirely.

Building on prior research (Phillips et al., 2010), we make explicit the implied assumptions – both managerialist and determinist – in stakeholder research. We argue that three elements – managerial discretion (Hambrick and Finkelstein, 1987; Shen and Cho, 2005), stakeholder orientation (Hosseini and Brenner, 1992; Berman et al., 1999) and nexus rent (Coff, 1999) – interact in important and under-examined ways. A firm's orientation toward its stakeholders determines how it will use the discretion accorded to it by external and internal circumstances. The interaction between these two factors affects a firm's ability to create value in the short term and influences the level of discretion available to the firm in the long term. We argue that the interplay of discretion and orientation create a vicious (or virtuous) cycle, in which the firm either creates or destroys goodwill with stakeholders, thereby making it more or less likely that stakeholders will grant discretion in the future. This argument suggests an account of stakeholder management that is sensitive to variation in managerial discretion, an account that is *more* constrained than typical moral and instrumental prescriptions about how firms should treat stakeholders and *less* constrained than descriptions premised on more deterministic theories.

Before developing this line of reasoning, it is important to put the status of managerial choice in stakeholder research into its proper context – our intention for the next section. Following that, we go on to describe the conceptual building blocks – managerial discretion, stakeholder orientation and nexus rent – which we use to build our model. The third and fourth sections advance lines of reasoning concerning the relationships among these constructs, these include testable propositions about the role of managerial discretion. We conclude by discussing the model's implications for future research.

MANAGERIAL CHOICE IN STAKEHOLDER RESEARCH

As we have described elsewhere, (Phillips et al., 2010) the question of how much managers' choices matter is not a new one. For decades, theories of strategy have tended towards either voluntarism or determinism, depending on how they handle the problem of managerial choice. Voluntaristic theories assume managerial decisions and actions are a substantial cause of the outcomes of firm activities. Deterministic theories situate managers and firms largely at the mercy of forces beyond their control with a decreased (even negligible) role for the effects of managerial actions on firm performance. This said, the most interesting theoretical insights often reside in the tensions and ambiguities that exist between these perspectives (Astley and Van de Ven, 1983; Hrebiniak and Joyce, 1985). For example, several voluntaristic approaches have emerged as explicit attempts to counter-balance the prevailing determinism of organizational sociology. The initial formulation of strategic choice theory (Child, 1972, 1997), the growth of the strategic management literature (Hoskisson et al., 1999; Harrison, current volume) and recent efforts to interject strategy into predominantly deterministic theories (Scott, 1995; Stevenson and Greenberg, 2000; Dobrev and Kim, 2006) all proceed from the hope that a well-developed understanding of strategic choice offers a starting point for a more robust view, which depicts managers as having 'degrees of strategic freedom' within constraining environments (Bourgeois, 1984).

From its inception, stakeholder research has largely rested on voluntaristic assumptions about managerial choice (Freeman, 1984). Though mindful of the power stakeholders wield over the firm – by definition, able to affect the achievement of its objectives – Freeman (1984: 74) explicitly frames his work as a contribution to the strategic management literature. Freeman (1984: 74) makes a clear 'plea for voluntarism' as 'the stakeholder philosophy' and much of the subsequent stakeholder research takes a similar voluntaristic perspective (see also Phillips et al., 2010). Thus, for example, some have argued that managerial decisions to engage (or not) in opportunistic behavior toward stakeholders can result in higher contracting costs and, ultimately, can impair firm performance (Jones, 1995). There is also empirical support for the hypothesis that how managers think about stakeholders, whether they value stakeholder relationships intrinsically or instrumentally, can affect the firm's performance (Agle, Mitchell and Sonnenfeld, 1999; Berman et al., 1999). There are also strong ethical criteria by which to judge the morality of managerial choices, as they manifest themselves in firm behavior (Evan and Freeman, 1993; Donaldson and Preston, 1995; Phillips, 1997). The resulting view of firm–stakeholder relationships, focused on what firms *can* and *should* do to manage stakeholder interactions, clearly rests on voluntaristic assumptions.

Of course, not all stakeholder research has subscribed unambiguously to these assumptions. A key dividing line in the literature is that between those who explore the impact of managerial choices on a firm's performance and those who study the antecedents of these managerial choices (Donaldson and Preston, 1995; see also Phillips et al., 2010). Departing somewhat from voluntaristic assumptions, the latter rely on more deterministic theories of organization, such as network (Rowley, 1997) and institutional theory (Johnson-Cramer, 2003a, 2000b), to account for the choices that firms and their managers make in regard to stakeholders. This is not to say that these theorists reject the possibility of managerial choice outright or ignore the role played by managerial action entirely. Rowley (1997: 887), for example, writes of the need not only to understand stakeholder influences on the firm but also 'how firms respond to these influences'. Nonetheless, the tendency of this second stream of research is to appeal to more deterministic supporting theories, with concomitantly underdeveloped notions of human agency. And, importantly, the assumptions regarding the sources and extent of constraints on managerial decision making are often left unstated and under-examined in these theories.

In framing the differences between voluntaristic and deterministic perspectives, Astley and Van de Ven (1983: 251) urge organization theorists to find insights in the tensions between different perspectives and to counterpose these perspectives in order 'to bring points of convergence into dialectical relief'. One straightforward approach to achieving such convergence is to treat the degree of managerial choice not as a steady state, assumed to be either present or absent, but rather as a continuous variable whose presence or absence can radically affect the importance of organizational strategizing (Perrow, 1986). Stakeholder research must, therefore, incorporate a respect for *both* the power of managerial action and the constraints and catalysts stakeholders create for managers.[1] To achieve this, we turn to the notion of managerial discretion. This concept provides a bridge between theories in which managerial choices play a significant role and those in which such choices play a lesser role (Hambrick and Finkelstein, 1987). Incorporating the varying levels of discretion afforded managers helps us to account more completely for environmental influences and constraints on managerial choice. In the next section, we offer some background on this and other key building blocks from which we construct our revised understanding of firm–stakeholder interactions.

CONCEPTUAL BUILDING BLOCKS

In this section, we elaborate three concepts – managerial discretion, stakeholder orientation and nexus rent – upon which our model will be built.

Managerial Discretion

Hambrick, Finkelstein and co-authors' elaboration of the concept of *managerial discretion* (Finkelstein and Hambrick, 1990; Hambrick and Abrahamson, 1995; Finkelstein and Boyd, 1998; Finkelstein and Peteraf, 2007) is explicitly intended to link voluntaristic and deterministic theories. They define managerial discretion as 'latitude of managerial action' (Hambrick and Finkelstein, 1987: 371). As originally elaborated, the level of managerial discretion may be a function of the task environment, the organization, the individual manager or any combination of these. Table 8.1 reproduces Hambrick and Finkelstein's (1987) figure of characteristics that influence discretion and adds the 'activity' level characteristics later identified by Finkelstein and Peteraf (2007). Taken together, these characteristics comprise a powerful set of possible limitations on – and catalysts for – managerial choice and firm strategy formulation. Of course, not all firms face the same level of constraint. We can view a firm as possessing more managerial discretion than another firm. For example, managers

Table 8.1   Sources of constraint on managerial discretion

Task environment	Internal organization	Managerial characteristics	Activity characteristics
Product differentiability	Age	Aspiration level	Complexity
Market growth	Size	Commitment	Uncertainty
Industry structure	Culture	Tolerance for ambiguity	Observability
Demand instability	Capital intensity	Cognitive complexity	
Quasi-legal constraints	Resource availability	Internal locus of control	
Powerful outside forces	Powerful inside forces	Power base Political acumen	

Source: Adapted from Hambrick and Finkelstein (1987: 379, Figure 2) and Finkelstein and Peteraf (2007).

in an older, large, highly regulated utility firm will have fewer strategic options at their disposal than managers in a firm with a highly differentiated product competing in a fast growing industry.

While Hambrick and Finkelstein's (1987) figure (and our reproduction of it) refers only to 'powerful outside' and 'powerful inside' forces, Hambrick and Finkelstein's (1987: 374, 378, original italics deleted) text explicitly defines discretion in terms of stakeholder acceptance, writing:

> To us, constraint exists whenever an action lies outside the 'zone of acceptance' of powerful parties who hold a stake in the organization. . .. Extending the concept to other types of stakeholders, one can think of board members, bankers, regulators, key employees, customers, as well as other parties, as all having their own zones of acceptance . . . A chief executive who is aware of multiple courses of action that lie within the zone of acceptance of powerful parties is said to have discretion.

This overlap makes the managerial discretion construct a particularly useful building block for a more sophisticated understanding of firm–stakeholder interactions, given that stakeholder behavior is, itself, a significant source of discretion or constraint. Managerial discretion offers a conceptually robust way to capture, in the aggregate, the constraints common to firms, without adopting the deterministic assumptions that accompany other notions of external control. Awareness of differentials in managerial discretion also allows researchers to compare firms with similar levels of constraint in order to better isolate the effects of proposed stakeholder-theoretic phenomena or better understand the moral challenges faced in managing stakeholder relationships.

Stakeholder Orientation

The concept of stakeholder management remains, for many purposes, only vaguely defined. Some studies point to the outcomes produced by firm action toward stakeholders (for example, Waddock and Graves, 1997) and 'good' stakeholder management is identified either by the priority afforded to particular groups (Mitchell, Agle and Wood, 1997). Others adhere to Freeman's original perspective, emphasizing procedural concerns such as communication, negotiation and monitoring (Calton and Kurland, 1996; Morris, 1997) or the thoroughness of procedural steps for managing stakeholder relations (Johnson-Cramer, 2003a) as the basis for describing a firm's approach to stakeholder management. Yet another approach focuses on the moral quality of firm behavior, with some positing a relationship between honesty and fair-dealing and firm performance

(Jones, 1995) or emphasizing the acceptance of particular moral claims (Phillips, 2003).

Among the various solutions that have emerged in response to the conceptual problem of specifying stakeholder management, the most promising for our purposes here is the notion of *stakeholder orientation* (Hosseini and Brenner, 1992; Berman et al., 1999). Stakeholder orientation can be defined as 'managers' attitudes and actions towards stakeholders' (Berman et al., 1999) consisting of the totality of 'a firm's overall approach toward managing stakeholder relationships' (Phillips et al., 2010: 178). It is a predisposition on the part of the firm and its managers to acknowledge (or not) and engage with (or not) stakeholders. Depending on whether they view stakeholders as means to an end or as having intrinsic worth, Berman et al. (1999) describe firms' stakeholder orientations as either instrumental or intrinsic. This predisposition may originate in the values of the firm's CEO and top management (Agle, Mitchell and Sonnenfeld, 1999), or it may reside in the overall cultural values and attitudes of the firm as a whole. Most notions of stakeholder orientation place some emphasis on the priority that a firm accords certain claims in distributing value among stakeholders. The simplest way to differentiate among firms by stakeholder orientation is to view them as either shareholder- or stakeholder-focused (cf., Friedman, 1970; Freeman, 1994). Firms may also adopt an orientation with a clear rank ordering of stakeholder claims (Mitchell, Agle and Wood, 1997). Though many firms prioritize in favor of shareholders, many others have built their reputation by prioritizing the claims of other stakeholders (for example, Nordstrom and customers, SAS Institute and employees). Detailing the myriad of prioritization schemes, however, produces countless orientations, which quickly become unwieldy and offer little hope of generalization.

We contend that a more useful standard is to categorize orientation according to the breadth of stakeholder claims recognized by a firm (Logsdon and Yuthas, 1997; Johnson-Cramer, Berman and Post, 2003). At one extreme, there are firms which hold a *narrow* orientation, these firms consistently privilege the interests of a single stakeholder (or a few stakeholders) over the claims of other stakeholders. The typical shareholder-centered approach to management, according to which all firm activities should be for the ultimate benefit of shareholders alone, represents one (though not the only) example of a narrow stakeholder orientation. At the other extreme lie firms that exhibit *broad* orientations and for which multiple stakeholders receive consideration in firm decisions. We can capture these extremes more formally by defining the breadth of a firm's orientation as the number of different stakeholder groups the firm purports to benefit or engage. Thus, a firm with a broad stakeholder orientation might be expected to expend more resources on employee benefits, community service and product quality or spend time pursuing the well-being of employees, the community or customers than would a firm with a narrow orientation – the latter generally preferring to maximize the benefits and well-being of a single stakeholder group, even if it comes consistently at the expense of the claims of other stakeholders.

Nexus Rent

The final theoretical piece in our model is performance. The most common dependent variable in empirical studies of firm–stakeholder relationships is some measure of firm financial performance. Much has been made of the need to establish a link between the way a firm treats its stakeholders and the resulting financial performance, though this line of research has produced few consistent results (cf., Griffin and Mahon, 1997; Margolis and Walsh, 2003). Jones (1995) and others have stressed the need for stakeholder researchers to develop a performance measure which does not separate financial performance from overall firm performance – shareholders and other financiers being important stakeholders in their own rights. He and others (Berman et al., 1999; Jones and Wicks, 1999) have argued that a proper estimation of firm–stakeholder relations requires a measure which does not assume stakeholders to be mere instruments of shareholder wealth generation but as having intrinsic importance.

Coff's concept of 'nexus rent' is a step in the direction of such a measure. Following Jensen and Meckling (1976) in defining the firm as a 'nexus of contracts', Coff (1999) developed the concept of nexus rent to describe the totality of rents generated by the firm and its stakeholders irrespective of whether they are reflected in profits, share price or other financier-specific measures. Nexus rent, 'is the sum of all the rent in the nexus regardless of which stakeholders appropriate it' (Coff, 1999: 121). A firm may perform very well in terms of having a competitive advantage in the marketplace, but this performance would not show up in standard measures of financial performance in cases where employees receive pay greater than their opportunity costs, customers receive value in excess of their best available alternatives, and so on.

This measure of performance is distinct from both measures of firm *financial* performance as well as firm *social* performance. Regarding financial performance, we would expect to see a relationship between nexus rent and narrower financial performance captured in net earnings or share price. The gains accruing to shareholders are an important subset of nexus rent and the magnitude of nexus rent will naturally influence the size of all stakeholders' shares – including those of shareholders and other financiers. However, as Coff (1999) points out, assuming that all rents will or *should* accrue to shareholders incorporates generally unstated normative assumptions. Unlike prior concepts such as organizational rent (Amit and Schoemaker, 1993, cited in Coff, 1999), nexus rent makes no assumption that all rents are or should be appropriated by shareholders.

However, the size of the nexus is not unlimited and nexus rent is thus also to be distinguished from concepts of corporate social performance (CSP). Nexus rent is the direct result of a firm's core business – the activities by which it creates value – rather than the broader social activities that are central to discussions of social performance (see Elms, Johnson-Cramer and Berman, current volume). Clarkson (1995) argues that firms have their primary impact on society through direct stakeholder relationships. Looking beyond these relationships to a firm's broader social impacts, he argues, serves only to muddy the conceptual waters. In order to avoid the difficulty that scholars of CSP have had in bounding their subject, we view nexus rent as more limited in scope than CSP. Many of the elements of nexus rent, such as working conditions for employees, may be a sub-set of CSP. But, dimensions of CSP, such as corporate philanthropy unrelated to the core business, would not be included in a measure of nexus rent.

While also marking a return to an older literature in strategic management on the nature of organizational effectiveness as performance toward multiple constituencies (Pickle and Friedlander, 1967; Friedlander and Pickle, 1968; Walsh, Weber and Margolis, 2003), nexus rent is also well-matched to the emergence of stakeholder theory in mainstream organization studies and strategic management literatures. A broader – but nevertheless delimited – set of variables is more conceptually consistent with the target phenomena of stakeholder theory than are historical measures of performance. Nexus rent is, as such, a better representation of the success or failure of stakeholder management activities (Rowley and Berman, 2000).

STAKEHOLDER ORIENTATION AND MANAGERIAL DISCRETION

Firm-level decisions interact with various constraints in shaping firm–stakeholder relationships. One outcome of these interactions is an effect on the magnitude of nexus rent, the total value created for the all stakeholders of the firm. Explaining why some firms outperform others is one of the main goals of any school of strategic management, and framing performance broadly invites scrutiny of a firm's decisions and actions toward a wide range of constituencies. Viewed in isolation, however, the relationship between how a firm behaves toward its stakeholders and the resulting performance is slippery at best (Griffin and Mahon, 1997; Margolis and Walsh, 2003). This has prompted demands for better theory about the relationship between stakeholder management and perform-ance (Rowley and Berman, 2000). The weakness of existing theory lies not merely in its being underdeveloped, but in the tendency to under-emphasize or ignore completely the constraints on managerial choice. These constraints limit the effect that stakeholder management can have on the amount of total value the firm produces.

In this section, we examine the interplay between choice (that is, stake-holder orientation) and constraint (that is, managerial discretion). The interaction between these two factors produces four possible states, each differs from the others in the degree to which managerial choices prove suitable for producing value for the firm's stakeholders. The propositions outlined here explain the likely patterns of variation in nexus rent across these four states.

Low Discretion–Broad Orientation

In a state of low managerial discretion, the firm has few available strategic options from which to choose. At the same time, top managers in a firm with a broad orientation hold an overarching view that the firm should have a broad commitment to satisfying the claims of a wide range of stake-holders. These conditions often give rise to at least two pressing concerns for managers. First, many of the constraints typically associated with low discretion relate directly to the level of resource munificence available to the firm (Boyd, 1990). Firms find themselves without the resources necessary to perform well. Second, low discretion is rarely a disembodied condition, but traces directly to the presence of a small set of powerful stakeholder groups seeking to satisfy their interests exclusively – often at the expense of the firm and its other stakeholders (Pfeffer and Salancik, 1978). Those strategic options which remain open to such a firm are likely to be those most clearly suited to serving the interests of this small group. How, managers wonder, can a highly constrained firm both spread the value it creates among multiple stakeholders and, at the same time, appease a narrow group of powerful stakeholders?

If genuinely committed to a broad stakeholder orientation, managers may find themselves awkwardly juggling this orientation with stakehold-ers' demands for focus by attempting to achieve numerous goals with too little discretion. The likeliest result will be a very low level of nexus rent. This comes about for one of two reasons. First, a broad stakeholder orientation places high demands on a firm's strategic decision-making process, as firms that consider the multiple stakeholder impacts of their strategies employ more comprehensive decision processes (for example, broader environmental scanning, engaging others to check presumed impacts of decisions, and so on; Fredrickson, 1984). In their study of strategic decision processes at 318 firms, Baum and Wally (2003) found a direct relationship between decision speed and performance, moreover, since decision speed also mediated the relationship between environmental conditions and performance, faster decisions are especially important in resource constrained environments, which usually afford firms little discretion.

Second, even if a firm can overcome the difficulties associated with strategy formulation, it still faces the problem of creating coherent strategy content. When successful, firms implementing a broad orientation succeed, in part, because market and non-market pressures on the firm align, and the strategic options for addressing each are complementary (Post, Preston and Sachs, 2002). A firm, for example, that undertakes 'green' activities (that is, actions friendly to the natural environment) often finds it possible to position these activities as customer – or employee – friendly, thereby reaping higher revenues and lower labor costs (Hart, 1995). Under low discretion circumstances, however, the likelihood of a coincidence between market-based and non-market claims is lower, by virtue of a more limited menu of strategic options of either sort from which to choose. In this condition, the activities of the broadly oriented firm closely resemble those of a firm which has diversified into unrelated activities. These activities often incur greater costs and lead to lower overall performance (Porter, 1987). Thus, even though many stakeholder groups receive some of the value generated by the firm, the total value available is not as large as it might be if the firm had simply chosen strategies to maximize value for a narrow set of stakeholders. Examples of how the low discretion–broad orientation condition influences nexus rent are found in the common experience of older firms in mature and commodity industries, especially those that are highly regulated. The recent headline-grabbing failures at British Petroleum (for example, Deepwater Horizon, refinery explosions, charges of market manipulation, and so on) on the heels of its 'Beyond Petroleum' campaign are suggestive of these challenges.

At first glance, this condition would seem an unlikely combination. How often do firms with relatively low levels of managerial discretion assume a broad stakeholder orientation? At least two groups have typically occupied this space. First, mature firms (for example, utilities, steel) with a long history of societal stewardship often find themselves committed to a broad orientation despite environmental shifts that leave them with little strategic choice. Second, firms in transition to another orientation/discretion combination may find themselves in this space, at least in the short term. For example, entrepreneurial ventures with explicit commitments to environmental or social causes may adopt a broad orientation despite low discretion. As we suggest later in this chapter, this combination need not always spell disaster for such firms. However, at any given point in time, and at least in the short run, we propose that a broad orientation, coupled with conditions of low discretion, leads to the inefficient investment of resources and a maladapted, mismatched strategy.

Proposition 1:   In a state of low discretion–broad orientation, nexus rent will be the lowest, relative to other states.

Low Discretion–Narrow Orientation

This state combines constrained managerial choice and a narrow view of which stakeholders merit the firm's attention and resources. In contrast to the low discretion–broad orientation firm, firms in this state essentially choose among limited strategic options the best strategy for providing value to a limited set of powerful stakeholders. In prioritizing stakeholders in this way, firms reap the benefits largely forfeited by broadly oriented firms. At a minimum, the firm avoids the costs of comprehensive decision processes and incoherent, mismatched strategies. The net effect on nexus rent is clear: under low discretion conditions, the narrowly oriented firm outperforms the broadly oriented one, at least in the short run.

At first glimpse, this argument might seem less germane to the matter of nexus rent than to the more common notion of shareholder value, or firm financial performance. How can it be better for all stakeholders, if the firm attempts only to maximize value for a narrow group of stakeholders? Understanding this requires us to distinguish between returns generated on behalf of the favored stakeholder groups and those generated on behalf of less favored groups. We argue that the tendency toward coherent strategies undertaken by narrow firms will generate the highest outcome possible in a low discretion circumstance for the favored stakeholders. At the same time, any actions undertaken by the firm on the behalf of less-favored stakeholder groups are more likely to complement the core strategies of the firm, since narrowly oriented firms only create value on behalf of these groups instrumentally (that is, if it promises greater returns for the privileged stakeholder group; see Donaldson and Preston, 1995). Many of the 'comparison companies' in Collins and Porras's (1994) *Built to Last* are characterized as relying on a 'classic profits-only perspective' (1994: 63), which results in adequate, but not 'visionary' returns. Thus,

Proposition 2:   In a state of low discretion–narrow orientation, nexus rent will be the second lowest, relative to other states.

High Discretion–Narrow Orientation

As we argued in an earlier section, the two states in which firms have high levels of discretion more closely approximate the voluntaristic context in which stakeholder researchers have usually imagined firms to operate. Many of the classic arguments concerning the relationship between 'doing good' and 'doing well' seem to apply in distinguishing between firms in these two states. In the high discretion–narrow orientation state, firms have wider latitude for strategic choice but tend to prefer those options that create and allocate value for only a few stakeholder groups. Of course, instrumentality in relationships is hard to mask over time (Frank, 1988), and these less favored stakeholder groups will distrust such firms, have deep concerns about the potential for opportunism in the relationship, mobilize more readily against them, and exact higher contracting costs as insurance against future dishonesty (Hill and Jones, 1992; Jones, 1995; Wicks, Berman and Jones, 1999; Rowley and Moldoveanu, 2003). These reactions will be more acute because stakeholder group members perceive that firms have a great deal of latitude in making choices.

What is missing from this picture, though, is the central role played by managerial discretion in exacerbating the effects of narrow stakeholder management. Many of the stakeholder reactions posited by existing research only manifest when these groups perceive the firm to have some measure of discretion. In a high discretion state, these attributions of discretion are well-founded, and the resulting distrust, conflict and contracting costs are even more likely to have their effect on performance. Here, the causal mechanisms associated directly with managerial choice, including both process features and strategy content implied by a firm's stakeholder orientation, have even more evident effects than in the low discretion state. For example, firms undertaking downsizing in profitable times are often perceived more negatively than those doing so in dire economic circumstances (Leana and Van Buren, 1999). Electronic Data Systems (EDS) announced it would cut 3000–4000 jobs even as its profits increased fourfold and the value of contracts signed doubled (Associated Press, 2006). Goldman Sachs added EDS to its list of five least favorite stocks in September of 2007.

Given the flexibility granted by high discretion contexts, the less comprehensive strategy formulation undertaken by narrowly oriented firms leads to missed opportunities and suboptimal results (Fredrickson and Iaquinto, 1989). Since high discretion environments afford so much more opportunity to find 'win–win' strategies that integrate across the interests of multiple stakeholders, narrowly oriented firms forego collaborative opportunities in their desire to create value for a narrow set of stakeholders. Nexus rent is likely to suffer both in the value created for the privileged group (due to the costs inflicted by less favored groups) and in the foregone value which might have been created for these other groups. Thus,

Proposition 3:   In a state of high discretion–narrow orientation, nexus rent will be the second highest – outperforming the low–narrow state but underperforming the high–broad state.

High Discretion–Broad Orientation

This state combines a high degree of managerial latitude with a view that stakeholders should share in the allocation of value created by the firm. In this state, managers likely feel driven to attend to stakeholders as intrinsically valuable, and this orientation, facilitated by a high discretion environment, translates into the highest level of overall nexus rent. As stated at the outset, this is the combination that most stakeholder researchers seem to have in mind in their writings and prescriptions. When these conditions occur, broadly oriented firms interact with stakeholders in ways that allow firms to capture the full benefits of trust and fair dealing (Calton and Lad, 1995). Even when the managers take actions that some stakeholders disagree with, they rarely privilege the same stakeholder consistently over time, thereby avoiding the penalties associated with opportunism and dishonesty (Jones, 1995). Many firms commonly cited as examples of 'good stakeholder management' operate with a wide degree of discretion. Firms such as Starbucks and Interface Carpet have successfully differentiated their products and services, allowing them substantial managerial discretion. Since these firms distribute the value created by the firm in a broad fashion – with all the process and content benefits already identified – the aggregate value creation of these firms will tend to be high. Thus,

Proposition 4:   In a state of high discretion–broad orientation, nexus rent will be the highest, relative to all other states.

A DYNAMIC MODEL

To this point, we have focused on the relatively short-term effects that the interaction between stakeholder orientation and managerial discretion can have on nexus rent. Most major studies of managerial discretion (Finkelstein and Hambrick, 1990; Hambrick, Geletkanycz and Fredrickson, 1993; Finkelstein and Boyd, 1998) similarly cast the concept in purely static terms. Finkelstein and Peteraf (2007) have recently begun to consider the dynamics of discretion. They convincingly claim that research emphasis should be directed primarily at the high-discretion manager: managers who, at the individual level, perceive themselves to have high discretion and act as such, sometimes despite constraints deriving from other sources. This is, in no small part, because managers who perceive themselves as having low discretion – irrespective of the magnitude of other constraints – are less likely to employ what discretion they have due to this perception.

Moreover, high discretion managers are, they argue, more likely to resist the constraints they do perceive – perhaps by selecting managerial activities that are complex, uncertain and unobservable (Finkelstein and Peteraf, 2007). We contend that constraint can be resisted in one of two ways. On the one hand, the firm can make strategic decisions that reduce the power of stakeholders and, concomitantly, increase the discretion of the firm. This notion of reducing the control exercised over the firm by external constituents is central to many schools of strategic management and organization theory (for example, Selznick, 1949; Stinchcombe, 1965; Pfeffer and Salancik, 1978; Porter 1980) and has begun to emerge as an option within managerial discretion theory itself (Finkelstein and Peteraf, 2007: 242).

Yet, this is not the only way that a firm's decisions regarding stakeholders can result in changes to managerial discretion. Rather than relying on the involuntary acquiescence of overpowered stakeholders, firms may also choose strategies to which stakeholders are likely to respond by voluntarily yielding discretion. As we argue below (summarized in Figure 8.1), constraint may also be diminished by adopting a cooperative orientation toward the actors who bear and wield the factors of constraint and latitude. A manager can rely on cooperation rather than coercion to convince stakeholders to lessen constraints of their own volition. Through the adoption of a broad stakeholder orientation managers can indirectly 'resist' constraint and thereby broaden their degree of discretion over time.

Because managerial discretion is so readily understood in stakeholder terms (recall Hambrick and Finkelstein's 'zone of acceptance' passage above) and because of normative stakeholder theory's emphasis on

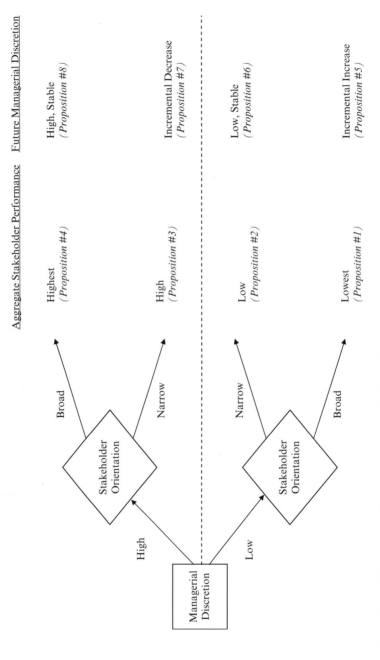

Figure 8.1   Managerial discretion and stakeholder orientation

cooperation (Phillips, 2003), it is especially fitting that we explain the evolution of a firm's discretion as a function of its stakeholder orientation. We argue that a firm's stakeholder orientation and its present level of discretion (aggregated across all levels for the purposes of this exploratory analysis) will interact to affect future levels of discretion by eliciting a combination of voluntary and involuntary reactions from stakeholders.

Low Discretion–Broad Orientation

It is axiomatic that underperforming firms often fail. Per our earlier discussion, firms in low discretion environments that adopt broad stakeholder orientations underperform those adopting narrow orientations in the short term, and many such firms will disappear. We contend, however, that those firms that survive will do so either by converting to a narrow orientation or by appropriating increased discretion *because they maintained a broad stakeholder orientation*. This occurs in three specific ways.

First, broadly oriented firms tend to monitor stakeholders more closely and position themselves to better understand stakeholder needs (Freeman, 1984; Post, Preston and Sachs, 2002). Such firms are more likely to introduce products, for example, that appeal to a broader range of customers, thereby expanding their industry segment and escaping previous industry constraints. Expanding its customer base in this way, the firm gains greater power over – and becomes more appealing to – extant and potential customers and thereby attains greater latitude. Second, a broad orientation can also attract new sets of stakeholders explicitly motivated by involvement with broadly oriented firms (Waddock, 2005; Arena, 2006). The appeal of green products, socially responsible investments, and employee-friendly work environments all attest to the market for virtue (cf., Vogel, 2005). Broadly oriented firms are well placed to satisfy this demand, to motivate non-participating groups, and thereby find another avenue for increasing future managerial discretion. Finally, while managerial choices may result in the expansion of the stakeholder set, broad orientation may also appeal to existing stakeholders, who appreciate the firm's values, find them more worthy of greater trust (Jones, 1995; Wicks, Berman and Jones, 1999) and reward them with greater discretion.

We contend that many stakeholder groups will afford this latitude despite the firm's current underperformance. Broadly oriented firms signal greater trustworthiness to stakeholders (Jones 1995). Trust leads these latter groups, in turn, to monitor firm behavior less (Wicks, Berman and Jones, 1999) thereby permitting firms greater latitude. Consider the role of trust in the evolution of eBay and other electronic commerce firms that emerged during the original internet boom (Cohen, 2003). These early days were characterized by shoestring budgets, long hours, a great deal of informational vulnerability, but with the promise of a lucrative future. Many firms did not survive the bursting bubble. But among those that did, high levels of stakeholder trust – generated by a broad stakeholder orientation – played a key role. And many of these firms now enjoy far greater managerial discretion than in those formative years. Thus,

Proposition 5:   In low discretion environments, a broad stakeholder orientation will lead to increased discretion in the long term.

Low Discretion–Narrow Orientation

Narrowly oriented firms in a low discretion environment elicit markedly different reactions from across their stakeholder set. A narrow orientation distinguishes sharply between the few groups receiving the greater part of the value generated by the firm (that is, the most favored stakeholder groups) and the many groups receiving much less value from the firm (that is, the non-privileged stakeholder groups). This distinction plays an important role in determining the future level of discretion available to the firm's managers. We argue that the net effect of a narrow orientation, given low levels of present discretion, will be a stable but low level of future discretion. Such a result arises from a combination of very different reactions from the firm's most favored stakeholder group(s) and the firm's non-privileged stakeholders.

For the most favored stakeholder group, the narrowly oriented firm is a fairly attractive partner. It outperforms similarly situated firms with a broad orientation, and it reserves the greater part of its returns for its most favored stakeholders. Having received a high proportion of the value generated by the firm, such stakeholders are likely to be satisfied. However, the question remains whether these stakeholders will seek to pursue a significant revision of the terms of the firm–stakeholder relationship. We contend that they have little incentive to do so. If future discretion, at least insofar as it is voluntarily given, represents a conscious investment of a stakeholder's share of the firm's rents, then two main considerations seem to determine the likelihood of a further investment. The first consideration is the natural inertia that comes with satisfaction. Stakeholders tend to respond when dissatisfied or underserved, when they perceive their interests as being violated or when they have urgent claims (Mitchell, Agle and Wood, 1997; Rowley and Moldoveanu, 2003). This tendency toward inaction not only ensures that the firm's most favored stakeholder groups will continue to afford the current level of discretion but also suggests that stakeholders will tend not to act (that is, to offer more or fewer avenues for discretion).

The second consideration is the dominant stakeholder group's evaluation of the firm's ability to extract greater rents from the least favored stakeholders. The return on a stakeholder's investment in offering greater latitude to a firm is that the firm can take advantage of that latitude to create greater value. Such value creation usually requires further investments from other stakeholders. For example, a firm's stockholders may elect not to demand greater dividends from the firm, allowing it greater discretion by permitting its managers to reinvest the funding in capital projects or new product development. The eventual return on this investment, however, also relies on employees' willingness to extend their efforts on the firm's behalf, customers' willingness to entertain new products from that company and so forth. Unfortunately, for the narrowly oriented firm, these investments by non-privileged stakeholder groups are not likely to be forthcoming (Frooman, 1999; Frooman and Murrell, 2005). Non-privileged stakeholders will have limited incentive to invest additional resources – or even limited additional resources – due to the firm's history of narrow orientation. This will be readily apparent even to the most favored stakeholder, making it less likely also that they will invest in offering the firm expanded discretion.

Consider, for example, a firm that has consistently maximized stockholder wealth at the expense of employees. The firm's narrow orientation may manifest itself in lower wages, less generous healthcare benefits, higher expectations for overtime and fewer opportunities for training and skill enhancement. These employees may resent the firm's treatment, but they lack both the incentive and the means to act against the firm. They realize that there will be little return to allowing the firm discretion at their own expense unless all stakeholders are equally willing to grant discretion similarly. At the same time, a group like this may also have a difficult time mustering the resources for collective action to further constrain the firm's current level of discretion (Olson, 1971; King and Soule, 2007). Such employees may have fewer job opportunities because they have not had opportunities to develop and less money saved to allow them to entertain a lengthy transition to another job. Together, these factors imply that such groups will have limited incentive to increase – and limited potential to reduce – the discretion available to the firm. These conditions often prevail in contexts of low-skill manufacturing and resource extraction – particularly in less developed nations (Sachs and Shatz, 1996). And the constant demand for lower prices by their contract buyers reduces the means and incentive to change. In sum,

Proposition 6:   In low discretion environments, a narrow stakeholder orientation will lead to stable but low levels of managerial discretion in the long term.

High Discretion–Narrow Orientation

The situation shifts somewhat when the focal firm inhabits a high discretion environment. The most favored stakeholders of a narrowly oriented firm may well behave here as they do in the low discretion case. Non-privileged stakeholders, however, have an incentive to further constrain the firm and somewhat greater resources to do so. Such non-privileged stakeholders in this circumstance will see that they are not benefiting from their relationship with the firm to the same degree as other, privileged stakeholders. Different from the low discretion situation, however, stakeholders' feelings of inequity or injustice are accompanied by the knowledge that broad discretion firms are *able* to distribute performance more equitably or fairly across stakeholders. These stakeholders will distrust the firm and will seek opportunities to shift current value distributions in their favor, through whatever constraints they have at their disposal, in a way that requires greater equity and fairness (Adams, 1965; Colquitt et al., 2001).

But, will non-privileged stakeholders be any more able to exert influence over the focal firm than similar groups in the low discretion environment? We contend that they will. As we have argued above, the combination of narrow orientation and high discretion evidences higher nexus rent than the low discretion–narrow orientation combination, *ceteris paribus*. Though the benefits of the firm's performance are concentrated on one or a few stakeholder groups, all stakeholders of a higher performance firm are better endowed with resources to overcome the barriers to collective action. A small proportion of a larger return is always bigger than the same proportion of a smaller return. An employee group (or any stakeholder) in a dynamic, growing industry – however small their allocation of the firm's value – will always be better placed to mobilize against the firm than corresponding groups in a shrinking market. If, as others have argued (Rowley and Moldoveanu, 2003), the resources for collective action merely constitute a minimum threshold for action, then it is the combination of resources, distrust and a heightened sense of inequity (that is, that the firm is not using available discretion in a fair manner) that results in the sort of collective actions that can decrease managerial discretion over time (Hayibor, 2005). Private security contractors such as Blackwater USA face a growing call for increased accountability, oversight and regulation due to an allegedly inadequate concern for employees and civilians. Thus,

Proposition 7:   In high discretion environments, a narrow stakeholder orientation will lead to decreased managerial discretion over time.

High Discretion–Broad Orientation

In the high discretion environment, it is the broadly oriented firm that is best placed to reap the benefits of stakeholder goodwill that, in turn, lead to high future discretion. After all, in the short term, as we argue above, managers who are relatively free from constraints can – whether for moral, instrumental or managerial reasons (Donaldson and Preston, 1995) – treat stakeholders as they wish. They can demonstrate wider breadth of concern for stakeholder well-being and, according to stakeholder theory, this will benefit both firm and stakeholders over time. The arguments for the relationship between these characteristics and nexus rent are well-known (Freeman, 1984; Jones, 1995; Jones and Wicks, 1999; Post, Preston and Sachs, 2002; Phillips, 2003) and include an increase in trust, lower costs of safeguarding, greater stakeholder commitment, moral obligation and greater feelings of fairness and equity. In the long term, higher nexus rent leads (asymptotically) to still greater trust and greater future latitude of managerial and firm activity (Wicks, Berman and Jones, 1999). This 'virtuous cycle' mirrors the 'vicious cycle' faced by the low managerial discretion–narrow orientation firm.

Evidence of this 'virtuous cycle' can be seen in the frequent overlap among the reputation lists that appear annually in various publications (for example, 'Best Places to Work', 'Most Trustworthy', 'Best Corporate Citizen', and so on). This overlap can be seen as indicative of a broad stakeholder orientation for those companies (for example, Starbucks, Costco, Merck, Google, Nike, and so on). Notably, many of these companies are in industries where one might expect to see limited managerial discretion (for example, health care, hotels, retail, financial services). Even so, an on-going commitment to a broad stakeholder orientation engenders on-going favorable perceptions among stakeholders leading, in turn, to this 'Best of. . .' overlap. Thus,

Proposition 8:   In high discretion environments, a broad stakeholder orientation will lead to increased managerial discretion over time.

IMPLICATIONS FOR FUTURE RESEARCH

Several important streams of inquiry in stakeholder theory appear to have reached an impasse. In recent years, researchers have continued their search for a relationship between individual stakeholder performance measures – often operationalized using data from the Kinder, Lydenberg and Domini ratings database – and measures of financial performance (for example Waddock and Graves, 1997). Yet, progress toward a deeper understanding of firm–stakeholder relationships has given way to calls for greater theoretical insight into why the social performance–financial performance relationship may or may not exist (Rowley and Berman, 2000; Margolis and Walsh 2003). Accounting for managerial discretion as a factor in firm–stakeholder relationships may shed new theoretical light on this stream of inquiry and open the door for advancement beyond this apparent impasse. We argue that the propositions developed in the previous section have at least three implications for future empirical research in this area.

Performance Variability

The model presented has implications for the study of the relationship between nexus rent, CSP^2 and financial performance. Recent meta-analyses suggest ambivalence in the findings, which at various times both support and refute the premise that relates 'doing good' and 'doing well'. However, the numerous studies and meta-analyses of the relationship between CSP and financial performance have uniformly ignored the differences in constraints facing firms (Griffin and Mahon, 1997; Margolis and Walsh, 2003). If, as we suggest, discretion interacts with orientation to determine performance levels for all stakeholders (including financial measures of shareholder return), then managerial discretion might be a hidden force which distorts the underlying relationship. Certain combinations of discretion and orientation will generate different levels of performance variability. In general, performance in low discretion environments will be more stable, performance in high discretion environments will be more variable. Future research might, then, start by seeking to confirm a more fundamental relationship between managerial discretion and the variability of stakeholder performance. Beyond this, future studies would be well-served to account for differences in managerial discretion among subjects.

Industry Effects

One growing area of research is the role that industry effects might play in moderating the stakeholder orientation–financial performance relationship. This is a promising avenue for future research but remains atheoretical, insofar as there are few insights into why the relationship between social and financial performance might vary so markedly from industry to industry. At best, those who have explored industry effects observe simply that, 'industries are different and have different stakeholder issues'. Our typology implies that useful theory could be developed suggesting systematic differences between low discretion and high discretion industries. Industry-level factors such as structure and attractiveness play no small role in determining a manager's level of discretion. So also may the nature of activities typical of an industry (that is, complexity, uncertainty and observability; Finkelstein and Peteraf, 2007) play an important role. If managerial discretion moderates the effects of stakeholder management, then we should not be surprised to find that, in general, controlling for industry helps to clarify the empirical results somewhat in studies of the impact of stakeholder management.

Beyond this basic proposition, future research might look even more closely at the multi-level nature of discretion for clues into how important industry effects really are. Managerial discretion derives from sources at multiple levels of analysis, of which industry level is but one (though arguably the most potent). The empirical findings on how industries matter in firm–stakeholder relations will become clearer still if future researchers parse the effects of discretion originating at the managerial, firm, industry and activity levels of analysis.

Perceived Discretion

An additional area of burgeoning interest is the question of why firms adopt certain stakeholder orientations. Stakeholder researchers have long been aware that how managers perceive their external environment can play an important role in how they address and prioritize various stakeholder claims (Mitchell, Agle and Wood, 1997). The managerial discretion literature also recognizes that how managers perceive their environments may influence the level of discretion they believe they have – and thus their behavior (Carpenter and Golden 1997). Though our arguments underscore how important it is to account for managerial discretion as a constraint on – and catalyst for – firm and managerial behavior, future researchers may also want to account for how managers subjectively assess the level of discretion available to them. By combining the four possible orientation/discretion combinations from our model with insights into how managers perceive discretion, we might find answers to two of the more compelling questions in stakeholder research. To wit, why do so many high discretion firms cling to a narrow stakeholder orientation despite the increasing calls for a broader allocation of value? And second, what accounts for those firms that press on with broadly oriented strategies despite significant environmental constraints?

The answers may lay in managers' tendencies to over- or under-estimate the discretion available to them. Carpenter and Golden (1997) suggest that managers' locus of control, a stable personality difference that reflects the extent to which individuals believe they are in control of, or are controlled by, their environment (Rotter, 1966) is negatively associated with their perceptions of discretion (cf. Key, 2002). Managers who believe that they are more or less constrained by the environment than they actually are may adopt inappropriate stakeholder orientations. Firms may underperform as a result of managers' misperceptions. The prevalence and persistence of narrow stakeholder orientations may, for example, be associated with systematic managerial beliefs that environments are more constraining than they are in reality. Misperceptions may also help to account for why some firms pursue broad orientations, even when they increase the risk of short-term underperformance. Managers who perceive less constraint than really exists may follow through on stakeholder-oriented values and press forward with a broad orientation despite the manifest dangers. Studies of entrepreneurs show that the entrepreneurial personality includes a high estimation of one's ability to control the external environment. We suspect that such managers will tend to over-estimate the discretion afforded them by industry and firm-level determinants. Should future researchers press forward with this insight, they might well discover why so many firms commonly associated with broadly oriented stakeholder management tend to be founder-controlled firms or those where the founding values have been particularly well assimilated into the firm's culture. Inconsistent, incorrect or ambiguous perceptions of latitude may confound the theorized relationships.

Additionally, although previous research has identified managerial perceptions of discretion as a key feature of their relationships with stakeholders, stakeholders' perceptions of managerial discretion have not yet been emphasized. These stakeholder perceptions may also play a role in stakeholder behavior, and thus in managerial discretion over time. Stakeholders who perceive higher levels of discretion than exist may be more susceptible to dissatisfaction with managerial behavior than stakeholders with more realistic perceptions of managerial discretion. The former may thus be more likely to attempt to intensify constraints on managers. Future studies might examine the interaction between managerial and stakeholder perceptions of discretion. If 'ought' implies 'can' (Danley, 1988) unrealistic perceptions of managerial discretion may result in unreasonable or irresponsible stakeholder demands. Managers who encourage such beliefs may be guilty of their own irresponsibility.

Finally, organizational ethicists who study stakeholders from a normative perspective and make moral prescriptions concerning how stakeholders should be treated must take greater consideration of the extent to which managers and firms are free to follow these prescriptions. The constraints of law (Ribstein, 2006; Hasnas, 2007), politics, history and path dependence, firm viability, and physical possibility all impinge upon the ability of firms and managers to act according to the moral ideals of stakeholder ethics. These constraints should inform future normative stakeholder scholarship and organizational ethics (Phillips and Margolis, 1999).

CONCLUSION

As stakeholder theory continues to mature, it grows more complex. Researchers have suggested many moderating and mediating variables between stakeholder management and performance. We argue that managerial discretion is an important variable in this chain. While managerial discretion may be a vital intervening variable in its own right, the propositions offered here suggest that explanations using discretion are even more powerful when discretion is combined with orientation. We explicate four combinations of discretion and orientation. Bringing managerial discretion into the conversation about firm–stakeholder relations gives an opportunity to bring further clarity into stakeholder research. We hope that future research explores this fruitful area.

ACKNOWLEDGMENTS

This chapter represents an extension of a previously published article: Phillips, R.A., Berman, S.L., Elms, H. and Johnson-Cramer, M.E. 2010. Strategy, stakeholders and managerial discretion. *Strategic Organization* 8 (2): 176–83. We have endeavored in this chapter to identify any overlap between the two texts, and thank *Strategic Organization* Editor Joel A.C. Baum for his support in publishing both of these related pieces.

We wish to thank Tom Donaldson, Megan Hess and Tom Jones for their helpful comments on earlier versions of this chapter.

NOTES

1. For the sake of simplicity and consistency with most of the prior literature, we refer throughout this article to the 'constraints' that stakeholders may impose. However, following our prior article (Phillips et al., 2010), we want to explicitly emphasize that in many cases, stakeholders also expand and catalyze the ability of managers to advance firm strategy.

2. As discussed above, we distinguish between nexus rent and historical conceptions of CSP. The 'social' in CSP implies a broader set of constituencies than denoted by aggregate stakeholder performance. Our model nevertheless has implications for the study of both.

REFERENCES

Adams, J.S. 1965. Inequity in social exchange. In L. Berkovitz (ed.), *Advances in Experimental Social Psychology*, Vol. 2. New York: Academic Press, pp. 267–99.

Agle, B.R., Mitchell, R.K. and Sonnenfeld, J.A. 1999. Who matters to CEOs? An investigation of stakeholder attributes and salience, corporate performance, and CEO values. *Academy of Management Journal*, **42**: 507–25.

Amit, R. and Schoemaker, P.J.H. 1993. Strategic assets and organizational rent. *Strategic Management Journal*, **14**: 33–46.

Arena, C. 2006. *The High-Purpose Company: The TRULY Responsible (and Highly Profitable) Firms That Are Changing Business Now*. New York: HarperCollins.

Associated Press 2006. Profit rises for E.D.S, but layoffs planned. *New York Times*, 2 August. Available online: http://www.nytimes.com/2006/08/02/business/02data.html, accessed 8 January 2011.

Astley, W.G. and Van de Ven, A.H. 1983. Central perspectives and debates in organization theory. *Administrative Science Quarterly*, **28**: 245–73.

Baum, J. and Wally, S. 2003. Strategic decision speed and firm performance. *Strategic Management Journal*, **24**: 1107–29.

Berman, S.L., Wicks, A.C., Kotha, S. and Jones, T.M. 1999. Does stakeholder orientation matter? The relationship between stakeholder management models and firm financial performance. *Academy of Management Journal*, **42**: 488–506.

Bourgeois, L.J. III. 1984. Strategic management and determinism. *Academy of Management Review*, **9**: 586–96.

Boyd, B.K. 1990. Corporate linkages and organizational environment: a test of the resource dependence model. *Strategic Management Journal*, **11**: 419–30.

Calton, J.M. and Kurland, N.B. 1996. A theory of stakeholder enabling: giving voice to an emerging postmodern praxis of organizational discourse. In D.M. Boje, R.P. Gephart and T.J. Thatchenkery (eds), *Postmodern Management and Organization Theory*. Thousand Oaks, CA: Sage, pp. 154–80.

Calton, J.M. and Lad, L.J. 1995. Social contracting as a trust-building process of network governance. *Business Ethics Quarterly*, **5**: 271–95.

Carpenter, M. and Golden, B. 1997. Perceived managerial discretion: a study of cause and effect. *Strategic Management Journal*, **18**: 187–206.

Child, J. 1972. Organizational structure, environment and performance: the role of strategic choice. *Sociology*, **6**: 1–22.

Child, J. 1997. Strategic choice in the analysis of action, structure, organizations and environment: retrospect and prospect. *Organization Studies*, **18**: 43–77.

Clarkson, M.B.E. 1995. A stakeholder framework for analyzing and evaluating corporate social performance. *Academy of Management Review*, **20**: 92–117.

Coff, R.W. 1999. When competitive advantage doesn't lead to performance: the resource-based view and stakeholder bargaining power. *Organization Science*, **10**: 119–33.

Cohen, A. 2003. *The Perfect Store: Inside eBay*. Boston, MA: Little, Brown, and Company.

Collins, J.C. and Porras, J.I. 1994. *Built to Last*. New York: HarperBusiness.

Colquitt, J.A., Conlon, D.E., Wesson, M.J., Porter, C.O.L.H. and Ng, K.Y. 2001. Justice at the millennium: a meta analytic review of 25 years of justice research. *Journal of Applied Psychology*, **86**: 424–45.

Danley, J.R. 1988. 'Ought' implies 'Can', or, The moral relevance of a theory of the firm. *Journal of Business Ethics*, **7**: 23–8.

Dobrev, S.D. and Kim, T. 2006. Positioning among organizations in a population: moves between market segments and the evolution of industry structure. *Administrative Science Quarterly*, **51**: 230.

Donaldson, T. and Preston, L. 1995. The stakeholder theory of the corporation: concepts, evidence, and implications. *Academy of Management Review*, **20**: 65–91.

Evan, W.M. and Freeman, R.E. 1993. A stakeholder theory of the modern corporation: Kantian capitalism. Reprinted in T.L. Beauchamp and N.E. Bowie (eds), *Ethical Theory and Business*, Englewood Cliffs, NJ: Prentice-Hall, pp. 75–93.

Finkelstein, S. and Boyd, B.K. 1998. How much does the CEO matter? The role of managerial discretion in the setting of CEO compensation. *Academy of Management Journal*, **41**: 179–99.

Finkelstein, S. and Hambrick, D.C. 1990. Top-management team tenure and organizational outcomes: the moderating role of managerial discretion. *Administrative Science Quarterly*, **35**: 484–503.

Finkelstein, S. and Peteraf, M.A. 2007. Managerial activities: a missing link in managerial discretion theory. *Strategic Organization*, **5**: 237–48.

Frank, R. 1988. *Passions Within Reason*. New York: W.W. Norton.

Fredrickson, J.W. 1984. The comprehensiveness of strategic decision processes: extension, observations, future directions. *Academy of Management Journal*, **27**: 445–66.

Fredrickson, J.W. and Iaquinto, A.L. 1989. Inertia and creeping rationality in strategic decision processes. *Academy of Management Journal*, **32**: 516.

Freeman, R.E. 1984. *Strategic Management: A Stakeholder Approach*. Marshfield, MA: Pitman Publishing Inc.

Freeman, R.E. 1994. The politics of stakeholder theory: some future directions. *Business Ethics Quarterly*, **4**: 409–21.

Friedlander, F. and Pickle, H. 1968. Components of effectiveness in small organizations. *Administrative Science Quarterly*, **13**: 289–304.

Friedman, M. 1970. The social responsibility of business is to increase its profits. *The New York Times Magazine*, 13 September.

Frooman, J. 1999. Stakeholder influence strategies. *Academy of Management Review*, **24**: 191–205.

Frooman, J. and Murrell, A. 2005. Stakeholder influence strategies: the roles of structural and demographic determinants. *Business & Society*, **44**: 3–31.

Griffin, J.J. and Mahon, J.F. 1997. The corporate social performance and corporate financial performance debate: twenty-five years of incomparable research. *Business & Society*, **36**: 5–31.

Hambrick, D.C. and Abrahamson, E. 1995. Assessing managerial discretion across industries: a multimethod approach. *Academy of Management Journal*, **38**: 1427–41.

Hambrick, D.C. and Finkelstein, S. 1987. Managerial discretion: a bridge between polar views of organizational outcomes. *Research in Organizational Behavior*, **9**: 369–406.

Hambrick, D.C., Geletkanycz, M.A. and Fredrickson, J.W. 1993. Top executive commitment to the *status quo*: some tests of its determinants. *Strategic Management Journal*, **14**: 401–18.

Hart, S.L. 1995. A natural-resource-based view of the firm. *Academy of Management Review*, **20**: 986.

Hasnas, J. 2007. Up from flatland: business ethics in the age of divergence. *Business Ethics Quarterly*, **17**: 399.

Hayibor, S. 2005. Understanding stakeholder action: equity and expectancy considerations. Unpublished dissertation, University of Pittsburgh.

Hill, C.W.L. and Jones, T.M. 1992. Stakeholder-agency theory. *Journal of Management Studies*, **29**: 131–54.

Hoskisson, R.E., Hitt, M.A., Wan, W.P. and Yiu, D. 1999. Theory and research in strategic management: swings of a pendulum. *Journal of Management*, **25**: 417–56.

Hosseini, J.C. and Brenner, S.N. 1992. The stakeholder theory of the firm: a methodology to generate value matrix weights. *Business Ethics Quarterly*, **2**: 99.

Hrebiniak, L.G. and Joyce, W.F. 1985. Organizational adaptation: strategic choice and environmental determinism. *Administrative Science Quarterly*, **30**: 336.

Jensen, M.C. and Meckling, W.H. 1976. Theory of the firm: managerial behavior, agency costs and ownership structure. *Journal of Financial Economics*, **3**: 305.

Johnson-Cramer, M. 2003a. Organization-level antecedents of stakeholder conflict. Unpublished dissertation, Boston University.

Johnson-Cramer, M. 2003b. Institutional antecedents of stakeholder conflict escalation. *Academy of Management Best Paper Proceedings*, Seattle, WA.

Johnson-Cramer, M., Berman, S. and Post, J.E. 2003. Reexamining the concept of 'stakeholder management'. In J. Andriof, S. Waddock, S. Rahman and B. Husted (eds), *Unfolding Stakeholder Thinking*, Vol. 2. London: Greenleaf Publishing, pp. 145–61.

Jones, T.M. 1995. Instrumental stakeholder theory: a synthesis of ethics and economics. *Academy of Management Review*, **20**: 404–37.

Jones, T.M. and Wicks, A.C. 1999. Convergent stakeholder theory. *Academy of Management Review*, **24**: 206–21.

Key, S. 2002. Perceived managerial discretion: an analysis of individual ethical intentions. *Journal of Managerial Issues*, **14**: 218–33.

King, B.G. and Soule, S.A. 2007. Social movements as extra-institutional entrepreneurs: the effect of protests on stock price returns. *Administrative Science Quarterly*, **52**: 413–42.

Leana, C.R. and van Buren, H.J. 1999. Organizational social capital and employment practices. *Academy of Management Review*, **24**: 538.

Logsdon, J.M. and Yuthas, K. 1997. Corporate social performance, stakeholder orientation, and organizational moral development. *Journal of Business Ethics*, **16**: 1213–26.

de Luque, M.S., Washburn, N.T., Waldman, D.A. and House, R.J. 2008. Unrequited profit: how stakeholder and economic values relate to subordinates' perceptions of leadership and firm performance. *Administrative Science Quarterly*, **53**: 626–54.

Margolis, J.D. and Walsh, J.P. 2003. Misery loves companies: rethinking social initiatives by business. *Administrative Science Quarterly*, **48**: 268–305.

Mitchell, R.K., Agle, B.R. and Wood, D.J. 1997. Toward a theory of stakeholder identification and salience: defining the principle of who and what really counts. *Academy of Management Review*, **22**: 853–86.

Morris, S.A. 1997. Internal effects of stakeholder management devices. *Journal of Business Ethics*, **16**: 413.

Olson, M. 1971. *The Logic of Collective Action: Public Goods and the Theory of Groups.* Cambridge, MA: Harvard University Press.

Perrow, C. 1986. *Complex Organizations: A Critical Essay.* New York: Random House.

Pfeffer, J. and Salancik, G. 1978. *The External Control of Organizations.* New York: Harper & Row.

Phillips, R.A. 1997. Stakeholder theory and a principle of fairness. *Business Ethics Quarterly*, **7**: 51–66.

Phillips, R.A. 2003. *Stakeholder Theory and Organizational Ethics.* San Francisco, CA: Berrett Koehler Publishers, Inc.

Phillips, R.A. and Margolis, J.D. 1999. Toward an ethics of organizations. *Business Ethics Quarterly*, **9**: 619–38.

Phillips, R.A., Freeman, R.E. and Wicks, A.C. 2003. What stakeholder theory is not. *Business Ethics Quarterly*, **13**(4): 479–502.

Phillips, R.A., Berman, S.L., Elms, H. and Johnson-Cramer, M.E. 2010. Strategy, stakeholders and managerial discretion, *Strategic Organization*, **8**: 176–83.

Pickle, H. and Friedlander, F. 1967. Seven societal criteria of organizational effectiveness. *Personnel Psychology*, **20**: 165–78.

Porter, M.E. 1980. *Competitive Strategy.* New York: Free Press.

Porter, M.E. 1987. From competitive advantage to corporate strategy. *Harvard Business Review*, **45**: 43–59.

Post, J.E., Preston, L.E. and Sachs, S. 2002. *Redefining the Corporation: Stakeholder Management and Organizational Wealth.* Stanford, CA: Stanford University Press.

Ribstein, L.E. 2006. Accountability and responsibility in corporate governance. *Notre Dame Law Review*, **81**: 1431–93.

Rotter, J. 1966. Generalized expectancies for internal versus external control of reinforcement. *Psychological Monographs*, **80**: 609–21.

Rowley, T.J. 1997. Moving beyond dyadic ties: a network theory of stakeholder influence. *Academy of Management Review,* **22**: 887–910.

Rowley, T. and Berman, S. 2000. A brand new brand of corporate social performance. *Business Society*, **39**: 397–418.

Rowley, T.J. and Moldoveanu, M. 2003. When will stakeholder groups act? An interest- and identity-based model of stakeholder group mobilization. *Academy of Management Review,* **28**: 204–19.

Sachs, J.D. and Shatz, H.J. 1996. U.S. trade with developing countries and wage inequality. *American Economic Review*, **86**: 234–9.

Scott, R.W. 1995. *Institutions and organizations.* Thousand Oaks, CA: Sage.

Selznick, P. 1949. *TVA and the Grass Roots.* Berkeley, CA: University of California Press.

Shen, W. and Cho, T.S. 2005. Exploring involuntary executive turnover through a managerial discretion framework. *Academy of Management Review,* **30**: 843–54.

Stevenson, W.B. and Greenberg, D. 2000. Agency and social networks: strategies of action in a social structure of position, opposition, and opportunity. *Administrative Science Quarterly*, **45**: 651.

Stinchcombe, A. 1965. Social structure and organizations. In J.G. March (ed.), *Handbook of Organizations*. Chicago, IL: Rand-McNally, pp. 142–93.

Vogel, D. 2005. *The Market for Virtue: The Potential and Limits of Corporate Social Responsibility*. Washington, DC: Brookings Institution Press.

Waddock, S.A. 2005. *Leading Corporate Citizens: Vision, Values, Value Added.* New York: McGraw-Hill/Irwin.

Waddock, S.A. and Graves, S.B. 1997. The corporate social performance–financial performance link. *Strategic Management Journal*, **18**: 303.

Walsh, J.P., Weber, K. and Margolis, J.D. 2003. Social issues and management: our lost cause found. *Journal of Management*, **29**: 859–81.

Wicks, A.C., Berman, S.L. and Jones, T.M. 1999. The structure of optimal trust: moral and strategic implications. *Academy of Management Review,* **24**: 99–116.

9. Stakeholders, entrepreneurial rent and bounded self-interest

Douglas A. Bosse and Jeffrey S. Harrison

Entrepreneurship may be envisioned as a process through which an actor (the entrepreneur) attempts to create rent by attracting and combining resources to satisfy a market need (for example, Schumpeter, 1934; Shane and Venkataraman, 2000; Alvarez and Barney, 2007). Throughout this process entrepreneurs must engage stakeholders to provide resources – such as prospective partners, employees, customers, suppliers and financiers – who are often uncertain about the entrepreneur's probability of success, and give them sufficient motivation to provide their resources to the venture (Freeman, 1984). This can be a challenge because in order to create and appropriate rent the entrepreneur must offer the stakeholders, as a group, less than the value of their combined resources, while at the same time trying to persuade them to engage in the venture (Rumelt, 1987; Coff, 2010).

A purely economic perspective to this entrepreneurial problem would suggest that the entrepreneur should seek out those initial stakeholders who are expected to provide their resources at the lowest cost, bargain to extract the lowest cost, and then withhold any information from them that might cause them to want a better deal in the future. The reasoning here is simple to understand if we assume that the entrepreneur is purely self-interested. Based on this assumption, the rational decision is to maximize each transaction without consideration of the interests of the stakeholders. We question whether this assumption provides an appropriate foundation upon which to understand the entrepreneur's resource acquisition problem and whether it is likely to lead to optimal decisions on the part of the entrepreneur. The efficacy of the pure self-interest assumption will be examined, followed by a discussion of how changing it alters our perspective of the behavior of entrepreneurs as they establish and manage relationships with resource-providing stakeholders. Related to Freeman's (1999) separation thesis, the logic we build based on the assumption of bounded self-interest explicitly recognizes the inseparability of ethical and economic behavior.

QUESTIONABLE ASSUMPTION

Entrepreneurs require the cooperation of a variety of resource providers in order to create entrepreneurial rent. These resource providers (stakeholders) typically include customers, materials suppliers, financiers, employees, managers and owners. Explaining the interactions among actors requires an assumption about what drives their behavior. Self-interest is the cardinal human motive that drives behavior in most economics-based theorizing (Schwartz, 1986; Miller, 1999). This way of thinking has a long tradition building at least from Bentham's (1780[1948]) philosophy of utilitarianism. Utilitarianism is based on the principle that humans are motivated exclusively by the pursuit of pleasure and the avoidance of pain. Jevons (1866), one of the co-founders of neoclassical economics, further specified that for economists self-interest refers only to the pursuit of satisfaction arising from the consumption of material goods (commodities).

> Economy investigates the relations of ordinary pleasures and pains thus arising, and it has a wide enough field of inquiry. But economy does not treat all human motives. There are motives nearly always present with us, arising from conscience, compassion, or from some moral or religious source, which economy cannot and does not pretend to treat. These will remain to us as outstanding and disturbing forces; they must be treated, if at all, by other appropriate branches of knowledge. (Jevons, 1866: 282)

The now-familiar assumption of self-interest is that people attempt to realize the greatest personal pleasure by picking the best combination of commodities they can afford given their income (Varian, 1999). A useful way to examine this phenomenon is in terms of the utility each possible combination might bring to the individual. Each combination of commodities, like a shopping cart, yields a certain number of underlying units of pleasure, which might be called 'utils'. An actor's utility function represents the trade-off calculations he/she makes when evaluating alternative courses of action. A utility function is applied to a set of expected material outcomes that might be consumed given each alternative course of action and a relative preference assigned by the actor to each outcome. The very concept of rent under this assumption, then, refers to the material value of commodities.

Although this hedonistic, individualistic assumption about human behavior has helped to explain many features of the collective economic behavior of society, the appropriate focus for explaining how entrepreneurs work with stakeholders to create entrepreneurial rent is on the level of individual actors (Freeman, 1984). Beyond the purely self-interested pursuit of commodities, what motivates the entrepreneur and the prospective stakeholder to engage with each other?

Scholars in a range of fields have found that the self-interest assumption is a poor description of human motivation because it abstracts from some of the subtler aspects of humanity and society that affect competitive market behaviors (Jevons, 1866; Keen, 2002). Extensive research in fields such as economics (Fehr and Gächter, 2000), philosophy (Becker, 1986; Rawls, 1999), sociology (Cropanzano and Mitchell, 2005), psychology (Rabin, 1998) and social psychology (Cialdini, 1984) shows humans are only boundedly self-interested. Bounded self-interest means actors' self-regarding behavior is bounded by the norm of fairness. When they experience something better (worse) than they expected they positively (negatively) reciprocate toward other actors in many competitive market situations (Fehr and Gächter, 2000). That is, economic actors regularly sacrifice self-interest to reinforce behavior they perceive as fair and to punish behavior they perceive as unfair (Thaler, 1991).

Self-interest is bounded because while people are motivated by the pursuit of personal pleasure and the avoidance of personal pain, this motivation reaches its boundary when it begins to violate their perceptions of what is fair. Concern for fairness means we are self- *and* other-regarding, not just self-regarding. Bosse, Phillips and Harrison (2009) provide a review of bounded self-interest that focuses on the work developed by labor economists, behavioral economists and organizational justice scholars. This work shows employees reciprocate positively to their employers when they perceive that they (and others) have been treated fairly. Positive reciprocity is demonstrated when employees provide more effort or more resources than originally expected. Employees also reciprocate negatively – by decreasing their effort or providing fewer resources than originally expected – when they perceive their employer has treated them (or others) unfairly. The difference between actual effort/resources provided and the expected effort/resources in an exchange can occur because employment contracts are incomplete. Bosse, Phillips and Harrison (2009) extend the application of bounded self-interest from the employee–firm context to all stakeholder–firm contexts.

The organizational justice literature contributes to the assumption of bounded self-interest by demonstrating that stakeholders' reciprocal behaviors are likely to be influenced by their perceptions of at least three types of fairness: distributive, procedural and interactional (for example, Colquitt et al., 2001; Bosse, Phillips and Harrison, 2009). In our context, distributive fairness refers to whether a stakeholder believes the distribution of material outcomes to the entrepreneur and the network of stakeholders is justified (Adams, 1965; Rabin, 1993; Nelson, 2001). Procedural fairness refers to whether a stakeholder believes the decision-making process is fair (Lind and Tyler, 1988; Phillips, Freeman and Wicks, 2003). This assessment can include aspects of the decision-making process such as the amounts of influence stakeholders have in decision making and the transparency of the decision criteria. Finally, interactional fairness refers to whether the entrepreneur treats stakeholders with respect and dignity or rudely and dismissively (Cropanzano, Bowen and Gilliland, 2007). Research demonstrates that people collectively consider all three of these types of fairness – and they consider tradeoffs among them – when enforcing the norm of fairness (that is, Greenberg, 1988, 1993; Blanchflower, Oswald and Sanfey, 1996; Ambrose, Seabright and Schminke, 2002; Brockner, 2006).

How does the bounded self-interest assumption change what is captured by the concept of rent? A venture has created rent when it compensates the actors, including the entrepreneur and all stakeholders, enough to keep them engaged in the venture, with at least one actor receiving compensation above that which is required to keep them engaged (adapted from Rumelt, 1987; Coff, 1999). Therefore, if concerns for distributive, procedural and interactional fairness affect the competitive behavior of entrepreneurs and stakeholders, *rent must refer to compensation that is both material and nonmaterial.* Part of an actor's compensation comes from the way they are treated by exchange partners. It even comes from the way their exchange partners treat third parties because fairness is not only enforced through reciprocity in dyadic exchanges, but also among third party actors in a network of exchanges (Ekeh, 1974). Nonmaterial compensation could come in many forms, such as better information, more voice in decision making, or better treatment during exchanges. These nonmaterial factors have value, too, because they motivate boundedly self-interested actors.

We now examine how shifting from the self-interest assumption to the bounded self-interest assumption changes three basic propositions for how entrepreneurs interact with their initial stakeholders to create entrepreneurial rent.

SELF-INTEREST AND STAKEHOLDER ENGAGEMENT

To obtain resources for their ventures, entrepreneurs must (1) search for parties to serve as stakeholders, (2) negotiate terms of exchange, and (3) manage exchanges after initiation (Larson, 1992; Gulati, 1998; Kale and Singh, 2009; Coff, 2010). Assuming economic actors are exclusively self-interested, we can deduce entrepreneurial behaviors in each of these stages that would seem to result in a greater amount of rent for the entrepreneur. For instance, based on this assumption we can predict that entrepreneurs will select stakeholders who are likely to charge the lowest cost, negotiate the lowest possible price required to engage those stakeholders and, after the initial exchange, withhold any information that could be used by stakeholders to opportunistically renegotiate for a larger portion of the rent that has been created.

Pure Self-interest and Engaging with Stakeholders

With regard to search, a prospective stakeholder who believes that the material outcomes from an entrepreneurial venture will be great will attempt to secure as many of those material benefits, *ex ante*, as possible. The lowest price, then, will tend to be charged by the stakeholder who has the lowest expectation of *ex post* material outcomes for the venture. The entrepreneur will select this stakeholder because it represents the lowest cost. Using this logic, we arrive at the following proposition:

Proposition 1:   Entrepreneurs generate more entrepreneurial rent by engaging stakeholders who possess the lowest expectations of ex post *material outcomes from the venture.*

After selecting an ideal prospective stakeholder, the entrepreneur must make an offer that entices them to engage in the new venture.[1] When evaluating an offer to enter a transaction, actors compare the offer to their opportunity cost – which is based on their expectation of the material outcomes they will receive from the best alternative use for the resources they control. Our proposition regarding an entrepreneur's offer to a prospective stakeholder under the self-interest assumption is simply derived from Rumelt's (1987) definition of entrepreneurial rent. The self-interested entrepreneur offers the lowest material compensation required to engage the stakeholder.

Proposition 2:   Entrepreneurs generate more entrepreneurial rent by offering stakeholders the minimum material value required to engage them.

After selecting and negotiating terms of exchange with stakeholders, entrepreneurs must carefully manage each stakeholder relationship. It is reasonable to expect that the existence of entrepreneurial rent relies on uncertainty regarding the outcomes of the venture (Alvarez and Barney, 2005; Kor, Mahoney and Michael, 2007), which drives entrepreneurs and prospective stakeholders to have different expectations of the value that will be created. Otherwise, resource providers would be more likely to appropriate much or all of the surplus value created by the venture, thus leaving little or no rent for the entrepreneur (Coff, 2010). Uncertainty exists largely due to a lack of reliable and verifiable information (Alvarez and Barney, 2005; Kor, Mahoney and Michael, 2007). As the entrepreneur successively forms exchanges with various stakeholders in pursuit of his/her opportunity, he/she begins to collect reliable and verifiable information about the expected value of the venture. If the entrepreneur is at the nexus of the stakeholder network, he/she may be the only actor with access to this information. What the entrepreneur does with this information can influence the entrepreneurial rent that is both created and retained.

Purely self-interested stakeholders seek the largest possible share of the rent. So if a stakeholder finds out their resource contributed material value that exceeds the cost they charged the entrepreneur, they will opportunistically renegotiate for a larger share of the rent (Coff, 2010). Purely self-interested entrepreneurs actively seek to appropriate a strictly larger share, too, so they will understate or withhold information about the actual underlying distribution of outcomes as it becomes available. This strategy of concealing information about the *ex post* value is executed until the entrepreneur can acquire isolating mechanisms (Rumelt, 1984, 1987; Mahoney and Pandian, 1992; Peteraf, 1993; Knott, 2003), which are factors that protect the value-producing aspects of the entrepreneur's venture from competitive imitation (for example, property rights, learning, buyer switching costs, reputation, organizational routines).

Proposition 3: Entrepreneurs generate more entrepreneurial rent by withholding as much positive performance information as possible from stakeholders.

While these three propositions are logical extrapolations based on the assumption of pure self-interest, they change when the assumption of bounded self-interest is introduced. The next three sections will examine these changes and provide alternative propositions.

Bounded Self-interest and the Search for Stakeholders

The first proposition that entrepreneurs should seek resources from stakeholders with pessimistic predictions regarding the economic success of the venture follows directly from the Rumelt (1987) definition of entrepreneurial rent and the assumption of self-interested actors. However, common observation suggests entrepreneurs often choose to engage stakeholders with high expectations for the new venture. We suggest that an assumption of bounded self-interest supports a more accurate depiction of entrepreneurial decision making in this regard.

Under the assumption of bounded self-interest, actors reciprocate positively or negatively based on perceptions of distributive, procedural and interactional fairness. This means some of the material outcome will be associated with the effort and level of resources provided by the stakeholders – and these things are determined in part by stakeholders in response to the entrepreneur's actions. Therefore, the material outcomes of a venture are partially endogenously determined by the interactions among the entrepreneur and his/her stakeholders. The entrepreneur in this model is unlikely to generate the most rent by selecting stakeholders with the lowest absolute expectations for the venture.

Reciprocal behavior is ultimately driven by mismatches between what an entrepreneur thinks is fair compensation for a given stakeholder and what that stakeholder thinks is fair. These expectations of fairness are not conceived exogenously in absolute terms. Evidence from the ultimatum game suggests expectations of fairness are relative (Fehr and Gächter, 2000). The ultimatum game is a popular experiment used by behavioral economists in which player A is given the right to propose a scheme for dividing a fixed sum of money with player B. This proposal is the 'ultimatum'. Player B has the authority to accept or reject the ultimatum. The result of a rejected offer is that both parties walk away with nothing; accepted offers are implemented. Findings across a wide range of subject populations show proposals that allocate less than 30 percent of the available money to player B are rejected (Fehr and Gächter, 2000). A ten dollar pot split $2/$8 is rejected as is a hundred dollar pot split $20/$80. Player B incurs a cost of twenty dollars, in this latter example, just to punish Player A for proposing an unfair split. A plausible interpretation is that people adjust their expectations of what is fair based on the relative allocation of compensation rather than on the absolute level of compensation they will receive.

Applying this logic to our context, we expect entrepreneurs to generate more rent when they engage stakeholders who possess complementary ideas about what is fair compensation for both parties. Because the level of compensation perceived to be fair is influenced by what the other party gets, searching for the stakeholder with the lowest absolute expectation (*ex ante*) for the venture can easily result in mismatched perceptions of fairness. Bounded self-interest characterizes entrepreneurs as well as prospective stakeholders, so the motivation of the entrepreneur (stakeholder) to engage with particular stakeholders (entrepreneurs) is influenced by his/her perceptions of fair and unfair treatment exhibited by those stakeholders (entrepreneurs). Thus, mismatching expectations for fairness likely leads to allocations of compensation that stimulate negative reciprocity from one of the parties. Negative reciprocity, in turn, is associated with less rent creation (Bosse, Phillips and Harrison, 2009).

The revised proposition is that entrepreneurs create more rent when they select stakeholders who share complementary (that is, matching rather than mismatching) expectations for fair compensation. This proposition, based on the bounded self-interest assumption, reflects a win–win scenario. The ideal strategy changes from 'get the largest slice of a fixed pie' to 'grow the size of the whole pie'. This approach is also appropriately seen as the 'names and faces' mental model of the startup venture (Werhane, this volume). This is because the entrepreneur believes stakeholders who hold complementary expectations of fairness will foster positive reciprocity, thus creating greater total value. A network of such stakeholders with complementary expectations of fairness will also help allocate the (now larger) material and nonmaterial value fairly. 'Complementary' here means the best stakeholder is the one most likely to reciprocate positively to the entrepreneur, given the entrepreneur's own expectations for distributive, procedural and interactional fairness. The revised proposition under the bounded self-interest assumption is:

Revised Proposition 1: Entrepreneurs generate more entrepreneurial rent by engaging stakeholders who possess expectations of distributive, procedural, and interactional fairness that are complementary to the entrepreneur's expectations.

One of the upsides of the logic associated with bounded self-interest is that it recognizes entrepreneurs' personal influence on the value created through new resource combinations. Entrepreneurs can influence expectations of fairness through the way they engage with stakeholders. For example, they can exhibit a high level of respect and courtesy for potential stakeholders during their contacts with them (interactional fairness). They can consider the needs and concerns of stakeholders as they develop plans for the venture, and can regularly communicate those plans and the way that stakeholder needs and concerns are accounted for (procedural fairness). They can also manifest a willingness to share the material outcomes from the venture fairly (distributive fairness), and to communicate regularly and openly with stakeholders concerning the particulars of the venture that are most important to them (interactional and procedural fairness). Indeed, we suggest that successful entrepreneurs do these things and that they help to keep the front-end costs as low as possible.

Consequently, our revised proposition suggests the lowest costs are not necessarily offered by stakeholders with the lowest expectations for *ex post* material outcomes from the venture. Rather, stakeholders with complementary fairness considerations may be willing to charge the entrepreneur comparatively low prices because they believe fairness considerations have value with regard to the size of the outcomes and the way they will be distributed.

Bounded Self-interest and Negotiating with Stakeholders

The components of cost and value under the bounded self-interest assumption include both material and non-material components. Furthermore, the material components do not just refer to distributions of value that can be monetized, but also the fairness of their distribution. So while actors hold different expectations of *ex post* material outcomes due to uncertainty (Kor, Mahoney and Michael, 2007), they can develop shared expectations (through reputation and discussion) of fair material and non-material outcomes. Astute entrepreneurs check references of potential stakeholders such as employees, financiers, and suppliers. A strong reputation for fairness enhances the desirability of the stakeholder. The parties can also discuss, for example, what role the stakeholder will play in decision making (a form of procedural compensation) or the way the entrepreneur will treat the stakeholder (interactional compensation). The upshot is that *ex ante* costs and *ex post* value are interdependent under the bounded self-interest assumption. Ex post value is positively related with ex ante cost because stakeholders reciprocate based on what they receive.

Entrepreneurs in a world of boundedly self-interested actors seek to manage the expectations for fairness among prospective stakeholders by demonstrating what levels of nonmaterial value they can expect in a proposed exchange. By explaining their relevant decision making processes and treating prospective stakeholders with dignity and respect during the offer negotiation process, entrepreneurs influence the basis for stakeholders' expectations for nonmaterial compensation.

These efforts put forth by the entrepreneur serve to mitigate some of the material outcome uncertainty that characterizes the entrepreneurial process (Kor et al., 2007). As stakeholders get better information about the nonmaterial compensation they can expect, even at the first point of contact, their uncertainty about the proposed exchange is reduced. As stated previously, people acknowledge tradeoffs in the three types of fairness. A distribution of procedural fairness that exceeds the norm, for example, can compensate for a potential distribution of material value that is below a stakeholder's (material) opportunity cost (Colquitt et al., 2001). Thus, a stakeholder who has reason to believe they will be treated fairly may be willing to reduce the price they charge the entrepreneur for access to their resource.

The revised proposition regarding an entrepreneur's offer to a prospective stakeholder under the bounded self-interest assumption builds on the endogeneity of *ex post* outcomes and *ex ante* costs. The entrepreneur crafts an offer to stakeholders such that the total material and nonmaterial value will be maximized. Because some of the value is endogenous to the fairness the entrepreneur distributes to stakeholders, the entrepreneur will seek to remove any nonmaterial uncertainty by promising (and demonstrating) a pattern of fairness toward stakeholders.

Revised Proposition 2: Entrepreneurs generate more entrepreneurial rent by offering stakeholders a total compensation including procedural, inter-actional, and material fairness that initiates a cycle of positive reciprocity.

Bounded Self-interest and Sharing Information with Stakeholders

As Proposition 3 suggested, the pure self-interest assumption leads to the idea that entrepreneurs should withhold positive information about the success of a venture so that stakeholders do not attempt to appropriate more of the value created. However, shifting to the bounded self-interest assumption, actors (both entrepreneurs and stakeholders) are expected to be more open with information about performance outcomes to the extent that they believe they can seek to make adjustments to their contracts where necessary.

If a stakeholder finds out the true value attributable to their contribution (material and non material) is greater or less than their perception of the fairness they have received, they will seek to remedy this unfairness. Stakeholders enforce fairness by either renegotiating for a fairer compensation or by adjusting the effort or value of resources they provide to the entrepreneur. The nature of the bounded self-interest assumption incorporates reciprocal rewards and penalties that occur after the initial agreement. Third parties that become stakeholders also reciprocate positively and negatively based on their perceptions of the entrepreneur's behavior, even if the second-party stakeholder they observe only engages in one transaction with the entrepreneur. The upshot is that norms of fairness are enforced over the course of multiple transactions between the entrepreneur and stakeholders. So even if the entrepreneur overpays a stakeholder at the initiation of their exchange, when that becomes apparent given the information that becomes available later, that stakeholder will either provide more value to justify the extra compensation they have received or give back some of the extra compensation. This is an example of boundedly self-interested actors willingly incurring cost to enforce their principles.

The revised proposition regarding entrepreneurs' information sharing with stakeholders builds on the assumption that fairness is enforced by stakeholders through both positive and negative reciprocity. The information-sharing strategy for an entrepreneur when actors are boundedly self-interested is to be transparent with stakeholders. They will openly share stakeholders' contributions to the rent that is created because openly sharing information with stakeholders stimulates positive reciprocity. For example, stakeholders may also be more disclosing with information that could be useful to the entrepreneur in creating even more value. Harrison, Bosse and Phillips (2010) argue that stakeholders are more likely to share nuanced information with firms that exhibit characteristics associated with what is considered fair and that this information can be used to increase the efficiency with which resources are allocated, spur innovation and better manage environmental uncertainty. These factors can also contribute to the success of an entrepreneurial venture. Even if a given stakeholder is purely self-interested, openly sharing this information with other stakeholders enables them to serve as fairness enforcers (positively and negatively) for the whole network of stakeholders (including the entrepreneur).

Revised Proposition 3:   Entrepreneurs generate more entrepreneurial rent by openly sharing performance information with stakeholders.

Taken together, the three revised propositions suggest that entrepreneurs will be more successful in generating rents from their ventures if they seek out stakeholders as resource providers who have similar values to their own with regard to fairness considerations (procedural, interactional, distributional), emphasize fairness characteristics as a component of the bargaining process and openly share performance information with them after the deal is struck. These propositions envision a scenario in which stakeholders and the entrepreneur are willing to strike a deal in which the costs of the resources may not be optimal in purely financial terms and from their own perspectives. In other words, the entrepreneur may not be getting the lowest possible price for a resource, in financial terms, but instead trades off this position for a situation in which he/she believes that the resource provider will exhibit fairness and that the terms of the agreement can be renegotiated *ex post* based on actual outcomes. 'I may not be getting the lowest price right now, but this stakeholder will be fair with me as our exchange (relationship) proceeds.'

Nevertheless, we do not expect that the entrepreneur will have to pay the highest prices for resources either. If the entrepreneur exhibits fairness characteristics during the bargaining process and promises disclosure of relevant information downstream, the stakeholder providing the resources is also expected to consider these nonmaterial forms of compensation as a part of the deal. 'We may not be getting the highest price possible, but this entrepreneur is going to be fair and open with us.'

Fairness considerations mean that the initial cost of resources provided by stakeholders may not be as important as they are considered to be under the assumption of pure self-interest. After all, fairness would suggest that initial contracts can be adjusted *ex post*. However, of equal importance to this discussion is the idea that fairness also influences the behavior of the actors through reciprocity (Bosse, Phillips and Harrison, 2009). Stakeholders reciprocate positively when they perceive that they (and others) have been treated fairly. Positive reciprocity is demonstrated through means such as providing additional effort or resources than originally expected. Stakeholders can also reciprocate negatively – by decreasing their effort or providing fewer resources than originally expected – when they perceive the entrepreneur has treated them (or others) unfairly. In our context, reciprocation means that fairness, as defined herein, will lead to a higher level of rent creation because of the motivation levels and actions of the actors in the venture.

If an entrepreneur is poorly matched with a stakeholder in terms of fairness considerations the optimal situation described above erodes, leading to less rent creation. Note that Revised Proposition 1 talks in terms of complementary expectations of distributive, procedural and interactional fairness between the entrepreneur and stakeholders. If the entrepreneur exhibits a high level of fairness and a stakeholder does not, then the stakeholder is likely to try to take advantage of the entrepreneur. Furthermore, procedural, interactional and distributive fairness come with costs, and those costs will not be compensated for unless they are associated with similar behaviors on the part of the stakeholder. From the opposite perspective, if the stakeholder exhibits a high level of fairness but does not perceive that the entrepreneur is of like mind, then the highest possible price will be charged for resources provided, recognizing that nonmaterial compensation factors are not likely to be realized *ex post*. Furthermore, additional effort and resources will not be provided. Either one of these scenarios will reduce the amount of total rent created by the venture.

The notion of matching entrepreneurs with stakeholders is similar to the concept of 'optimal trust' espoused by Wicks, Berman and Jones (1999). Indeed, trust is essential to the expectations of fairness we have been discussing. Wicks et al. argue that it is possible to overinvest or underinvest in trust. For instance, companies can invest too many resources in establishing trust, thus eroding profitability, and too much trust can also lead to opportunistic behavior. Similarly, companies may not expend sufficient resources to establish the trust that is needed for productive relationships with their stakeholders. In our situation, an entrepreneur who exhibits more fairness than the stakeholder is using the additional resources needed to create that level of fairness unproductively, at least in that particular stakeholder relationship. Also, an entrepreneur who does not exhibit fairness to the stakeholder will have to pay what is essentially a premium for resources provided in order to compensate for the lack of nonmaterial consideration. As explained by Hartman (this volume), entrepreneurs and stakeholders can efficiently come to agreement about what is fair through conversation (rather than bargaining).

DISCUSSION

This chapter examines three propositions regarding the creation of entrepreneurial rent under the common assumption that actors are driven by a cardinal human motive of pure self-interest. For each proposition we also derive a revised proposition by assuming actors are boundedly self-interested. While the assumption of bounded self-interest is believed by many scholars to be a more accurate depiction of human behavior (Cialdini, 1984; Becker, 1986; Rabin, 1998; Rawls, 1999; Fehr and Gächter, 2000; Cropanzano and Mitchell, 2005), our objective is not to prove the accuracy of this assumption. Instead, we have sought to draw attention to the face validity of these contrasting propositions about how entrepreneurs behave when creating entrepreneurial rent. The result is a set of explanations that extend important concepts of stakeholder theory to the initial resource acquisition behaviors of entrepreneurs.

The first proposition explains selection criteria entrepreneurs use when identifying prospective stakeholders. Under the purely self-interested assumption the ideal stakeholder, *ceteris paribus*, is the one that expects to receive the lowest payment for the use of his/her resources. Because stakeholders have divergent expectations regarding the value a venture will create, entrepreneurs search for the lowest price resource provider (stakeholder) based on who has the lowest expectations of future material outcomes.

In contrast, we explain that under the assumption of bounded self-interest the entrepreneur and the prospective stakeholders will use more than material costs and benefits in their evaluation of who to engage in transactions. We argue that entrepreneurs and stakeholders will choose to engage with actors who possess expectations of distributive, procedural and interactional fairness that are complementary to their own expectations. When two parties in an exchange have complementary expectations of fairness, neither party is motivated to negatively reciprocate toward the other. So the best strategy for an entrepreneur is not to pick the stakeholder who has the most divergent future expectation to his/her own, but to pick the stakeholder who has the most convergent expectation of fairness.

Many new entrepreneurs select family and friends as their stakeholders. We see this as an example of Revised Proposition 1. Friends and family, by definition, have preexisting relationships with the entrepreneur so they have knowledge of his/her pattern of fairness, exhibited in terms of distributive (for example, generosity), procedural (for example, patterns of decision making) and interactional fairness (for example, respect). Likewise, knowledge of how potential friends and family stakeholders behave enables the entrepreneur to judge which ones are ideal prospective stakeholders for the new venture. This compensates for a portion of the exogenous uncertainty about material outcomes for both parties. The entrepreneur is highly motivated to behave in a manner that will be perceived as fair to the stakeholders, and they are highly motivated to do what they can to make the venture a success. In a sense, family and friends offer an extreme case of complementarity, although we expect the phenomenon to be evident to a lesser degree in most entrepreneurial decisions regarding selection of stakeholders.

The second foundational proposition is about what entrepreneurs offer prospective stakeholders in order to generate more rent. Pure self-interest suggests that entrepreneurs provide only material value to stakeholders and that they should therefore offer the minimum material value required to engage them. However, under the assumption of bounded self-interest this would not generate the most rent possible. Instead, offering the least possible material value while ignoring procedural and interactional value considerations could initiate negative reciprocity from a stakeholder that would be costly. In a world of boundedly self-interested actors, entrepreneurs can reduce the uncertainty of 'returns' to a stakeholder by promising procedural and interactional fairness that he/she can determine, and he/she offers a fair distribution of whatever material value they ultimately create together. Stakeholders who are uncertain about the material outcome, but comfortable that they will receive procedural and interactional fairness, are likely to accept a lower price for their resources, all else being equal. This revised proposition provides a plausible explanation for why so many entrepreneurs with limited resources are, in fact, able to access the resources necessary to pursue an opportunity and generate rent.

This line of reasoning also implies that the *ex post* distribution of value is not entirely established *ex ante* in a bounded self-interest world. The material value that is created by the entrepreneur depends in part on the way stakeholders are treated. Stakeholders give more effort and resources when they are treated fairly, and less effort and resources when treated unfairly. As a result, entrepreneurial rent is larger when the entrepreneur can get stakeholders to reciprocate positively. This logic emphasizes the collective nature of entrepreneurial opportunity creation, suggesting that the entrepreneur and his/her earliest stakeholders have highly interdependent roles in creating and exploiting an opportunity together (Harper, 2008).

Our theory underscores the importance of the reputation of the entrepreneur, even in the early stages of a first venture (Fischer and Reuber, 2007). A reputation for fairness can facilitate acquisition of resources and reduce their material costs (Barney and Hansen, 1994). Alternatively, a tarnished reputation can make resources very expensive or even make impossible the acquisition of sufficient resources to initiate the venture (Zahra, Yavuz and Ucbasaran, 2006). The ideas in this chapter suggest that an entrepreneur should be very careful about projecting the right image with regard to fairness considerations. This argument may partially explain the existence of serial entrepreneurship. An entrepreneur who exhibits fairness towards stakeholders in a first venture will be in a much stronger position to obtain resources for the next venture. Furthermore, those resources may cost less because of his/her earned reputation for fairness.

After the entrepreneur has begun collecting market feedback about the actual material value of the venture, the third proposition formed under an assumption of pure self-interest is that being opaque with stakeholders about this information results in more rent creation for the entrepreneur. Under bounded self-interest, however, entrepreneurs do not withhold information about the true value of their stakeholders' contributions because this is an unfairness that providers will penalize upon discovery. Instead, entrepreneurs openly share information about the true value of their stakeholders' contributions and information about the venture as a whole. This reduces uncertainty and can motivate stakeholders to share nuanced information with the entrepreneur that can lead to still higher levels of rent creation.

The revised propositions included in this chapter are consistent with a statement from Baker and Pollock who, during a review of the literature at the intersection of the entrepreneurship and strategic management fields, suggest 'research in entrepreneurship has consistently provided empirical support for the continued importance of values and goals besides maximizing short-term profitability in shaping entrepreneurial activity' (2007: 300). We have deliberately avoided a normative perspective; however, we openly acknowledge that the values associated with fairness have a strong moral foundation. We suggest that this chapter provides a foundation for future research on how nonmaterial considerations affect entrepreneurial rent creation.

On a broader scale, we question whether a comparison of *ex ante* costs and *ex post* material outcomes really captures the success of an entrepreneurial venture. In a world of bounded self-interest, two major things can happen to distort this measurement. First, according to distributive fairness, an entrepreneur may distribute more of the material outcomes to stakeholders who have contributed the most to the success of the venture if the *ex post* material outcomes are great. In essence, rent appears smaller than would otherwise be the case because it is widely distributed (Coff, 1999). Second, actors accept nonmaterial outcomes associated with procedural and interactional fairness as a part of their compensation. Rent itself would tend to have a nonmaterial dimension as the entrepreneur gains satisfaction from reciprocating with certain stakeholders. The entrepreneur may also justify such behavior as building relationships to facilitate acquisition of resources for future ventures.

Another potentially fruitful area for future examination is the application of the bounded self-interest assumption to the question of managerial discretion and nexus rents presented by Phillips et al. (this volume). If the entrepreneur chooses to interact with potential stakeholders in the ways described above under the pure self-interest assumption, our analyses and theories likely underestimate how much stakeholders can constrain those entrepreneurs. The bounded self-interest assumption, because it draws attention to the initiation of reciprocal behavior among stakeholders, helps to highlight stakeholders' influence on the entrepreneur's discretion (or the constraints on his/her behavior).

Moving forward, in-depth study of entrepreneurial resource acquisition can help shed light on these issues. Case studies and surveys that include an examination of fairness issues would be useful in ascertaining the decision-making processes of entrepreneurs and their stakeholders during and after venture formation (also suggested by Jones, this volume). Which nonmaterial factors do entrepreneurs and stakeholders consider as they decide who they will engage? How do entrepreneurs and stakeholders trade off material and nonmaterial costs and expected outcomes? How and to what extent does full performance information disclosure influence the behavior of stakeholders *ex post*? These questions provide fruitful areas for future empirical research.

In conclusion, this chapter questions some of the fundamental propositions that can be derived from the assumption of pure self-interest on the part of entrepreneurs and stakeholders as a venture is formed to pursue an opportunity. The underlying premise is that nonmaterial considerations are a potent force in the resource acquisition process and in the management of performance information after the venture is initiated. We suggest that reciprocity and fairness considerations are important to the decisions that entrepreneurs make regarding their stakeholders as well as the material and nonmaterial outcomes of the venture. Consequently, entrepreneurs should be very careful about the stakeholders they choose, their first interactions with those potential stakeholders, and how they manage performance information after the venture is started. Entrepreneurial rent may increase as a function of the fairness exhibited by both entrepreneurs and their stakeholders although such increases may be hard to detect because fairness also means that more value is likely to be allocated back to stakeholders.

NOTE

1. We control for differences in prospective stakeholders' resource quality in a given category (i.e., raw materials suppliers, employees, etc.) in this discussion to highlight the relevant differences arising from the assumptions of pure self-interest vs. bounded self-interest.

REFERENCES

Adams, J.S. 1965. Inequity in social exchange. In L. Berkovitz (ed.), *Advances in Experimental Social Psychology*, Vol. 2. New York: Academic Press, pp. 267–99.

Alvarez, S.A. and Barney, J.B. 2005. How do entrepreneurs organize firms under conditions of uncertainty? *Journal of Management*, **31**: 776–93.

Alvarez, S.A. and Barney, J.B. 2007. The entrepreneurial theory of the firm. *Journal of Management Studies*, **44**: 1057–63.

Ambrose, M.L., Seabright, M.A. and Schminke, M. 2002. Sabotage in the workplace: the role of organizational injustice. *Organizational Behavior and Human Decision Processes*, **89**: 947–65.

Baker, T. and Pollock, T.G. 2007. Making the marriage work: the benefits of strategy's takeover of entrepreneurship for strategic organization. *Strategic Organization*, **5**: 297–312.

Barney, J.B. and Hansen, M.H. 1994. Trustworthiness as a source of competitive advantage. *Strategic Management Journal*, **15**: 175–90.

Becker, L. 1986. *Reciprocity*. Chicago, IL: University of Chicago Press.

Bentham, J. 1780[1948]. *The Principles of Morals and Legislation*. New York: Hafner Press.

Blanchflower, D.G., Oswald, A.J. and Sanfey, P. 1996. Wages, profits, and rent-sharing. *Quarterly Journal of Economics*, **111**: 227–52.

Bosse, D.A., Phillips, R.A. and Harrison, J.S. 2009. Stakeholders, reciprocity and firm performance. *Strategic Management Journal*, **30**: 447–56.

Brockner, J. 2006. Why it's so hard to be fair. *Harvard Business Review*, **84**(3) (March): 122–9.

Cialdini, R.B. 1984. *Influence: The Psychology of Persuasion*. New York: William Morrow and Company.

Coff, R.W. 1999. When competitive advantage doesn't lead to performance: the resource-based view and stakeholder bargaining power. *Organization Science*, **10**(2): 119–33.

Coff, R.W. 2010. The coevolution of rent appropriation and capability development. *Strategic Management Journal*, **31**: 711–33.

Colquitt, J.A., Conlon, D.E., Wesson, M.J., Porter, C.O.L.H. and Ng, K.Y. 2001. Justice at the millennium: a meta analytic review of 25 years of justice research. *Journal of Applied Psychology*, **86**: 424–45.

Cropanzano, R., Bowen, D.E. and Gilliland, S.W. 2007. The management of organizational justice. *Academy of Management Perspectives*, **21**: 34–48.

Cropanzano, R. and Mitchell, M.S. 2005. Social exchange theory: an interdisciplinary review. *Journal of Management*, **31**: 874–900.

Ekeh, P.P. 1974. *Social Exchange Theory*. Cambridge, MA: Harvard University Press.

Fehr, E. and Gächter, S. 2000. Fairness and retaliation: the economics of reciprocity. *Journal of Economic Perspectives*, **14**: 159–81.

Fischer, E. and Reuber, R. 2007. The good, the bad and the unfamiliar: the challenges of reputation formation facing new firms. *Entrepreneurship Theory and Practice*, **31**: 53–75.

Freeman, R.E. 1984. *Strategic Management: A Stakeholder Approach*. Marshfield, MA: Pitman Publishing Inc.

Freeman, R.E. 1999. Response: divergent stakeholder theory. *Academy of Management Review*, **24**: 233–6.

Greenberg, J. 1988. Equity and workplace status: a field experiment. *Journal of Applied Psychology*, **73**: 606–13.

Greenberg, J. 1993. Stealing in the name of justice: informational and interpersonal moderators of theft reactions to underpayment inequity. *Organizational Behavior and Human Decision Processes*, **54**: 81–103.

Gulati, R. 1998. Alliances and networks. *Strategic Management Journal*, **19**: 293–317.

Harper, D.A. 2008. Towards a theory of entrepreneurial teams. *Journal of Business Venturing*, **23**: 613–26.

Harrison, J.S., Bosse, D.A. and Phillips, R.A. 2010. Managing for stakeholders, stakeholder utility functions, and competitive advantage. *Strategic Management Journal*, **31**: 58–74.

Jevons, W.S. 1866. Brief account of a general mathematical theory of political economy. *Journal of the Royal Statistical Society*, **XXIX**: 282–7.

Kale, P. and Singh, H. 2009. Managing strategic alliances: what do we know now, and where do we go from here? *Academy of Management Perspectives*, **23**(3): 45–62

Keen, S. 2002. *Debunking Economics: The Naked Emperor of the Social Sciences*. Australia: Pluto Press.

Knott, A.M. 2003. The organizational routines factor market paradox. *Strategic Management Journal*, **24**: 929–43.

Kor, Y.Y., Mahoney, J.T. and Michael, S.C. 2007. Resources, capabilities and entrepreneurial perceptions. *Journal of Management Studies*, **44**: 1187–212.

Larson, A. 1992. Network dyads in entrepreneurial settings: a study of the governance of exchange relationships. *Administrative Science Quarterly*, **37**: 76–104.

Lind, E.A. and Tyler, T. 1988. *The Social Psychology of Procedural Justice.* New York: Plenum.

Mahoney, J.T. and Pandian, J.R. 1992. The resource-based view within the conversation of strategic management. *Strategic Management Journal*, **15**: 363–80.

Miller, D.T. 1999. The norm of self-interest. *American Psychologist*, **54**: 1053–60.

Nelson Jr., W.R. 2001. Incorporating fairness into game theory and economics: comment. *American Economic Review*, **91**: 1180–83.

Peteraf, M.A. 1993. The cornerstones of competitive advantage: a resource-based view. *Strategic Management Journal*, **14**: 179–91.

Phillips, R.A., Freeman, R.E. and Wicks, A.C. 2003. What stakeholder theory is not. *Business Ethics Quarterly*, **13**(4): 479–502.

Rabin, M. 1993. Incorporating fairness into game theory and economics. *American Economic Review*, **83**: 1281.

Rabin, M. 1998. Psychology and economics. *Journal of Economic Literature*, **36**: 11–46.

Rawls J. 1971[1999]. Justice as reciprocity. In S. Freeman (ed.), *John Rawls: Collected Papers*. Cambridge, MA: Harvard University Press, pp. 190–224.

Rumelt, R.P. 1984. Toward a strategic theory of the firm. In R. Lamb (ed.), *Competitive Strategic Management*. Englewood Cliffs, NJ: Prentice-Hall, pp. 556–70.

Rumelt, R.P. 1987. Theory, strategy, and entrepreneurship. In D. Teece (ed.), *The Competitive Challenge*. Cambridge, MA: Ballinger, pp. 137–58.

Schumpeter, J.A. 1934. *The Theory of Economic Development*. Cambridge, MA: Harvard University Press.

Schwartz, B. 1986. *The Battle for Human Nature*. New York: Norton.

Shane, S. and Venkataraman, S. 2000. The promise of entrepreneurship as a field of research. *Academy of Management Review*, **25**: 217–26.

Thaler, R.H. 1991. *Quasi Rational Economics*. New York: Russell Sage Foundation.

Varian, H.R. 1999. *Intermediate Microeconomics: A Modern Approach*, 5th edition. New York: W.W. Norton & Company.

Wicks, A.C., Berman, S.L. and Jones, T.M. 1999. The structure of optimal trust: moral and strategic implications. *Academy of Management Review*, **24**: 99–116.

Zahra, S.A., Yavuz, R.I. and Ucbasaran, D. 2006. How much do you trust me? The dark side of relational trust in new business creation in established firms. *Entrepreneurship Theory and Practice*, **30**: 541–59.

10. Some thoughts on the development of stakeholder theory

R. Edward Freeman

The ideas behind the stakeholder concept are as old as commerce itself. No one can possibly deny that from its earliest beginnings in barter, business has been a matter of trade between buyers and sellers so that both were at least perceptually better off because of the exchange. Exchange created value between the partners and led to specialization of labor, more knowledge and innovation, and hence more exchange. Eventually, employees were added, though during ancient times they had relatively little freedom. While the separation of ownership and control may well be rooted in feudal society,[1] the emergence of wealthy merchants who often earned their profits on the backs of others has a long history. Where value is created, value can be destroyed. Commerce affected customers, suppliers, and employees and the owners of the business, even if value was sometimes destroyed for some.[2]

Even communities and governments have long been involved in value creation and trade. Fernand Braudel's magisterial history of capitalism shows us the fiction that is free-floating markets disconnected from the rest of society.[3] Markets emerged as town fairs, then moved outside the gates of towns to avoid governmental taxes, much in the way that some multinational companies incorporate off shore to minimize tax exposure. 'Managing the government or community relationship' has been a part of value creation and trade from the very beginning. According to Braudel, door-to-door peddlers were outlawed in England during the seventeenth century because they prevented the government from collecting their fair share of the tax. One can think of the emergence of such peddlers as an innovation to deliver products and services to customers more efficiently, much like Internet shopping, or one can think of it as one more innovative way to manage the interface with government, community and supply chains, much like some have suggested that Internet commerce be free from sales tax.

Move to the Industrial Age and we find a clearer delineation of the role of employees, as well as customers and suppliers. Managers were hired to run large operations, and communities often existed partially in the squalor that was produced by inhuman working conditions. The story of the emergence of the dominance of business as a social institution is often littered with the cruel strategies some businesses used for dealing with key stakeholders.

For instance, in the panic of 1873, investment banker Jay Cooke and Company went bankrupt after putting too much money into the fast growing railroad business and financing the second transcontinental route, in particular, with Northern Pacific Railroad.

According to Michael D'Antonio (2006: 31),

> Thousands of paper millionaires lost everything, and many banks went under as depositors withdrew their cash. Those lenders who survived simply stopped giving credit, which made it impossible for firms to buy supplies or finance expansion and new equipment . . . Nearly ninety railroad companies disappeared. More than 18000 other businesses, many of which depended on the railroads went bankrupt. Unemployment surged to 14%.

The effects of this recession and subsequent deflation on workers and communities were enormous. There were fewer jobs, so that many firms could pay workers less, demand more work, and often provide very difficult conditions. It set the stage for class warfare in the industrial revolution, and a focus on the very nature of capitalism as a struggle between owners and workers, with Marx pitted against Adam Smith as an argument that continues till the present day. I want to suggest that even in this more dire time of panic and struggle, we still need to understand business as an institution that is creating (or perhaps destroying) value for stakeholders.

Some tried to do better. Milton Hershey[4] and other progressives tried to take care of their employees and build communities for them to live in. Some of these experiments are often called 'social experiments', but that is a testament to the separation of 'business' and 'social' in the dominant narrative. One might even see the confessional of the so-called 'robber baron' Andrew Carnegie's (1901) *Gospel of Wealth,* as a way to atone to communities and societies for any damage that had been done by pursuing profits at the expense of the underlying social fabric. This point of view still holds sway today under the guise of corporate philanthropy and sometimes, corporate social responsibility (CSR).

If you want to understand business, from the dawn of commerce, understand that the unit of analysis should be something akin to 'stakeholders'. For starters, we can specify that almost any business affects customers, suppliers, employees, financiers/owners and communities/governments. How can we understand the emergence of trade routes, wholesalers, retail shops, the crafts and craftsmen, the factory, the labor unions, the social unrest around company towns and mistreatment of employees, and the like, without understanding how value is created (or destroyed/reallocated) to customers, suppliers, employees, communities and financiers, at a minimum?

To make this claim should be entirely uncontroversial, but it is set against a very different background story that we have come to accept. This background story takes as the unit of analysis, neither a particular business nor the set of value-creating/value-destroying relationships in which it is engaged. It sees the idea of 'markets' as the dominant metaphor for understanding business. Further, it has a quite stylized view of 'markets' in terms of many buyers and many sellers, each with an undifferentiated product, with prices that reflect all relevant information that everyone knows. In other words it focuses on 'competitive markets' where marginal revenue is driven to marginal costs, and with enough assumptions, profits are on average, zero.

Much of what I have come to call 'stakeholder theory' has been taken as a counterweight to this 'business as competitive markets' narrative. In principle, however, there is very little direct conflict between these narratives. There is little of what *au courant* social scientists would call 'competing theories approach'. There are no hypotheses that could be tested that would favor one over the other. The conflict lies in a more subtle disagreement about the most useful way to think about business.[5]

Surely for some purposes 'business as markets' is most useful. For instance, if we are trying to understand how complex trading scenarios worked, like the Wall Street market for securities, or even the Dutch tulip market during the Golden Age, or how bubbles and crashes occurred, then business as markets is surely compelling. Likewise for some concrete business decisions around how to deal with highly competitive and undifferentiated products, business as markets may well yield real practical insights.[6] Many theorists in the field of strategic management have taken these insights and developed them into theories of competitive advantage and competitive strategy that can be useful to managers and theorists alike. And, of course, much of the powerful edifice of modern economics would not exist without the 'business as markets' narrative.

There are many forms of this narrative, many of which are familiar to those who would be interested in stakeholder theory. Stakeholder theory is often juxtaposed with 'shareholder theory' or with 'agency theory' or with 'the resource based view of the firm', all of which rely primarily on economics and economic language for their appeal. I am a great admirer of economists[7] and economics. But, there is a problem, especially in modern schools of business.

These modern schools of business have come to be schools of economics and economic reasoning, often narrowly construed. The danger here is that we come to see markets as the primary, indeed the only, metaphor in business. This runs the risk of ignoring the fact that businesses are populated by human beings in all of their complexity, and have been so since the dawn of commerce. It runs the risk of ignoring that business has always been deeply embedded into the societal fabric, wherever it has risen and flourished. It also runs the risk of seeing 'economic' language in too narrow a fashion, certainly contra to its founder, Adam Smith. The recent rise of behavioral economics and finance is a positive direction in recognizing the complexity of human behavior.

I want to call the alternative to 'business as markets' something like 'business as creating value for stakeholders' with the caveat that many times in the past and present, value has been destroyed as well. The academic study of business using the idea of stakeholders as the primary unit of analysis, I have come to call, 'stakeholder theory'. I believe that stakeholder theory has developed explicitly over the past half century as a sometimes more useful explanation for how business actually works. In particular if one wants to see how to manage and lead a business, how to create value that can be sustained over time in a responsible way that is at once profitable and deeply embedded in the societal fabric, then the metaphor of 'stakeholders' is a more useful starting point. To understand how to manage a business as a success or as a failure is to understand how value is created or destroyed for customers, suppliers, employees, financiers and communities.

Yet, there is a more subtle danger here for stakeholder theorists. The dominant narrative of 'business as markets' has many tentacles that are embedded in the ways that we talk about business. It is often tempting to latch onto some of those tentacles that express a partial insight in the real business world of stakeholder relationships embedded in society. Nothing is more tempting than to latch onto the concept of 'social' or even 'social responsibility' or even 'social performance' or even 'corporate social responsibility' to articulate the societal embeddedness of business. In what follows I want to suggest that such vestigial limbs of the old narrative are best dropped, and re-conceptualized in stakeholder theoretic terms. Such has been the fate of stakeholder theorists for the last 30 years, arguing among themselves, failing to appreciate that they have created what theorists such as Richard Rorty would call a new 'geistesgeschichte', a new grand narrative about business. The time for that grand narrative is now long overdue, and hopefully the next 30 years will prove its usefulness. Stakeholder theory is about developing such a new story about business, or more precisely, retrieving a very old story about business and making it fit for the twenty-first century.

A PERSONAL REPRISE

In June of 1982, I sat down at my home in Princeton Junction, New Jersey to begin to write *Strategic Management: A Stakeholder Approach* (*SMASA*). I had agreed with Bill Roberts, CEO of Pitman US to write it as a textbook for courses in strategic management. I had met Professor Ed Epstein of Berkeley at the Academy of Management, and he encouraged me to submit the proposal for the book to a series at Pitman, of which he was the editor. The series was called Business and Public Policy. Of course, I had no experience with writing books, textbooks or teaching strategic management with any kind of textbook. I simply wanted to write a systematic account of how to think about businesses by taking seriously the idea that businesses needed to pay much more attention to stakeholders. There was a fair literature on the stakeholder idea at the time, and in Chapter 2 of the book, I tried to sort that literature into some streams. But, at the time, no one had thought too much about how to use the stakeholder idea as a more fundamental idea about how to understand and manage a business.

I had spent much of the previous six years working with companies, alongside colleagues such as Jim Emshoff[8] and Gordon Sollars, and helping them to use the stakeholder idea to understand their business, to become more externally focused. However, I was trained as a philosopher in ethics and decision theory. I had no real idea about the 'do's and don't's' of social science, especially as practiced in the business schools of our time. As I went around giving seminars to various universities, I found that I had struck a nerve with the comprehensiveness of the stakeholder idea. I will never forget a session at the University of Pittsburgh where Bill Frederick simply took me aside and told me to write a book, that I had something to say that could be important. I certainly wasn't sure about that, but it seemed like good advice, so I took it.[9]

Eight weeks later, I turned in the first draft of the manuscript to Pitman. I spent most of the next year revising and responding to criticisms from Roberts, Epstein and Edwin Hartman, a fellow philosopher in business. The book came out to no acclaim. I don't think it received any reviews, except for one by a friend of mine named Jim Webber in a hospital management newsletter. It just lay there. Pitman did give away a number of copies in order to build its brand. Over the years, it became an easy way to reference stakeholder theory, and occasionally someone would actually read the book and write about it.

I am humbled that 25 years later a group of scholars has taken the trouble to re-read this book and assess both its arguments and the progress of 'stakeholder theory'. They raise a number of important questions and themes, and I will take each of them in turn. First of all, several raise the issue of what exactly is stakeholder theory about. Is it about how businesses can be more socially responsible? Is it about how businesses can be more strategic by taking stakeholders into account (Elms, Johnson-Cramer and Berman)? Is it about how strategic management, as a field, should evolve (Harrison)? Or, does it raise more systemic issues that ultimately must be conceptualized in other than stakeholder terms (Werhane)? Second, they raise issues of what kind of a theory stakeholder theory is. Does it ultimately have to rest on some normative foundations (Donaldson)? Can we understand it in terms of a kind of pluralism or is that its conceptual undoing (Scherer and Patzer)? Third, what kind of assumptions are made in strategic management about why people do what they do (Bosse and Harrison)? And, what is the role of managerial discretion in those assumptions (Phillips et al.)? Finally, Jones and Hartman raise some important philosophical issues about where the future of stakeholder theory might lie.

WHAT IS STAKEHOLDER THEORY ABOUT?

When I wrote *SMASA*, I thought I was very clear about the nature of the task. I now believe that clarity was the reward for ignorance. I self-identified as a philosopher in a business school who was thinking broadly about strategy or 'strategic management' as it was being called. I wanted to write a book about what strategic management would look like if one were to take the stakeholder idea seriously. I wanted to see what I could say about the hundreds of executives I had given seminars to, and worked with over the previous six years, who were actually out using the stakeholder management idea to make decisions about their businesses. I had been pretty lucky to work with companies on very small, mostly political decisions, for instance, trying to deal with a particular regulatory environment, and very large decisions with wide ranging implications, like the repositioning of a multi-billion dollar line of business. I was writing from this experience because that was all I knew, never having had a business course, and never having been 'schooled' in the proper conceptual/theoretical niceties of the social sciences.

Strategy or Corporate Social Responsibility?

Elms, Johnson-Cramer, and Berman are determined to hold *SMASA* to this original intent by finding a 'strategy only' interpretation of the book. They seem to want an interpretation that is devoid of any inkling of CSR or even of ethics. This is certainly faithful to the spirit in which I wrote *SMASA*, perhaps to a fault. Their analysis of three mischaracterizations of *SMASA* is interesting. These mischaracterizations are that (1) *SMASA* approves of CSR; (2) *SMASA* is about society; and (3) *SMASA* is normative. I would amend Elms, Johnson-Cramer and Berman in the following way.

It is not so much that I disapproved of CSR, I just did not think it was very useful, and I would now argue that it gets in the way of adopting a stakeholder based narrative. It seemed to me to be peripheral to the underlying business model, which needed to be interpreted in stakeholder terms. My argument was, and still is: get the stakeholder issues right, and the need for CSR vanishes.[10] It is an argument about the right unit of analysis for strategy, or as I would prefer to say it now. . .Stakeholders are the right unit of understanding for any business. Elms, Johnson-Cramer and Berman want to delineate the boundaries between strategic management and CSR. I am not opposed to such a delineation, but I do think it is really beside the point. I want to simply stop talking about CSR unless we can replace 'social' with 'stakeholder'.

As for (2), of course society is an important part of understanding a business in stakeholder terms, and the book is full of ways to build that understanding in, but fundamentally I was trying to say something about how to run a successful business in turbulent environments. I would now call this the 'Problem of Value Creation and Trade' (Freeman et al., 2010).

(3) is more problematic. It simply never occurred to me to keep out the language of ethics. Even in that early work, I was anti-separation thesis, though it took me a number of years to be able to articulate in a reasonable way.[11] *SMASA* is full of the language of ethics. Enterprise strategy is about purpose, and the analysis of values, social issues, societal trends, all play central roles in the processes in the book, and played important roles in my work with companies. And, what I thought was a sequel to *SMASA*, *Corporate Strategy and the Search for Ethics*, explicitly argues that what is wrong with strategic management is a lack of integration of the language of ethics. Dan Gilbert and I jokingly referred to this book as 'son or daughter of Stakeholder', and, in fact, it had very little impact on either strategic management or business and society.

While Elms, Johnson-Cramer and Berman focus on so-called 'mischaracterizations' in the academic literature, there is an interpretation of the stakeholder idea which exists in practice that I believe is compellingly wrong, and it is connected to their arguments. In many places, both geographic and academic, when you begin to talk about 'stakeholders', managers, policy makers and academics immediately think that this is a more fine-grained way to talk about society, community or civil society organizations. I want to insist that whatever the merits of considering these interests, a stakeholder view of business, and hence stakeholder theory, must give an account of customers, employees, suppliers, communities and financiers. I believe this is connected to Elms, Johnson-Cramer and Berman's idea about the boundaries between strategy and CSR. I am less interested in the academic boundary issue and more interested in how we can construct a more useful narrative about business.

More interesting is their discussion of the criteria for boundaries. They suggest, first of all, that stakeholder theory is 'business centric' rather than 'society centric'. This is surely the flavor of *SMASA*, but I would put it differently today. I think that we need a 'business in society' centric view. The global financial crisis has demonstrated the inherent flaw in seeing business as separate from society. And, I do not believe we can leave the construction of a 'business-in-society' centric narrative to the hands of either strategic management or CSR scholars. We need the disciplines of business to be embedded in society. There is much work to be done here. Freeman and Newkirk (2008) have suggested how we can come to see the disciplines of business and business schools themselves as embedded in society, and thus, as deeply human. Freeman et al. (2010) have identified this issue as the 'Problem of Managerial Mindsets', and I believe that it must be a central part of stakeholder theory.

Second, Elms, Johnson-Cramer and Berman have suggested that the boundaries of stakeholder theory be delimited in terms of identifying stakeholders. My view here is that there are different uses of the stakeholder idea for different purposes. For some purposes, it is useful to define 'stakeholder' very widely, and for some uses very narrowly. I take this boundary condition to say that we need to keep clear what the uses are of the theories that we construct. Some have suggested that we need to define 'stakeholder' once and for all, and marry it to a theory of which groups are legitimate and which are always merely instrumental. We pragmatists believe that such a theoretical move is not very useful.[12]

The third condition, texture, is particularly interesting. I agree that the texture of CSR research is different from my own ideas about stakeholder theory. There are times when CSR research is just anti-business, or it accepts what I once called 'the business sucks story'. However, the more I read in the mainstream of the strategy literature, the more I become convinced that most of it also accepts the same story. The difference is that CSR research seeks to build a better world, while the strategic management literature often seems to celebrate the fact that it can give a purely narrowly economic rationale for what looks like complex behavior.[13] Thinking about texture is akin to what literary theorists would call 'tone', the author's attitude towards a text. We desperately need to do a reading of both the strategy and the CSR literature from the standpoint of literary theory. Such a reading would reveal, I believe, a deeply anti-humanist view in strategy, and a deeply anti-business view in CSR. I believe that such narratives are not useful in trying to solve the underlying problems of stakeholder theory.

The final boundary condition is on the source of normative claims. I agree with much of their argument here, however, I do want to suggest that 'Freeman (1984) makes no moral claims . . .' is a very particularized reading that depends on the separation thesis. Business and ethics are inextricably entangled, to use Hilary Putnam's language. It has always been so, and it is time to give up the descriptive and normative distinction, as telling us anything more than the politics of the author.

The Politics of Strategic Management

It is the politics of strategic management as a discipline that concerns Jeffrey Harrison in his personal account of becoming a stakeholder theorist. I was recently struck by the admission of one stakeholder theorist that working on these ideas was 'risky' and one could only do so after accruing academic weight and title through more traditional means. It is difficult to disengage the emergence of strategic management as a discipline in business schools from the development of a rather narrow positivist, economic orientation. One need only go to academic meetings to wonder what happened to the cornucopia that is real business, enmeshed in a set of relationships with customers, suppliers, employees, communities and financiers. Slowly the academic discipline is shifting. There are more and more papers published in the so-called, 'A Journals' on stakeholder theory, and the Strategic Management Society recently approved interest groups on both 'Stakeholder Strategy' and 'Human Capital'.[14]

Much of the difficulty with the lack of traction in strategic management for these ideas has been diagnosed by Elms, Johnson-Cramer and Berman. Many strategic management scholars have simply identified stakeholder theory with CSR, making it easy to marginalize. But Harrison suggests a deeper analysis. By focusing the main question of strategy as how do firms find and build competitive advantage, the field actually adopts a kind of ideology that closes off ideas about value creation. By searching for academic legitimacy it overspecializes in a particular kind of empiricism, long discredited in philosophy.

Giles Slinger's rewrite of the history of stakeholder theory is instructive here. Slinger suggests that the early connections of the stakeholder idea to the theorists at Tavistock such as Bion, Trist and others, and their connections to the psychoanalytic schools of thought such as object–relations theory, put a premium on the clinical approach. This certainly rings true for me writing *SMASA*. I did not think about how to find propositions that would describe all firms at all times in all circumstances. After Freud, this idea just seemed ridiculous, not worth considering. The stakeholder idea was too fine grained for such theorizing. It tried to give an account of how this business was successful or not, rather than all businesses. Consequently, it had a great deal of traction with executives. The theory of strategic management, as it developed was much more influenced by a set of economists who were trying to explain how competitive markets emerged. While the idea of 'markets' is an important part of theorizing about business, it is not the only useful trope.

Harrison suggests that there are many points of contact between the developed field of strategic management and stakeholder theory. He is surely correct here, and I confess to simply giving up on the field of strategic management for a number of years. I found it ironic that when I left the Wharton faculty to go to Minnesota, Harbir Singh actually moved into my office. At roughly the same time, Charles Fombrun, Bala Chakravarthy and Graham Astley also left Wharton, soon to be followed by Russell Ackoff and his students. Most of the ideas about stakeholder theory and collective strategy seem to have left with us, for there is very little mention of the stakeholder idea in either the resource-based view or the relational view of the firm. I have always attributed this to a lack of either interest in clinically based concepts like stakeholder theory or our particular interpersonal skills.

Yet, despite the language of 'struggle' and 'battle', Harrison remains optimistic about the future, as do I. Strategic management as a discipline has reached a critical point. Either it decides to deal with the global realities of business today, or it will rather quickly become irrelevant to students, as well as practitioners. Those global business realities include a diverse set of complex and interconnected problems, which only something like stakeholder theory can address.

Stakeholder Theory or Systems Theory?

Patricia Werhane suggests that stakeholder theory, as it has been depicted, creates a way of looking at business that is too much centered on the firm or organization. When the traditional hub and spoke diagram of stakeholder theory is taken as the only depiction, she is surely correct. She suggests a number of interesting depictions that can be useful for a variety of purposes. I have several additions to Werhane's argument, while acknowledging her substantial contribution to the development of both stakeholder theory and my own personal development.

First of all, her insistence on taking a systems point of view is, of course, correct. Stakeholder theory was born in systems theory, and lived there for many years at Wharton under the care of Russell Ackoff, Eric Trist, Howard Perlmutter and others. The difficulty with 'systems thinking' is not the broader view of how various elements are connected. Nor is it Ackoff's insistence on synthetic and holistic thinking rather than just the breaking down of systems into their component parts (analysis, which comprises much of the academic literature on stakeholder theory). The difficulty is in practice. There is much temptation to try and 'manage the system' because focusing on any one part risks 'sub-system optimization'.

My version of stakeholder theory depicted in *SMASA* was opposed to such temptations to 'manage the system'. These too easily lead to totalitarian regimes, whether in private business or public policy. Rather, one appreciates the complexity of system, but must recognize that action has to be taken at a subsystem level, so that order is an emergent and revisable property, as Hayek would conclude. The world is littered with failed projects, all well-meaning, all trying to 'change the system' with incomplete knowledge, bounded rationality and a great deal of complexity.

Several early versions of papers written at Wharton contain these more complex system diagrams. My take on them today is that for some purposes they are very useful, but for other purposes they are not. Many critics have accused stakeholder theory of claiming that corporations are the center of the universe, by depicting them in the middle of a hub-and-spoke diagram. I believe I was careful to say that this is not the case. Indeed, in the little read chapters of the book on how to understand stakeholders, I suggested that each stakeholder be placed in the middle, in turn, and that managers needed to understand the world from the stakeholders' point of view. However, I was mainly interested in developing a more useful theory about good management, and I thought at the time that such a depiction of the manager in the center was most appropriate. Today I would broaden this depiction along the lines that Werhane suggests, and indeed we began this process in *Managing for Stakeholders*, especially with the picture devised by Novo Nordisk (see Freeman, Harrison and Wicks, 2007: 97).

Werhane's argument for decentering the firm also has an interpretation in stakeholder theory. By moving from 'stock' to 'stake', the very idea of stakeholder theory is decentering. By redrawing stakeholder maps, and trying to be clear about which map for which purpose, we can remake our organizations so that they are more reflective of their very human purposes.

WHAT KIND OF A THEORY IS STAKEHOLDER THEORY?

The temptation with systems thinking is to try and find a normative ground, or a set of depictions that will work for all possible combinations of stakeholders in a business. While Werhane stays rooted in the real world, simply trying to improve the way that companies are currently managed, both the Donaldson and Scherer and Patzer papers demand more from stakeholder theory. Both want to ground stakeholder theory in something more philosophical than the pragmatist roots it has developed in the hands of my colleagues and I.

Donaldson's Search for the Bottom Turtle

Tom Donaldson sets out to fix a problem created by a misinterpretation of his paper with Lee Preston. In that now famous paper, they suggested that stakeholder theory could be divided into four parts: descriptive, instrumental, normative and managerial, though Donaldson's paper in this volume fails to mention the managerial level.[15] In fact, he follows most of the literature here, and in doing so falls prey to his own misinterpretation. Donaldson suggests that there is a firm philosophical ground underneath stakeholder theory, and it is something like the theory of property, as conceptualized through integrated social contracts. Donaldson says that it is a mistake to argue that there can be a stakeholder theory that is not based somehow on normative notions.

Of course, I am in 100 percent agreement with him here. The problem is that by dividing up stakeholder theory into normative, descriptive and instrumental, Donaldson has created his own problem. It is almost like the famous story about the philosopher's student who asks, when told that the world is held up by an elephant, 'what holds up the elephant?' When told that a turtle holds up the elephant the student persists with 'what holds up the turtle?' The philosopher, perhaps an early pragmatist, responds with, 'It's turtles all the way down'.

In their original article Donaldson and Preston suggest that, at its core, stakeholder theory is managerial, and therefore it is very difficult to separate out normative, descriptive and instrumental, since managerial theories combine all of them. There simply is no 'bottom turtle'. Again, I couldn't agree more, but since many find this typology quite useful, I want to propose the following pragmatist interpretation for it.

Sometimes it is very useful to talk about how we understand what our businesses are actually doing. Our main task is to write fairly descriptive prose and narrate who is doing what to whom. Of course, this is not really 'non-normative', especially when we use the very idea of 'stake-holder', which is itself a partially normative move. I believe I have made this point repeatedly over the years in places too numerous to mention. Sometimes it is useful to focus on how we could make our organizations better, more just, more human and so forth. In that part of stakeholder theory we would expect to find more explicitly moral language. Of course, this is related to how organizations actually conduct themselves. There is no pure case. Facts and values are inextricably entangled. Nowhere is this clearer than in the instrumental case. Putnam (2002) has given us an excellent example of how this process works in language, in general and in economic theory, in particular.

Donaldson's search for the normative ground wants to rule out some of these ways of talking as derivative from others. I believe that this misunderstands the nature of the language that we owe to Wittgenstein, Quine, Davidson and others. Language is an unbroken whole. The pathway from agency theory to Kant may well be a tortured one, but it might be interesting to explore, as we try and find new and different metaphors for understanding our organizations. Donaldson suggests that shareholder value theory is morally laden, and of course he is right. The interesting question is to try and diagnose why anyone would think otherwise.[16] Shareholder rights include a nest of moral claims about property rights, and sometimes it is very useful to examine these claims in explicitly moral language as Donaldson suggests.[17]

Equally true is Donaldson's reliance on an argument by Charles Fried (1981) about the Coase Theorem. Fried suggested many years ago, that one could not bargain away one's right to bargain, on pain of selling oneself into slavery. Donaldson seems to approve of this old argument when he invokes the rights theory of Henry Shue. I would respond that Fried has already done this work in a much less controversial framework.

Rights talk has limits. For many purposes, it is not very useful. The same may be said for every tradition in philosophical ethics. The difficulty is not that philosophical ethics is not useful, but that there is no certainty that the frameworks will always produce useful results. Judgment is always required. Our freedom and our ability to choose is always at stake, as is our ability to engage in self deception and bad faith. There are no guarantees provided by ethical theory. And, ultimately, Donaldson and I may well have different views of what it means to do ethics and philosophy. I am very glad to see that Donaldson has argued that there can be no descriptive or instrumental stakeholder theory without normative theory. I would add that the inverse is also the case. We can no longer afford a view of ethical theory that pretends that human beings are creatures of the state, first, and value creators and traders somewhere well down the line. In fact, in their important book, *The Ties that Bind*, Donaldson and Dunfee (1999) go a long way towards rectifying such an arid view of ethical theory. The now well-known Donaldson–Preston typology can be useful, but I believe we should read it along with Putnam's *The Collapse of the Fact/Value Dichotomy* (2002). The role of ethics in stakeholder theory is too important to leave to the neo-positivists who are looking for bottom turtles.

Scherer and Patzer's Middle Turtle

Andreas Scherer and Moritz Patzer seem to understand why stakeholder theory does not need a 'bottom turtle' or ultimate ground. Nonetheless, they worry about the opposite problem from Donaldson; namely, that there are too many grounds. We do not need a bottom turtle but we need some 'middle turtle' on which to base our analysis. The pluralism of stakeholder theory, they argue, as interpreted by my pragmatist colleagues and I, leads to an unsatisfactory state of affairs. They worry that the road from pluralism to relativism is a short one. And, they rightly point out that many stakeholder theorists do not really understand the dangers.

Scherer and Patzer suggest a method of meta-analysis and a sorting of paradigms as a way to understand the different positions of stakeholder theorists. While the application of Kuhn's notion of paradigm may well be useful, I share Kuhn's own skepticism, which he expressed in the postscript to the second edition of *The Structure of Scientific Revolutions* (1970). I had the pleasure, as a doctoral student at Washington University in the mid-1970s, to actually hear Professor Kuhn talk about what a mess many social scientists had made of his idea of paradigms. While I am sure he would not have read it, I believe that Gibson Burrell and Gareth Morgan's use of the term would itself have been, to Kuhn, a 'paradigm' of misuse.

The idea of paradigm doesn't so much involve a choice of foundations, or even an awareness of differing foundations. Overlaying traditional philosophical dualisms such as realism and nominalism, positivist and interpretive and so forth assumes the relevance of the very kind of philosophy that we pragmatists want to suggest isn't very useful. Andrew Wicks and I (1998) explicitly made this argument a number of years ago, and we suggested that a philosophical pragmatism was very different from the kind of relativism that one finds in *Images of Organization* (Morgan, 1986). While Scherer and Patzer quote this paper, they seem to have a different interpretation. I suspect that is because they find pragmatism unacceptable for some reason. Their philosophical language at times approaches a kind of Kantian foundationalism that can be found in at least the early Habermas. They seem to pine for 'comprehensive theory building', which is difficult in stakeholder theory, they argue, due to 'paradigmatic incommensurability'.

I would rather say that different ways to talk have different uses, and we need to be cognizant of how these different vocabularies work, as well as the connections among them. I am not sure we can aspire to more. Using their technique of meta-analysis, we may find a useful way to talk in the same vein that structuralists in literary studies gave us some useful ways to sort out nineteenth-century Romantic Poetry. The proof will be in Scherer and Patzer's narrative, their re-description of stakeholder theory along these 'paradigmatic' lines.

In short, my differences with Scherer and Patzer are roughly the same differences between Rorty and Habermas. I think that terms like 'communicative rationality', 'unity of practice', 'comprehensive theorizing' and so forth are nice honorifics that theorists pay to others whose theories they approve of. I don't yet see the usefulness of talking this way, nor do I see how it helps us to remake our businesses in a way that solves the problem of the ethics of business. However, if by 'a procedural concept of communicative rationality' they mean that we need to understand ethics as a conversation about how to describe and re-describe our world, and hence enact a better one, then I count them as pragmatists. Our door is always open to new and better ways to talk. There is much more interesting dialogue to be had putting together the ideas of pragmatists like Rorty, Putnam, Davidson and so forth, with the substantial body of work of Habermas and his followers. I do believe that this is one of the most fruitful lines of research in business ethics, and Scherer and Patzer have done stakeholder theorists like myself a real favor by beginning this dialogue.

WHAT ARE THE ASSUMPTIONS THAT STAKEHOLDER THEORY MAKES ABOUT PEOPLE?

In my graduate studies I was heavily influenced by John Rawls, *A Theory of Justice* (1971), and by the fact that Rawls had built his theory in a way that was consistent with some of the best economic thinking of the time. My dissertation, under game theorist, Edward F. McClennen, explored the rational decision models under complete uncertainty, one of the major arguments for justice as fairness, known as the veil of ignorance argument. At the same time I was beginning to read the existentialist novels of Sartre, de Beauvoir and others, as well as the psychoanalytic theories of Freud and his followers. Even the best economic thinking is only a partial truth. Now I would say it has limited usefulness.

When I wrote *SMASA* I didn't think too much about the question of what makes human beings tick. I wasn't sure I had any insight into this question, and I thought that regardless of how we answered it businesses had stakeholders that had to be addressed. I now think that one cannot address the issues of stakeholder theory without addressing the question of the assumptions about human behavior. I believe that most of stakeholder theory is in fact consistent with a lot of economic theory, but that economic theory offers limited insight into the vast reservoir of the human psyche. There is much more work to be done here.

In the chapters by Bosse and Harrison, and Phillips, Berman, Elms and Johnson-Cramer, there are ample demonstrations that by understanding 'economic' in slightly broader terms, we can make most of stakeholder theory consistent with, and an improvement over, most of what might be called 'standard strategic management thinking'.

Bosse and Harrison continue to develop a line of work begun with Robert Phillips in two papers in *Strategic Management Journal* that outlines a somewhat broader notion of choice, which they dub here 'bounded self-interest'. They argue that such an idea can accommodate ethical concerns such as reciprocity and fairness. Hence, there is no need to commit to the separation fallacy.

Their argument is consistent with what we know from decision theory and the line of work that I referred to above with respect to Rawls. There is a long history of solving decision theoretic puzzles such as Prisoner's Dilemma, Ulysses and the Sirens, Newcomb's Problem, Ellsberg's Paradox and the like with broader ideas about rationality. Bosse and Harrison's idea is much like 'constrained maximization' developed by David Gauthier in *Morals by Agreement* (1986), and Ned McClennen's (1988) idea of 'resolute choice'. I, for one, am very happy to see these ideas from choice theory begin to appear in the strategy and entrepreneurship literature as they offer more robust ideas about human behavior.

Phillips et al. seem to have a similar project in that they want to show that a stakeholder theory that is more carefully constrained and stated can offer insights into mainstream organization theory and strategy. They rightly see stakeholder theory as having been developed resting on the notion of voluntary choice. While recognizing constraints, stakeholder theory depends on the idea that organizations will be better off if they voluntarily choose to manage stakeholder relationships. It is fundamentally a libertarian view as Phillips and I set out some years ago (Freeman and Phillips, 2002). Their project is also connected to the work in choice theory mentioned above, however there is a nuance here to consider. In trying to give a more careful statement of the continuum from choice to constraint, the temptation is to try and do 'purely descriptive' work. The entanglement of stakeholder theory in a theory about freedom and responsibility, however, is impossible to ignore. Let me illustrate.

They claim: 'For example, managers in an older, large, highly regulated utility firm will have far fewer strategic options at their disposal than managers in a firm with a highly differentiated product competing in a fast growing industry' (pp. 167–8). However, if those same managers understood their responsibility to create value for their stakeholders, they might well create new choices for themselves and those stakeholders. It is tempting to say that managers who do not create such choices are not to be held responsible because they had little discretion. This would ignore any entrepreneurial imperative that we may find in every business. AT&T invented the technology for cellular telephones in the 1960s. One could argue that it was a colossal mistake to wait until deregulation to deploy the technology, both from the standpoint of the business and of society as a whole. We can easily explain their choice using Phillips et al.'s framework, but it is difficult to evaluate the choice. Ironically, they seem to endorse this explanatory framework when they identify stakeholders with the constraints they 'impose' rather than the value creation opportunity they represent.

Both chapters make substantial contributions in linking work in stakeholder theory to more traditional management theory. Both deepen our understanding of what it means to make 'rational' and 'self-interested' choices, and how issues of ethics are connected. I hope that both chapters inspire others to open up the line of work in philosophy and decision theory. I believe this has great future promise.

WHAT IS THE FUTURE OF STAKEHOLDER THEORY?

When I wrote *SMASA*, I had no idea that the arguments in it would be relevant 25 years later. If Tom Jones and Ed Hartman are correct, the work done by stakeholder theorists during the last 25 years has set an agenda for many years to come. While my colleagues and I have tried to outline what we see as a number of fruitful research questions in the last chapter of *Stakeholder Theory*, which I do not want to repeat here, both Jones and Hartman point to some even broader issues that need to be addressed.

Jones locates the future of stakeholder theory in the integrative understanding of business, rather than in the fields of strategic management or corporate responsibility. We need a much more fine-grained understanding of stakeholder roles than we currently have. Customers, suppliers, employees, communities and financiers simply mirror the functional disciplines of business. We know that in the real world there is a high degree of overlap among these roles. There is no reason to believe that the stake of an employee who is a customer, employee and owner is equal to the sum of those individual stakes. Likewise we need a more nuanced understanding of the idea that stakeholder interests are joint, and that creating the most value for stakeholders does not involve trade-off thinking.

However, as central as these issues are to stakeholder theory, Jones' chapter raises one of the most important questions to business scholars, namely, 'What is the total performance of a business'? Since I do not think that the standard financial measures actually answer this question, and since Jones' critique of CSR measures is compelling, I believe that we need to start anew in answering this question.[18] It is much like the situation depicted in Michael Lewis' *MoneyBall* (2003). In that book, Billy Beane understood that the standard measures of performance in baseball failed to capture central features of performance. He was able to demonstrate that there were better measures of performance. We need a *MoneyBall*-like revolution in understanding business. For instance, it might turn out that an overall measure of employee engagement and one of customer satisfaction are better indicators of performance than profitability. I made several ham-handed attempts to address this question in *SMASA* (pp. 177ff.), but I simply couldn't articulate the question in as clear a way as Jones has done. I hope that answering this question about the total performance of a business occupies stakeholder theorists for some time to come. Unfortunately, there are temptations to simply use whatever data is available.

If Jones causes us to think deeply about the integrative nature of business and the question of its total performance, Ed Hartman does a similar job for ethics. Hartman's chapter raises the question of how we understand ethics itself as a conversation that cuts across institutions in society. He grounds this analysis in the work of stakeholder theorists who claim that thinking about how value gets created for multiple stakeholders is one of the key insights of stakeholder theory. He identifies what I have called the jointness of stakeholder interests with Aristotle's notion of the common good in general, and the depiction of the so-called Prisoner's Dilemma problems in particular.[19] He suggests, rightly, that sometimes tradeoffs must be made, that win–win solutions are not always possible. Hartman then suggests that we want 'real pros' making these tradeoffs so that we know they will 'play the game the right way', preserving value for the future.

While Hartman relies on my love of baseball and the experience of watching baseball games (and having many conversations about the game with Hartman and Dan Gilbert) a better analogy is my more recent turn to martial arts. The 'Do' of Tae Kwon Do is simply about the way one lives. The art of martial arts is less about being a 'real pro' and more about one's commitment to purpose, of living in a way that embodies the values of respect, integrity, perseverance and continuous improvement. Purpose is an underutilized concept in business, and in stakeholder theory. Not every purpose is the same, and not every purpose has the same moral weight. Much evil has been done in the world under the rubric of 'the common good'. It is the underlying values of the 'common good' or 'purpose' or 'jointness of stakeholder interests' that must be held to some scrutiny. Yet, Hartman is surely right that these values, which he identifies with Aristotelian virtues, and which I would call the Buddhist Way, are central to a workable notion of stakeholder theory.

The chapters in this volume are proof that surpasses any expectations I had to write a useful book, those many years ago. I believe that stakeholder theory is a much more useful way to think about business, and about business schools. The jury is out as to whether the disciplines of business can re-conceptualize themselves along stakeholder terms, and whether strategic management theorists, CSR theorists, and business ethicists can stop fighting among themselves and begin to celebrate the fact that they have fomented a conceptual revolution in business. The actual proof will be in our students and the kinds of businesses and theories that they are able to conceive.

The philosopher John Wisdom (1953) once said, 'the halo that surrounds the head of a saint does not become visible until we know he has paid the rent'. Stakeholder theory is one way for businesses and business theorists to pay the rent and to retake the moral high ground for capitalism, the greatest system of social cooperation we have ever invented.

ACKNOWLEDGMENTS

I am grateful to many co-authors and collaborators over many years for the ideas expressed in these pages. The very existence of this volume proves the claim that I get far too much credit for what many people have done for a long time. For a more complete history of the stakeholder idea see Giles Slinger, Essays on Stakeholders and Takeovers, Ph.D. Dissertation, Cambridge University, and Chapter 2 of Freeman, Harrison, Wicks, Parmar and de Colle, *Stakeholder Theory: The State of the Art*, 2010, Cambridge University Press. I have learned a great deal in conversations with many, but especially noteworthy are Professors Robert Phillips, Edwin Hartman, Patricia Werhane, and Gordon Sollars and their conversations over many years. None of this would have been possible without James Emshoff, John Lubin, Ram Charan, the late William Evan and others too numerous to name.

NOTES

1. Ironically, the principal–agent distinction so popular in modern finance theory, and in business schools generally got its impetus in the law from the question of whether masters were responsible for the actions of their slaves. This master–slave metaphor was present in the law of agency until very recently. For a discussion see Bowie and Freeman (1990).

2. My colleagues, Jeff Harrison, Andrew Wicks, Bedpan Parmar and Simone de Colle and I have tried to make this somewhat clearer in the first chapter of *Stakeholder Theory: The State of the Art* (2010). I am grateful to them and to other collaborators and co-authors for allowing me to develop many of their ideas and share them here.

3. See F. Braudel, *Civilization and Capitalism, 15th to 18th Century*, especially *Volume 3, The Perspective of the World*, p. 619.

4. Michael D'Antonio (2006) is an excellent example of why business schools must reconsider their anti-historical bias.

5. We pragmatists often find little direct conflict between ways of talking that seem to be opposed. Most of the time we argue that a particular vocabulary, say, the vocabulary of stakeholder relationships and managing for stakeholders, is more useful for many purposes than the vocabulary of only creating value for shareholders. This pragmatist move is not well understood in management theory, but is the potential source of making much of management theory more useful to real managers.

6. However, we want to be cautious here. Many would argue that there is no more competitive or undifferentiated market than the market for concrete and cement. However, the famous case of CEMEX belies such an analysis. It is not the only such story.

7. I have had the privilege of meeting three Nobel economists before they were so recognized. As a young doctoral student studying ethics and decision theory, I had the opportunity to meet Amartya Sen and Thomas Schelling in the mid to late 1970s. Their powerful work, later acknowledged in Nobels for each, had a profound impact on my thinking about Rawlsian ethics at the time. On the other hand, both were paragons of humility who did not believe that modern economics held the only keys to building a better world. Later, I met James Buchanan whose discourse on the centrality of what he called 'the attitude towards freedom', had a large effect on my embracing of some kind of libertarian principles.

8. Emshoff's and Sollars' roles in the development of stakeholder theory cannot be underestimated. Emshoff was the force which directed me to try and develop what Sollars and I called 'stakeholder management'. Sollars kept up my interest in philosophy and ethics, and helped figure out how we could apply these ideas in client companies. I have recently come across some early papers that we wrote, some of which were never published, and I appreciated even more how much of my early work was really due to Emshoff. Emshoff's own book, *Managerial Breakthroughs* (1980) summarizes some of the work we did at the Wharton Applied Research Center. Much of the managerial apparatus I wrote about in *Strategic Management: A Stakeholder Approach* (1984), and later in *Managing for Stakeholders* (2007), was in fact invented by Emshoff, and perhaps refined by Sollars and I, as we tried to make it work with clients.

9. Little did I know that social scientists simply did not write books. Of course, I knew that philosophers and others in the humanities would think of nothing else. If I have broken any new ground with this early book, I am afraid that it would be scarcely possible in today's business school environment.

10. Phillips and I were fairly clear about this in a paper on corporate citizenship in 2008.

11. See especially Chapter 2, footnote 3 of *SMASA*, 49.

12. My colleagues and I try to address this point in Chapter 3 of *Stakeholder Theory*.

13. Indeed the behavior looks complex only if one has a very narrow view of human behavior that does not admit complexity or tries to reduce such complexity to simply economic terms.

14. However, this is surely a curious term for humanists and libertarians, and those few of us who claim the heritage of both groups.
15. See Donaldson and Preston (1995: 67) for their discussion of Thesis 4, that stakeholder theory is managerial in the broadest sense.
16. Phillips (2003) addresses this issue as well.
17. I owe my understanding of this claim to Gordon Sollars.
18. Indeed Jones and I have begun a line of work to try and answer this question or at least ask it in a more interesting way.
19. In *SMASA*, I originally thought that Prisoner's Dilemma problems held a key to building a more useful stakeholder theory. See page 74ff. for my discussion of the 'stakeholder dilemma' game. I was unable to find an interesting way to pursue this claim in the subsequent years, except for Chapter 5 in Freeman and Gilbert (1988).

BIBLIOGRAPHY

Ackoff, R.L. 1971. Towards a system of systems concepts. *Management Science*, **17**(11): 661–71.

Bosse, D.A., Phillips, R.A. and Harrison, J.S. 2009. Stakeholders, reciprocity, and firm performance. *Strategic Management Journal*, **30**(4): 447–56.

Bowie, N. and Freeman, R.E. (eds) 1990. *Ethics and Agency Theory*. Oxford, UK: Oxford University Press.

Braudel, F. 1992. *Civilization and Capitalism, 15th to 18th Century, Volume 1: The Structures of Everyday Life*, 1992; *Volume 2: The Wheels of Commerce; Volume 3: The Perspective of the World*. Berkeley, CA: University of California Press.

Buchanan, J.M. 1975. *The Limits of Liberty*. Chicago, IL: University of Chicago Press.

Carnegie, A. 1901. The *Gospel of Wealth and Other Timely Essays*. New York: The Century Co.

D'Antonio, M. 2006. *Hershey: Milton S. Hershey's Extraordinary Life of Wealth, Empire, and Utopian Dreams*. New York: Simon and Schuster.

Donaldson, T.L. and Dunfee, T.W. 1999. *The Ties that Bind*. Cambridge, MA: Harvard Business Press.

Donaldson, T.L. and Preston, L. 1995. The stakeholder theory of the modern corporation: concepts, evidence and implications. *Academy of Management Review*, **20**: 65–91.

Emshoff, J. 1980. *Managerial Breakthroughs*. New York: American Management Association.

Freeman, R.E. 1984. *Strategic Management: A Stakeholder Approach*. Boston, MA: Pitman.

Freeman, R.E. and Gilbert, D. 1988. *Corporate Strategy and the Search for Ethics*, Englewood Cliffs, NJ: Prentice-Hall.

Freeman, R.E. and Newkirk, D. 2008. Business as a human activity. In Witherspoon Institute (ed.) *Rethinking Business Management*. Princeton, NJ: Princeton University, pp. 131–48.

Freeman, R.E. and Phillips, R. 2002. Stakeholder theory: a libertarian defense. *Business Ethics Quarterly*, **12**(3): 331.

Freeman, R.E. and Phillips, R. 2008. Corporate citizenship and community stakeholders. In A.G. Scherer and G. Palazzo (eds), *Handbook of Research on Global*

Corporate Citizenship. Cheltenham, UK and Northampton, MA, USA: Edward Elgar Publishing, pp. 99–115.

Freeman, R.E., Harrison, J. and Wicks, A. 2007. *Managing for Stakeholders: Survival, Reputation, and Success*. New Haven, CT: Yale University Press.

Freeman, R.E., Harrison, J., Wicks, A., Parmar, B. and de Colle, S. 2010. *Stakeholder Theory: The State of the Art*. Cambridge, UK: Cambridge University Press.

Fried, C. 1981. *Contract as Promise*. Cambridge, MA: Harvard University Press.

Gauthier, D. 1986. *Morals by Agreement*. Oxford, UK: Oxford University Press.

Habermas, J. 1991. *Moral Consciousness and Communicative Action*. Cambridge, MA: MIT Press.

Harrison, J.S., Bosse, D.A. and Phillips, R.A. 2010. Managing for stakeholders, stakeholder utility functions, and competitive advantage. *Strategic Management Journal*, **31**(1): 58–74.

Kuhn, T.S. 1970. *The Structure of Scientific Revolutions*, 2nd edition. Chicago, IL: University of Chicago Press.

Lewis, M. 2003. *Moneyball: The Art of Winning an Unfair Game*. New York: W.W. Norton & Company.

McClennen, E.F. 1988. Constrained maximization and resolute choice. *Social Philosophy and Policy*, **5**(2): 95–118.

Morgan, G. (1986). *Images of Organization*. Newbury Park, CA: Sage.

Phillips, R.A. 2003. *Stakeholder Theory and Organizational Ethics*. San Francisco, CA: Berrett-Koehler Publishers.

Phillips, R.A. 2003. Stakeholder Legitimacy. *Business Ethics Quarterly*, **13**(1): 25–41.

Putnam, H. 2002. *The Collapse of the Fact/Value Dichotomy and Other Essays*. Cambridge, MA: Harvard University Press.

Rawls, J. 1971. *A Theory of Justice*. Cambridge, MA: Belknap Press of Harvard University Press.

Slinger, G. 2001. Essays on Stakeholders and Takeovers. Ph.D. Thesis, Department of Applied Economics, Cambridge University.

Wicks, A.C. and Freeman, R.E. 1998. Organization studies and the new pragmatism: positivism, anti-positivism, and the search for ethics. *Organization Science*, **9**(2): 123–40.

Wisdom, J. 1953. *Philosophy and Psychoanalysis*. Oxford, UK: Blackwell.

Index